Biggest thing that bothers me is human relations

Interpersonal Dynamics in the Small Group

Interpersonal Dynamics in the Small Group

GERALD M. PHILLIPS The Pennsylvania

RANDOM HOUSE / NEW YORK

State University EUGENE C. ERICKSON Cornell University

Dedication

Our thanks to our wives, Ann and Nancy, for their patience and cooperation while we worked through this project, and to our children, Dean, Kenyon, Judy, Steve, Ellen, Jeff, Abigail, Kirsten, and Amy, for putting up with our hostilities and frustrations. Our thanks also to the institution out west where the authors first met and discovered that people in different disciplines really aren't so far apart, and where they found that it is a delight for people to share their specialities and come up with something that is, hopefully, new and stimulating.

Contents

The Impact of Communication on Human Behavior   160

Introduction

How to Use This Book

Learning about small groups is something like learning about love. Somehow, people have managed to fall in love and sustain that feeling without ever having read *Sonnets from the Portuguese,* and a great number of people who know a good deal about the biophysical, socioemotional, and psycholinguistic characteristics of that human emotion classified as "love," have been quite unable to form any sort of viable liaison with the girl of their dreams. There is, in short, quite a gap between the theory and the practice, as every lover knows.

Most complex human activities are very difficult to describe and even more difficult to generalize about. About the fourth century B.C., Aristotle, for example, wrote a book called *The Rhetoric* in which he described, in essence, the speechmaking behavior of the great orators of the Athens of his day. Note, he DEscribed what he saw; he did not necessarily PREscribe a way to do it. Unfortunately, humans seek the easy way out most of the time only to discover at the end that it was a most uneconomical mode of procedure. Consequently, generations of teachers attempted to disseminate the findings of Aristotle's "study" in the form of prescriptive advice to speakers, without very much success. It has only been a recent pedagogical discovery that the act of learning how to carry on a human activity is best learned by carrying on that human activity, and further, that it is possible to act effectively without knowing the theory behind the acting. Speakers like Winston Churchill, Franklin Roosevelt, Adlai Stevenson, and others were not firmly rooted in the theoretical bases of the art of "rhetoric," yet they were able to become models of its use. And all of us know that on every campus there are any number of young men who are "great lovers" and cannot write a poem and a great number of frustrated poets who cannot get a date.

We find essentially this same pattern emerging in books and writings about small groups. On one hand we have men known as sociologists, who write the results of their experiments in small group interaction, or summarize what they have seen in a live group engaged in discussion. On the other hand, we have "speech people" who attempt in the classroom to teach the "techniques" of group discussion. It is interesting that many of the men who know the most about theory of the small group are quite unable to participate in one, and many of the men who perform very effectively with others in small groups are unable to say very much about the "theory" under which they operate.

Those who seek to discover "law" or "scientific principles" may do so for various reasons. Some men study a phenomenon because "it is there." Others hope to discover some generalization that, when applied, will improve the state of the phenomenon they are studying. Both are perfectly legitimate reasons for study. What is illegitimate, however, is the assumption that *study about* confers *skill in*. The man who studies about may, through practice, cultivate skill, and he may have a deeper understanding of his skill because he understands some of the generalizations. The man who has skill may find himself better able to transmit some of the components of his skill to others

if he can develop a theoretical framework into which he can
fit his practical propositions.

It is perhaps for these reasons that sociologists and rhetoricians are coming somewhat closer together in their approaches
to the small group.   Sociologists are becoming more concerned
about the doing, and speech experts are becoming more concerned about the reasons why.   It almost appears now that in
most cases the parts are interchangeable, and what we have
developed is a cadre of people who are concerned with the
phenomenon of people interacting with each other, regardless of
their own home base discipline.   They want to know both how
to improve it and what its essential nature is.

This book, written by a "sociologist" and a "communication
expert," purports to be a possible solution to the problem of
combining theory with practice.   The writers were somewhat
startled and also encouraged by the areas in which they agreed
—despite the fact that they had trained in different disciplines
at different universities, and despite the different courses they
had taught, and the different texts used for apparently different
purposes.   The agreements indicated that the phenomenon was
worthy of attention in and of itself.   The two contrasting focuses
were not so different after all.   It seemed it might be possible
to approach the problems of the small group independent of
academic limitations, and to attempt truly to coordinate the
particular academic "grooves" of speech and sociology.

The book combines generalizations derived from experimentation and observation with controversial questions drawn
from the literature of a number of fields.   It is written without
footnotes, as though the authors were expert enough to speak
on their own authority, but it is clear that they both owe a
considerable debt to the men they spoke to and the books
they read, all of which are honored in a final chapter.   Since
within each discipline, and for that matter between and among
them, there is considerable agreement on many generalizations
about the small group, it was hard for them to discover precisely where their ideas came from.   It seemed dishonest to try
to attribute them to particular sources.   Where identifiable
sources are used they are referred to in the text.   But it is
recognized that there are particular statements with which some

persons, arguing from different premises and circumstances, might find exception. We hope this does not reduce the effectiveness of the whole book. We think not. For those interested, we will try to cite the ten or so men or works that have most influenced our thinking. We humbly request that the readers (teachers and students alike) accept this deviation from the formalities of the academic function called "textbook writing."

The generalizations and controversial questions supply, hopefully, a theoretical basis for understanding the small group. The problem of improving participation is a bit more difficult. In the bibliography chapter a number of works are cited that present methodologies for participation in the small group. Both authors question, mildly, the effectiveness of these books, despite the fact that they have been used for many academic generations to the satisfaction of the professors. There is so little feedback from the students about how the books "changed their whole lives" that we cannot be sure that the methodologies presented were of any use at all. Since at least one of them was written by one of the present authors, at least one of the stones cast turned out to be a boomerang. But since there are so many books available, and so little we could add to the various methodologies, no attempt will be made here to offer a system to follow to improve participation.

The essential philosophy about participation presented in this book runs as follows:

1. The act of discussing problems with others in groups is a real and vital act, essential to success in our society.
2. The traditional modes of teaching participation in society were somewhat detached from its realities.
3. The activity can be best learned by participation under "real" conditions where you have a stake in the outcome, in other words, will either profit by or suffer from what is decided.
4. It is possible to generate such discussions in the classroom without being accused of detached simulation or spurious roleplaying, provided both teachers and students are willing to risk a little.
5. The generalizations about group discussion and group inter-

action are much better understood if they are studied during
a time of participation, rather than in isolation.

6. A pedagogy based on a combination of theory and practice
offers the most learning potential to the student, and is the
most efficient for the teacher.

From these propositions, we offer a method of teaching a
course in the "small group" based on somewhat traditional
activities and a few new ones, which may startle the austere and
ivy-covered, but that not only provide solid answers to the
question of how to teach the small group, but peripherally deal
with the question, "how can students be given a greater share
in the planning and operation of their own education?"

This is a book for the beginning student in the social sciences. Libraries are replete with books filled with general
conclusions on the small group. But, since they are so often
based on controlled observations, these are difficult to use as
companions to the classroom sessions that deal with understanding the small group.

In attempting a book aimed at the students' behavior in a
small group we have of course chosen a very complex subject.
In fact, it is a subject as complex as social science itself. In
attempting to make the material manageable we may have over-
simplified or distorted data. This can hardly be avoided in a
beginning book for students in different disciplines. But we
hope that students, in their first exposure, will have a little
better understanding of the complexity of their roles as they
actually participate in social interaction.

A Teaching Philosophy

Almost all of the teaching done in colleges is cognitive. Students learn *about* things. They may study the history of their
country without living it, they may learn about the political
process without participating in it, and they may learn about
their society and experience none of it. It is the basic premise
of the authors that it is relatively worthless to learn *about*
small groups. The phenomenon of small group interaction is
so personal that most of the propositions really make little

sense unless the student has had some real participation. Anyone who doesn't believe this should try to generate an "objective" test on small groups, or try to come up with some firm
criteria for grading an essay test.

On the other hand, the propositions available about human
interaction in small groups become exquisitely simple once the
student has experienced the tension of interaction. The problem is that in the classroom it is very difficult to simulate
reality sufficiently so that the student will feel that he has
enough at stake to make the kind of commitment he will have
to make to groups he experiences in "the life outside." One
way to "beat this rap" is to permit the student to take the lead
in generating and evaluating the course in small groups. Small
groups can be used to generate assignments and to develop a
method of evaluating them. Small groups can be used to present substantive material. Small groups can carry on projects
in the community in which they actively attempt to exert their
influence on events. One of the authors experienced this less
than a year ago. He told his students to discover a problem
on campus and do something about it. The result was that one
group organized a continuing seminar with the local merchants,
resulting in publication of a pamphlet of advice on how to get
along with local merchants. A second group generated a
proposal for improvement of registration procedures that is
now in the hands of a select faculty committee. A third group
discovered that there was very little that could be done about
law enforcement on the campus. A fourth carried on a public
relations campaign to explain procedures at the university
health center, and a fifth discovered that the drug problem on
campus was as bad as stated. Every student in the class
received a first-hand experience in small group interaction,
complete with the frustrations that go along with it. Not all
the groups succeeded. They took delight in sharing their experiences and relating them to the theoretical material offered
in the classroom. They did not care about their grades. When
the instructor gave them the task of parceling out the A's, B's
and C's, they did not hesitate at all, and came up with something resembling a normal curve. Their decisions were based
on their perception of the amount of contribution each made

to the completion of the selected group task. The whole business was a pleasant experience for teacher and students alike, and the teacher was convinced that this class not only learned something about small groups, but they learned small groups as well. Most important, they learned something about themselves and their reactions under conditions of interpersonal stress.

Examination of the exercises at the conclusion of the chapters will indicate that we have recommended assignments similar to this throughout. We have also provided assignments that can be administered in a more traditional way. It is, of course, the choice of the students and their instructor. Instructors should be cautioned that private study and classroom-based activities do not generate the empathy and clarification of values that are necessary to real understanding. More to the point would be to suggest that this learning problem be shared with the class. Perhaps they, working in small groups, can come up with some exercises that simulate small group interaction and work in the most traditional of classrooms. If they do, please communicate those ideas to the authors, so they can be shared.

Just before this book went into final production, the instructors were treated to another example of what students working together to learn about groups can do. A group of twelve students decided to simulate a public relations firm and perform a task of publicity on a national scale for less than $50.00. They decided to attempt to get a word into the dictionary. The word, created by one of the professors, was "khulyages." It was a word without definition, for the students declared that the public ought to be offered an opportunity to play some role in defining this new word.

Planning together, they developed a series of staged events: a fund drive, a button sale, a publicity table, a half-time demonstration at the football game, and publicity photos. They also disseminated the results of their activities to the press, and their story has appeared in more than 100 newspapers. Interviews were conducted with ten radio and television stations. To date they have received more than 500 contributions of possible definitions. They had a great deal of fun with the "Khulyages Khonspiracy," and they also learned the power and impact that people working together in groups can have. They did this without injuring anyone; indeed, their project brought smiles to a great many people. Most important, they are now able to converse intelligently about what goes on in a group, what their own capabilities are, and the impact people can have on people. They are now ready to acquire understanding of theory. It is to this kind of learning that this book is addressed.

Interpersonal Dynamics in the Small Group

Among the Primary Uses of the Small Group are
Problem Solving, Policy-Making, and Program Administration!

Uses
of the
Small
Group

In our society, people do quite a bit of "getting together" but it is often not clear to us why we do it. When we are with others it is rarely clear whether we are sharing time and space because of the pleasure we derive from it, because of the way it helps us release tensions, or because there is some task for us to do. The way we behave will differ in each case. For example, we do not behave in a businesslike fashion when we carry on normal socialization. When people stand around with cocktails in their hands and swap stories or discuss children or window drapes, their objective is to derive what pleasure they can from the experience.

Fred Wilson stood at the country club, drink in hand, looking out across the golf course. Andy Stanton asked him who he thought would win the Super-Bowl, and Fred was noncommittal, although he knew perfectly well that the A.F.L. team didn't have a chance. After all, Stanton was the boss. Fred had to play it cool.

Bill Martin was quite definitive in his response. He

declared for the Colts and, despite Stanton's argument about
how the Jets were "up for the game," wouldn't budge an
inch. Fred was bewildered by Bill's truculence. After all,
he worked for the same company. It looked like a real
opportunity.

"I agree with you Andy," Fred declared with vigor. "I
think the Colts have it made." But by the time he made the
comment, the conversation had shifted to a discussion of the
relative merits of Dewar's versus Justerini and Brooks as a
preferred Scotch whiskey. Once again, Fred tried to psych
out which way Andy was going to fall, but he seemed to
be playing the middle road. And once again, Fred was
bewildered when Bill declared that neither suited him, that
he would remain faithful to Haig and Haig, thank you.

When his wife called him away, Fred hadn't said more than
ten words. Bill commented to his wife that he had had a
pleasant conversation with the boss. The boss commented
to his wife that Fred Wilson didn't have much to say for
himself.

The problem in this encounter is that Fred had an agenda
that he was trying to work through. In consciously weighing
his words so that he could support his boss, he found himself
excluded from the conversation, unable to "play" according to
the rules. What he did not recognize is that the social game sets
its own rules. While it is perfectly true that many business
deals are consummated in the locker room of the country club,
their accomplishment is more dependent on the totality of
feeling about the encounter than on conscious analysis of problem solving. Thus, in any transaction, the social requirements
must be observed, for to attempt to play out an agenda without
reference to social imperatives defeats the opportunity to win a
social victory. There is little doubt that the boss would remember Bill Martin as a worthy social companion, an evaluation
that could not help but influence any business transaction between them. On the other hand, Fred Wilson would emerge
with an image of "wishy-washy," hardly calculated to assist
materially his corporate advancement.

In this book, we are not concerned with listing methods of
acquiring conversational skills for all occasions. Rather, we
hope to examine the commonalities and differences of various

social situations and various group "structures" and "processes" including casual conversation, formal problem solving, and formal and informal group therapy. We hope to look at talk—or exchange—in various ways to obtain an understanding of how it can be used to facilitate both individual and group satisfaction and possible improvement. We will avoid, however, presenting lists of behaviors required for "success," for it is our belief that orientation to the group is a personal matter, deeply rooted in personality and not amenable to "skills" type instruction.

We shall begin by examining the various functions that small groups can perform. For the moment, let us not be too precise about defining the word "small." We will temporarily regard a small group as several people, but not so many that it is impossible to know all their names conveniently. Later on we will examine larger and smaller units of interaction and even inquire into an optimum size for effective interaction. The word "interaction," incidentally, merely means sharing meanings with each other face-to-face. And we might remember that usually these meanings are shared through "talk" or conversation. Most of us encounter interaction through social conversation, which is a good type of experience to examine for an opener.

Social Conversation

Social conversation is often loose and apparently aimless. When we talk to our friends and acquaintances in our homes or at the club, we have no formal agenda of topics to deal with. We may flit from topic to topic, so long as the topic is approved by the people discussing it. If the topic is not approved, the subject can change or individuals can move away from the conversation group and go on to find another one. Individuals may have some goal, perhaps to establish an acquaintanceship that might be useful at business or to suggest that a friend return the book he borrowed, but these individual goals need not become the agenda for the entire group. In a sense, each participant can go his own way: the topics employed show considerable anarchy.

To suggest, as we are, that topics may be approved or disapproved by a particular group at a particular time is to suggest that there are *standards* under which the group functions. These standards may be called *norms*. Though the topics under discussion may seem flighty, there are norms operating just the same. It might be more helpful to ask what is not being discussed than what is.

Social conversation is often employed for "testing" purposes, to determine how deep a relationship might become with people that we don't know very well. For that reason, among others, social conversation remains on a relatively superficial level, and avoids controversial topics until it is indicated that the relationship is strong enough to broach them. Even then, solutions need not be found. Any device may be employed to protect the feelings of the participants. Furthermore, formal discussion of business matters in the presence of those not involved is scrupulously avoided.

It is possible for an individual to move out of a social conversation at any time he chooses. Any obligation to the conversation is individually assumed, perhaps in order to earn the title "good conversationalist." In order to avoid participation, it is only necessary to fall silent or make a polite excuse and move to another group.

It is customary in social conversation to keep deep feelings concealed. To expose them might disturb the pleasant aura of the interaction. If someone feels a bit disturbed by what is said, his most frequent recourse is to move away, rather than attack ideas that he finds unpleasant. Most skilled conversationalists, however, attempt to avoid topics that people *could* find threatening.

If the conversation turns into a problem-solving discussion, it will only be after some clear signal has been given by a person with the authority to do so. For example, a group of employees carrying on a conversation at the water cooler during a break in a business meeting can be returned to business merely by the boss saying, "let's go, it's time to finish up."

Problem Solving
At another extreme and quite different from casual social conversation is the problem solving activity of the "small group."

Normally, what is referred to as a small group is two or more persons sitting face-to-face in a defined space dealing with a specific agenda that states some goal like solving a problem, feeling better, or procuring enjoyment. Each participant, normally, has some stake or interest in the process and stands to gain or lose personally by the outcome. Each has the opportunity to develop some sort of relationship with each other person present. Furthermore, every participant has the opportunity to take on a distinct role or roles designed to implement or impede group process. Usually, there is a formal leader of some sort. (Other leaders are also likely to emerge.) While there may be digressions, the agenda of the meeting serves as a formal magnet to keep participants on the subject. Finally, there is some hope held by one or more participants that something worthwhile will come out of the conversation. In short, the small group may be considered as a social or informal transaction *and* a rhetorical interaction—social in that it brings people together to talk with one another; rhetorical in that it is purposive. Social conversation may be considered as interaction in which rhetorical business sometimes gets done, but is incidental and not necessary to social group process. In the problem solving group, interaction supports rhetorical business and is of concern only as it facilitates or impedes the doing of business.

Rhetorical Function of the Small Group

"Rhetoric" refers to purposive communication carried on by a person to alter the beliefs or behaviors of others. Small group discussion is rhetorical on two levels. First, each participant has personal needs and goals congruent with his stake and interest in the problem discussed. He seeks, through his participation, to convince other members of the group that his goals are worth adopting, or he may seek to persuade himself that his personal goals are compatible with those of the group. On the second level, once a group has agreed on goals and methods of achieving them, it becomes a rhetorical organization concerned with gaining sufficient acceptance from relevant authorities that the program or plan can be put in operation.

In order to meet the rhetorical requirements of small group discussion, participants must submit to a modicum of organization, curb their individual tendencies to digress or fight, and engage in face-to-face interaction with others to achieve both personal and group goals.   Participation in any kind of small group discussion, of course, calls for some engagement in group interaction for the satisfaction of personal goals, for it is difficult to conceive of a group of humans coming together without getting some satisfaction out of it.   It is neither possible nor desirable to force a small group to start and remain on a basis of "strictly business."   There must be ample opportunity given for the members to test each other out, to estimate reactions, and to familiarize themselves with the communication styles of the other people.   In this sense, informal, nonpurposive conversation becomes part of all small group discussion.

The following three conversations will illustrate the crude differences in interpersonal interaction in the group.

Situation One: informal, nonpurposive conversation:

"Hi!"

"How have you been?"

"What did you think of that movie the other night?"

"Great! I don't care if Bardot is thirty-three. She still turns me on. Did you get your car fixed the other day?"

"I guess so. But I'm so totally unmechanical I couldn't tell if it was fixed or not."

. . .

Situation Two: problem-solving conversation:

"The next item on the agenda is the question of expenditure of funds for new office furniture. Mr. Abrams, could you give us the budget picture?"

(Budget presented.)

"It is clear we have the funds to spend. But some items have been more expensive than we had planned. Those funds allocated to new furniture could be reallocated this year. What do you think, Charlie?"

"Frankly, I'd like my program on ——— expanded a lot

more than I'd like a new chair to sit in. I'd vote for the
reallocation of funds."
  "Irv. How do you feel?"

. . .

Situation Three: problem solving interspersed with interaction language:

  "Let's not kid ourselves, we've got a lot to do today. Let's
see, where shall we start? . . ."
  "Speaking of kidding, I remember a story . . ."
  (Tells story.)
  "Back to business. How's that new promotional program
coming?"
  "It's going great. We just spent our first hundred
thousand. The steam roller is underway . . ."
  "You're going to squash 'em I bet."
  (Laughter.)
  ". . . I think in about two weeks we'll have all the first
mailings finished."

. . .

Sometimes it is hard to distinguish purposeful talk from
social-emotional discourse. In certain cases, the sensitivities of
the issues or of the people involved make it necessary to make
decisions in semiformal or informal surroundings. Many business luncheons exemplify this kind of dual activity.
Consultations, for example, at United Nations headquarters are
often carried on over the dinner table. The combination of
purely social-emotional functions with a formal business agenda
provides more options to the participants. If the business
seems to be getting sticky, it is possible to reduce interpersonal
tensions by paying attention to social interaction, returning to
business when the time seems right. Social-emotional ex-
changes permit the participants to test the willingness of the
others to interact equitably. In any case, failures at a luncheon
need carry no stigma since no one actually expects great decisions to result. Such situations afford each participant the
opportunity to do "business," accomplish a task, as he can—
without losing face. This, in turn, permits subsequent interac-

tion, formal or informal, to occur when necessary. Diplomats recognize that the formalization of an agenda carries with it the tacit responsibility of producing a solution.

This kind of dual activity has become more and more frequent in business. The fluidity of the combination, apparently, permits a wider range of interaction and solution capability. Furthermore, it is often necessary to know more about the people with whom you must work than can be discovered over the conference table. The social capability is extended even in formal discussions by making refreshments available and by taking frequent breaks. It is rather difficult to do battle with a man with whom you have had coffee and certainly more difficult to fight in comfortable surroundings.

In spite of the moderately blurred context of much discussion, however, small group discussion can be identified by its purposiveness either expressed or implied. A social conversation may develop purpose for one or more of the people involved, but the main reason for informal interaction is the pleasure of spending time together. When there is an expressed purpose for people coming together, results are expected. When problems are solved during a social conversation, it is an increment. It is most distressing to expect goodwill and social camaraderie from purposive group discussion to the point where problem solving is sacrificed to the pursuit of friendship.

How Groups Come Together

Small groups form for many purposes:

1. *People who feel a common concern about a problem use groups to devise a solution for or take some action about that problem.* Civic groups responding to needs in the community fall into this category. A group of parents who come together to make rules for their children, or a group of volunteers who gather to support a candidate, illustrates this use of the small group.

Our society has witnessed the rise of voluntary action groups: the activities of college students on behalf of Senator Eugene McCarthy in the 1968 primary elections were not centrally coordinated and represented interested individuals planning to-

gether how best to mobilize their resources, citizens committees
have banded together in various communities to control the
influx of pornography into their area, and a variety of neighborhood pressure groups have sprung up in our central cities to
barrage governmental bodies with proposals for action.

2. *Groups are used to bring together people of various professional capabilities to investigate a problem and propose solutions to some body or person with the power to implement
them.* The use of select committees has been on the increase.
Various governmental subdivisions have discovered that their
own view of problems is clouded by their regular work. To
obtain a more objective view they have adopted the practice of
calling in panels of experts to focus study on specific problems
and to propose lines of policy or methods to resolve them. One
such committee was appointed by the legislature of the state of
Pennsylvania to examine the problem of competition between
community colleges and the branches of larger universities.
They were charged to make an independent study of the problem and they produced a variety of proposals. The regular
units of government were then responsible for deciding on what
specific actions to take.

Business and industries also utilize such small groups.
Management consultant teams are now a feature of industrial
operation and often businesses will commission independent
studies of problems with which they are faced.

3. *Regularly designated legislative and decision-making
groups deal with public issues.* The committee system is one of
the most frequent uses of the small group. Most decision-making bodies recognize that the parliamentary process is only
useful when there are clear-cut alternatives to be examined and
debated. The alternatives have to come from somewhere. For
this reason, committees are established and either regular or
special problems are assigned to them. Sometimes the committees are charged with the responsibility of investigating a problem and making recommendations about how to deal with it,
and sometimes they are asked to explore broad areas to isolate
problems for future investigation.

Boards of directors also function as small groups in their
decision-making processes. The establishment of lines of policy

by a board of directors functioning as an executive and a legislative body simultaneously call upon the members to function in a small group format.

4. *Groups are used by established organizations, companies, schools, governmental units, and so forth, to deal with problems as they arise on a regular basis.* Most organizations have groups of experts established to handle problems as they come up. Sometimes these groups can anticipate their work, as, for example, those charged with the responsibility of developing a merchandising campaign for each season. Sometimes the groups function as trouble shooters to handle customer or citizen complaints. Regardless of the type of problem handed them, their organization procedures give them facility to function as problem-solving groups, sometimes with executive ability. In this case, they would not only develop solutions to the problems but would implement them as well, and would face the added responsibility of preparing an implementation plan.

5. *Groups may also be used to prepare implementation plans for previously designated programs or policies.* The problem of executive administration is falling more and more into the hands of groups of administrators. Most government and industrial problems are far too complex to be handled by only one person. Consequently, a number of schemes have been devised to bring together administrators for the purposes of coordination of activities and the development of optimal implementation plans.

Innovations like PERT (Program Evaluation and Review Technique), which was developed by the federal government, have permeated industry, and most executives are now trained in techniques for bringing together experts to examine an implementation procedure and to anticipate problems and obviate them.

The Group as a Teaching Strategy

The small group can also be used to support educational goals. When used in this context, the kind of output expected is different than in problem-solving discussion. Instead of programs or solutions, appreciation and understanding are sought. Often in teaching small group behavior in the classroom, students are asked to attach themselves to problems like "American foreign policy" or the solving of some social issue like "open housing." Although the students generate statements of "solutions" to the problems, these cannot be considered relevant solutions since the students have neither stake nor authority for the solution of the problem. The students have gone through an academic exercise which, if properly done, helps them to examine their own behavior in a simulated problem-solving situation. They may also gain deeper understanding of the problem area. But they do not get a real sense of the pressures involved in small group decision making since their solution is binding on no one and they can neither gain nor lose as a result.

If performance in a classroom discussion is being graded, students focus more on individual behavior and personal goals. That is, they seek to discover what behavior the teacher evaluates highly so that they can behave that way in order to influence the grade. What is commonly called "discussion" in the classroom is not discussion in the sense of problem solving or decision making. It might better be termed interchange of ideas. For example, in dealing with a work of literature various members of the class might talk about the impressions that a poem or an essay made on them. Or they might say words about what they think the author was trying to express in a written work. Even if a group of such discussants agrees on a meaning or an interpretation, this does not represent output, for there is no action to be taken. The problem the group is really attacking is the sharing of ideas and the heightening of perceptions, both of which are individual matters. The group, as a group, might make recommendations to other readers or learners, but output would be represented by a planned program to get the book widely read.

It would be useful to novices at the group discussion process if they could learn early the distinction between sharing of ideas in a group and focused problem solving. A relevant approach to the teaching of problem-solving discussion in the classroom, for example, would necessarily involve permitting the students to deal with questions about how the class should be conducted, what performances should be, and how they should be evaluated and graded. They might even be given the problem of determining what will happen in the classroom on each day. This sort of discussion would give each participant a personal stake and would accurately simulate the small group discussion process.   The group would, at least part of the time, be concerned with generating output on matters that affected them.

The small group process is an effective device to simulate interest and motivate unsupervised work in any classroom.   In this context, it bridges the gap between social conversation and group problem solving.   But only actual grappling with problem issues that affect the individual will provide the real sensation of involvement in group problem solving.

The Small Group in Therapy

Small groups are also used in a number of therapeutic contexts. Of late there has been a tendency to utilize techniques applicable to groups to "improve" the functioning of problem-solving groups.   A number of authorities have devoted their attention to how the problem-solving group could be used for therapeutic effect on the participants.   It is important to understand that participation in problem-solving discussion may result in positive emotional feeling, provided the group has achieved a consensus and has generated a successful solution to the problem. It may also result in considerable frustration when agreement cannot be reached or when the solution that emerges is clearly ineffective.   The emotional state of the participant is a function of and a result of problem solving, but it is not the end goal of problem solving.   As a matter of fact, it would be reasonable to assume that an aura of goodwill should be a desirable by-product but it is unreasonable to sacrifice the quality of problem solving to achieve it.   The goals of therapeutic discussion are sufficiently different, however, from those of problem solving to preclude the possibility of blending them.

The goals of therapeutic discussion are primarily personal. While "outcomes" are desired, they are measured in the improvement of the single individual rather than by the effectiveness of the whole group at the performance of some task. Often, in therapeutic discussion, tasks are employed to enable the personality to improve.   The welfare of the individual is the

main goal, however, and the task is incidental, while in problem-solving discussion, the emphasis must continually be on
group action. The individual role is subordinated to the group
welfare, and success is measured in terms of group activity.

Furthermore, therapeutic discussion seeks some behaviors
that would be disruptive if they occurred in problem solving.
The therapist conducting the sessions, for example, may be
seeking personal exposure, in other words, to have the individual lay open some facet of his personality previously concealed
so that in subsequent private therapy sessions the therapist can
have more information on which to base his activities. Such
personal exposures could be quite embarrassing were they to
happen in normal problem solving, or, if the exposures were
accompanied by cathartic outbursts, they could well stimulate
personality clashes which would prevent the group from functioning. The therapist can, of course, shift his personnel when
it is clear that they can no longer work together, but business
establishments do not have this facility of movement.

In addition, group therapy sessions often seek to stimulate
the patients to work through a transference process. The affective relationships which exist between participants are very
important in the treatment of the illness. This is an attenuated
process and the dependencies and hostilities that feature shifts
of transference must be dealt with by a trained professional.
The normal problem-solving group has neither the time nor the
professional skill to deal with them, and furthermore, there is no
reason to believe that the output of the group would be materially affected by changes in affinity patterns that are quite as
drastic as those that occur in therapy groups. Of course, the
attitudes that members of groups have toward each other are
important, and if there is too much hostility the progress of the
group can be impeded. On the other hand, if the hostilities are
minor, it would be specious to devote much time to working out
the problems.

Another feature of the behavior of individuals in the therapeutic group is the catharsis. Therapists often seek strong,
sometimes violent, outbursts on the part of their patients.
These may provide emotional releases and may reveal information to the therapists, but they are emotionally draining for all.

There is no reasonable purpose that could be served by stimulating such action in the normal problem-solving group.

The therapeutic group is also used to assist patients to understand that they share common problems, to achieve some insight into their own problems, and to develop some techniques in dealing with them. Normal problem-solving groups may be confronted with vaguely similar kinds of individual problems. It may be necessary to take some time to analyze personal problems that impede the group, to achieve some insight into defective problem solving, or to work out methods to improve the process. Though similar, however, it is not at all clear that utilizing techniques that are clearly therapeutic would result in an improvement of the problem-solving process. If commonalities are to be explored and utilized, they should be superficial. Therapy simply should not be practiced by anyone without credentials, and hopefully, successful experience.

There are, however, a number of authorities that regard the small group as a method by which normal people can work out their personal problems. Success in group participation or participation in a successful group might provide reward and ego prop for the person who has a low regard for his personal capability. But to structure the group in such a way that a timid individual was rewarded by having his ideas accepted would subvert the goals of group problem solving. Such manipulations, consequently, cannot be considered legitimate in problem solving.

Exactly as it is possible within the framework of therapeutic treatment to develop discussions that simulate problem solving but which are really devoted to personal improvement of the participants, so is it possible to develop therapeutic activities within the framework of a problem-solving discussion. The problem-solving context represents a manipulation and there should be no illusion about the therapeutic capability of the group. To alter a normal problem-solving group so that it can deal with personal problems disrupts problem-solving capability. Yet, it is often necessary to deal with emotional problems of people in problem-centered groups.

In any face-to-face discussion, confrontation with the ideas of others may induce a highly emotional state, which, if uncontrolled, may result in an explosion in the group. Few groups that deal with real and pressing problems avoid going through some rather stormy periods in which the participants face each other down, confront each other with considerable hostility, argue, battle, call names, and in other ways express their strong feelings. This is a necessary concomitant of face-to-face interaction, particularly if participants have some stake in the outcome. In social conversation, when frustration levels become too high it is possible to move away and seek another partner. But in the problem-solving group it is necessary to remain in face-to-face contact. Theoretically, the mores of the group will seek to prevent such conflict or at least to end it quickly. It is neither socially nor practically desirable to have a great number of personal explosions or catharses. Among the emotionally disturbed, however, there are a number of people who bottle their emotions tightly in themselves. The first requisite of therapy is to release this internal tension, and it has been discovered that seating people face-to-face, ostensibly to deal with common problems, often stimulates such cathartic reactions. Under therapeutic conditions, once the outburst has taken place, the resources of the group can be mobilized to treat it. A normal problem-solving group, however, has no such facility for treatment, nor can it disband to escape the tension for this would mean failure at the task.

The main question we must deal with here is how to deal with the emotional context of small group discussion. Should potential emotional disturbances be prevented? Can they? When and if they arise, should they be dealt with directly as a main item of business or should they be evaded or glossed over? Perhaps this question may be resolved by examination of two possible approaches, sensitivity training and systems analysis.

The diagnosis and treatment of emotional illness is very largely bound up with understanding human speech patterns. Many patients may develop skill and competency in their psychiatrists' offices. However, they find it harder to maintain inhibitory control when confronted with less familiar people. For this reason many psychiatrists are not willing to trust judgments derived from office interviews and they will place patients face-to-face in a group and observe their behavior under more natural circumstances. The topic of discussion is irrelevant. The small group is employed as a device to enable the psychiatrist to observe the differences in communication behavior in a small group as opposed to office behavior. The relatively unpredictable nature of small group activity will often trigger the type of behavior about which the patient is concerned and will give the psychiatrist the opportunity to see it in action in a relatively real context. The problem being discussed is likely to be spurious. The face-to-face interaction is real. It is the response to face-to-face interaction that the psychiatrist wishes to examine.

One of the requirements of rehabilitating the emotionally disturbed is to retrain them in the use of language so that their communication behavior returns to the limits acceptable to society. For this reason mental patients are often assigned small group activities so that they may practice acceptable communication styles. These kinds of activities usually center around simple tasks and minimal problems, though as therapy proceeds the participants may be assigned legitimate problems to discuss. One technique, for example, calls upon a group of patients to plan an evening's activity or a day's outing outside the institution and then confronts them with the responsibility not only of implementing their plan but of taking the consequences of their planning. In this case, group problem solving is used to readjust the behavior of the individual away from egocentric needs and wants, directing it once again toward group-centered behavior. Apparently it is assumed that the normal, adjusted person is capable of working with others in groups. At this point in therapy, there is considerable concern about what happens within the group, but even more concern about how well the group accomplishes its task. Presumably, if it gets the job done with minimum confusion, it could be inferred that each of the participants had made a reasonable adjustment at least to the point where he no longer disrupted group activity, and undoubtedly even made some contribution to the quality of the solution. The question raised here is: can this procedure be reversed? If problem solving can be used as a vehicle for ameliorating individual behavior, will concentration on improving individual behavior result in more effective problem solving?   Given a small problem-solving group with some personality clashes between some unhappy people, would it materially assist the problem-solving process to take time out for the rehabilitation of the individuals who seem to be disrupting the group process?   Furthermore, if such personality disturbances could be prevented by a program of training, would it not be useful to take the time and make the effort to obtain the training, particularly with a group of people who work together regularly and for whom, as a consequence, interpersonal combat would be quite destructive?

Sensitivity Training

The foregoing seem to be the assumptions of sensitivity training. The designation sensitivity training or "T-grouping" has been applied to a system of techniques and strategies that purport to make individuals more understanding of their own needs and wants, adequacies and inadequacies, and to improve their understanding of such matters in others.   Sensitivity training utilizes both stylized and natural events to bring people into "confrontation" with each other and with themselves.   A good deal of feedback and commentary about behavior is employed so that participants are confronted with a constant stream of information about their own behavior.   The assumption is that becoming aware of how others perceive them will enable them to control those behaviors which tend to antagonize and alienate, thus permitting the development of more cooperative and, therefore, more desirable behaviors.   There has been a reasonable body of evidence arrayed to indicate that there is an immediate gain in positive personal behavior from this kind of training, but not much to indicate a great deal of carry-over from it into the normal group life of those who participate.   In fact, it sometimes appears that those people most captivated by sensitivity training are those who are moderately disturbed themselves and are seeking some kind of personal therapy.

This does not mean that it is unwise to seek reflections of self from others in order to gain better understanding, but merely that too large a dose of such exposure may be more disruptive than it is helpful.   There are some things about every man that are better not made known even to the self and particularly not to others. Furthermore, satisfactory participation in the world of interaction demands a fairly strong image of self. Feeding in of much negative data may make the individual more sensitive to the needs of others, but it also may render him unfit to participate or compete, perhaps denying him the opportunity to earn his livelihood, or to make the contribution he is capable of making to his personal growth, his family, and his community. It is certainly clear that sensitivity techniques should not be used without the presence of an experienced and highly skilled trainer who understands the wide range of behavior that might be evoked by the use of sensitivity techniques. The use of these techniques in the hands of amateurs or even semiprofessionals may result in disruptive and unpleasant behavior on the part of the participants and make no real contribution toward learning or progressive problem solving. There is a vast literature on sensitivity training that should be examined with care before any personal commitment is made to the activity. The question that must be asked about sensitivity training is: will it make a real contribution in a given context? That is, if applied to a group of organization executives, will they be able to live with each other and work together after the training is over? Will the new awareness of adequacies and inadequacies help the problem-solving capability of the group? Will it provide both personal benefit and benefit to the organization? Finally, it might well be asked whether the sensitivity training is being introduced to provide variety and excitement for the individual introducing it. It is entirely possible that it is suggested because of a kind of voyeur's interest in the personal lives and affairs of the participants. It is obvious that mere participation in problem-solving discussion provides much information about the capabilities of individual members of the group. By observing and evaluating individual behavior as it interferes with or fosters group progress and output, remedies can be found for destructive interpersonal behaviors as well as defective group procedure. It is not necessary for small group experts to become quasi-therapists in order to do an effective job of leading, participating, and evaluating the problem-solving group. While this is a strong and direct statement that appears opposed to sensitivity training, the authors of this book are not implacably hostile to it.   The best recommendation seems to be that sensitivity training should be introduced to meet a specific need within the group if it has been determined by group decision that there is reason to believe that it is the most effective way of meeting the need.   If individuals wish to take training on their own for their own personal reasons, this, of course, is a matter of personal choice.

An Alternative to Sensitivity Training

Another method of improving group behavior is concentration on the specific techniques of group procedure, attempting to stylize agenda items so that the group is compelled to concentrate on systems rather than on personal wants.   The American Public Health Association has developed a format for group behavior that embodies PERT programming, which it has found quite useful when applied to small agency problem solving. The following chart is an adaptation of this system developed by James Bemis, Eugene Erickson, and Gerald Phillips and published in the American Public Health Association Monograph, *Health Program Implementation Through PERT* (San Francisco, 1966).

The advantage to be gained by adherence to a specific agenda is the tendency of the system to become a foil for the antagonisms of the participants.   It is somewhat less harmful, if there are hostilities latent in particular members, to have the hostilities reflected against the requirements of a system rather than against other people.   A system can be modified without injury to personality, and usually with very little disruption to the group.   A tight system can be made looser without sacrificing the benefits of the system.

Those who have worked with this method have found it quite useful in minimizing interpersonal antagonisms of the sort that may evoke calls for sensitivity training were they allowed to materialize in the group.   It is important that participants in small group problem solving recognize that the main purpose of their activity is the development of solutions to problems. Personal dilemmas may need treatment, but it should not be

Problem-Solving Technique Flow Chart

I Specification of the Problem
II Fact-Finding
   A. Factual Statement of Problem
   B. Factual Analysis of Causes
III Goals and Criteria for Solutions
IV Evaluation of Solutions
V Implementation

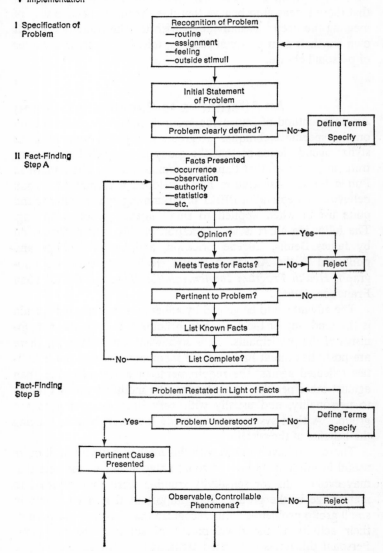

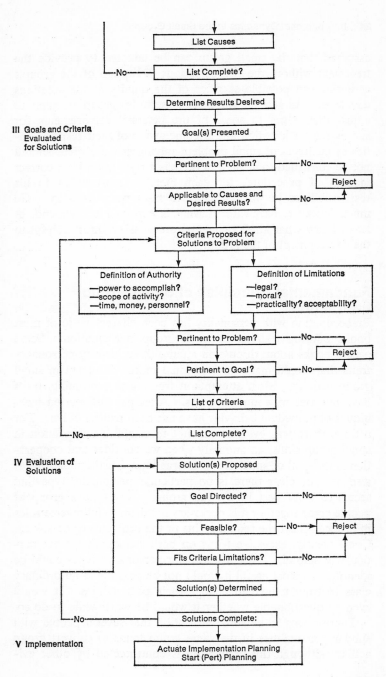

III Goals and Criteria
Evaluated
for Solutions

List Causes

List Complete? —No

Determine Results Desired

Goal(s) Presented

Pertinent to Problem? —No→ Reject

Applicable to Causes and
Desired Results? —No

Criteria Proposed for
Solutions to Problem

Definition of Authority
—power to accomplish?
—scope of activity?
—time, money, personnel?

Definition of Limitations
—legal?
—moral?
—practicality? acceptability?

Pertinent to Problem? —No→ Reject

Pertinent to Goal? —No

List of Criteria

List Complete? —No

IV Evaluation of
Solutions

Solution(s) Proposed

Goal Directed? —No

Feasible? —No→ Reject

Fits Criteria Limitations? —No

Solution(s) Determined

Solutions Complete: —No

V Implementation

Actuate Implementation Planning
Start (Pert) Planning

23

assumed that the small group can be adapted to provide the treatment without the risk of serious disruption of the group's activities and possible sacrifice of the quality of the solutions developed. In general, it might be useful for group members to adjust themselves to some of the personal requirements for successful participation and become aware of their responsibilities as members of small problem-solving groups. This should not be construed to mean that there is a right attitude or correct manner of procedure, for each member must adapt to his responsibilities in ways suitable to his own personality. He must, however, be aware of what is expected of him and, at least, know what kinds of mental attitudes are most helpful to the development of the group.

Fundamental Principles of Small Group Interaction

Preoccupation with personality has been characteristic of most books offering training in small group participation. Some earlier books about discussion attempted to identify personality traits that would make an individual more competent in small group activity. Most attempts at training in personality traits have not met with much success. Attempts to focus on techniques of individual behavior have not been fruitful either. For a time, there was even an attempt to establish competition in small group skills, an anomaly when we consider that cooperation is the goal of small group interaction. Furthermore, it has also become clear there is no particular personality type that seems to work best in a small group. Any time a group of people come together it is necessary for them to fill diverse roles in order to meet the requirements of the problems to be solved. Consequently, excessive focus on basic personality is not particularly helpful. Even if particular personality types could be identified as most useful it would not be possible in an ordinary class to train people to change their personalities. It would even be questionable whether it would be worthwhile to do so.

There seems to be some indication that several people with similar personalities in the same group tends to subvert group activity although this contention is contradicted by other evidence. For example, it appears that when people of high intelligence and strong personality and motivation are put together in a small group there is considerable dissension and conflict and group output is materially weakened. On the other hand, putting relatively average people in small groups appears to improve individual output materially. Perhaps the best policy to follow, if one even seeks a policy, is to allow small groups to develop as they may and not pay particular attention to either personality traits or assessments of capability. The nature of the problem as it is perceived by the participants and the extent to which they as individuals feel involved in the solving of it, as well as their affiliation with the group goal, are the most important considerations in determining the role that individuals will play in improving group output.

While we cannot identify personality traits that insure satisfactory outcome there appear to be certain states of mind that seem to enhance small group interaction. We are not asserting that adoption of these attitudes and behaviors will guarantee satisfactory outcomes. We are stipulating that these attitudes and behaviors usually make it more possible for satisfactory outcomes to emerge. Once again it must be repeated that the quality of the output of a discussion depends on the extent to which the problem dealt with is solvable, as well as on the amount of personal involvement that participants have with it. Given a solvable problem to which the individuals in the discussion are reasonably strongly committed, they may assist themselves in their decision making by adopting four premises about their personal and group activity.

1. *It is useful to be able to suspend verbalizing judgments about the contributions of others.* It is virtually impossible to avoid making some kind of evaluation of the remarks another person makes. It is not necessary to the progress of the group, however, to verbalize these evaluations. It does not matter whether the remarks were affirmative and supportive or hostile and destructive. The group proceeds best when the ideas of the greater number of people can be heard and enough can be said so that areas of agreement and disagreement can be identified with precision. Evaluative comments about the quality of a man's speaking or skill at research are not material or relevant

to the problem-solving process. If participants can successfully withhold them, then extraneous threats need not materialize in the group. Regardless of how strongly you might feel about a person and his ideas, any expression of these ideas carries with it the danger of being interpreted as a personal attack. If it is desirable to avoid personal conflict and clashes of personality and to restrain conflict in the group to problem issues, then comments directed to personal behavior must be curbed. The very natural and very human desire to respond quickly and immediately to remarks as they are made can be held in check. We can all train ourselves to hold back our evaluations. Many who are successful in small group activities have already learned that to the extent they can suppress their desire to evaluate and criticize they improve their chances of bringing about a desirable result within the group.

2. *It cannot be assumed in any case that an individual comes into the group without personal motivation.* People come into groups as people. They have their own commitments to greater or lesser degrees. In real problem-solving situations, people stand to gain or lose depending on the way the problem is solved. In addition, they carry with them into the group all of their beliefs, biases, and personal commitments, and these cannot be cast off in favor of total commitment to the group goal. Therefore it should be expected that some statements made by participants will appear to be biased or selfish. Accusations of personal interest are not at all helpful, for personal interests will and must be present. Consensus is indeed a process of reconciling personal interests. No one could reasonably ask participants in a problem-solving discussion to abandon totally their personal goals but it is reasonable to require that they be suppressed, at least temporarily, so that the widest possible range of commitment can be revealed before attempts at resolution are made. Using strategies designed to implement personal goals too early in discussion can often lead to digression or may resolve the group into a polarized conflict and thus become a debate. Once the group has polarized it has been blocked from examining the widest possible range of problem-solving potentials. The group is restricted to reconciling hostile factions. Once a decision is made on one of two alternatives, the

minority may be implacably hostile in subsequent problem solving.

Consequently, one way to evaluate potential in a small group would be to examine the extent to which participants are willing to withhold expression of personal goals and, better yet, be willing to avoid conflict about those goals, at least until it is clear that the decision the group is about to make puts them in jeopardy. There is no question about a man's right to fight for what he believes in and holds dear, but to start out by assuming that the group solution would necessarily jeopardize personal goals is begging the question. It leads to excessive defensiveness, which, in turn, leads to head-on collisions between group members.

3. *Sitting and talking is often boring.* There are posterior pains and internal anguish felt by those who attend committee meetings regularly. It is a strain on both body and mind to sit and listen to droning conversation for hours and hours. Even the most fascinating problems with which we are vitally concerned can become dull. When this happens we may tend to jump at the wrong solutions just to get the meeting over. A great many participants tend to leap rapidly for a solution, remembering, perhaps, some of the discomfort they felt the last time they worked with a group and hoping to avoid some of the discomfort by getting to the point quickly.

But there is no such thing as a group memory or a group wisdom that can be transmitted in time from one group to another. The present group is not the same as the past group and it is perhaps necessary that the present group make all the mistakes the past group made. What one learns about discussion from Group A is probably applicable to Group B, but only after the fact. Different participants must follow the same blind alleys, the same false leads. They must work through the same red herrings and unravel the same red tape that was done in the group before. Consequently, willingness to devote sufficient time to the group solution can materially enhance group output. Most often, coming to agreement swiftly indicates that the group is approaching its task uncritically or perhaps that the group is afraid to face up to the basic issues in the problem. Issues must be clarified before they can be delt with. Frequently the deeper and more relevant issues do not emerge until the superficial and irrelevant have been thoroughly sorted out.

Impatience and the desire for speed can be curbed largely by taking "deep breaths" throughout the discussion or by cultivating the art of doodling. Periodic coke or coffee breaks are helpful. The wise discussion leader encourages this type of diversion by permitting periodic breaks and giving the participants time for sufficient social interaction to break the tension of problem solving. While the group must take responsibility for seeing to it that sufficient time is spent on the problem, it is impossible to do it without providing some recreation. Perhaps this is why so many business conferences are combined with dinner. A general caution might be offered to the civic-minded student that participation in community-oriented activities requires considerable expenditure of time. Personal discomfort that results from spending this time is not a legitimate excuse for avoiding participation, but it should be recognized as a hazard, and some effort should be made to cultivate patience, or at least to anticipate frustration.

4. *There is a tendency to attempt to substitute personal satisfaction for solid solutions.* Many feel that, somehow, participation in a small group will confer benefit on them in the form of personal well-being or euphoria or that participation will have some sort of salubrious effect upon personality. "Happiness" is really not a relevant goal in small group problem solving; satisfaction, however, might be a justifiable goal for the individual personality concerned, but satisfaction can only be obtained after a solution to a problem has been put in operation and tested for efficacy against the problem.

For example, certain student governments may be examined. There is constant frustration in student government because committees tend to work on excessively broad problem areas and then do not allow sufficient time to work through them. One such committee recently became concerned about the availability and price of textbooks. They found seven local bookstores catering to student and faculty needs in textbook supplies. These books were all sold at retail price. A very elaborate apparatus was maintained for the purchase and resale of used textbooks and special order services were maintained to provide for special needs of faculty members and students in more esoteric classes. A student government committee jumped immediately to the conclusion that a college bookstore on campus would solve all the problems and proceeded to develop a plan and a budget so that such a store could be set up. They were quite proud of themselves for doing such a complete job and particularly proud of the fact that they had taken the time and the trouble to develop such a complicated budget. Unfortunately, however, when it came time to present their plans to the faculty group with the power to deal with such matters they were unable to answer basic questions like, "What was the policy on other campuses and how well did it work?" They could not answer simple and fundamental questions about the resale price of textbooks and amounts paid for used books. The committee did not take the time to explore the essential facts of the case and consequently all of their elaborate budget planning was wasted since the faculty committee was not ready to recommend a new bookstore without some significant presentation of need. The zest for achieving the satisfaction of a solution pushed the group into jumping to conclusions and avoiding the more difficult aspects of their problem.

It is difficult for small groups to foresee the rhetorical requirements of problem solving but time taken to explore the relevant facts of a situation will at least arm the group with some of the data needed to defend their solution. In most places, for example, groups that plan the program do not have responsibility for administering it. Some executive with the power to make decisions must be convinced of the necessity and practicality of the proposed program. Any group that has taken adequate time for investigation and planning should be capable of defending their solution before the decision maker.

Groups tend to avoid detailed program planning. An example is the committee that decided it would be culturally enriching to have a certain musical group appear on campus. They scheduled the group and signed the contract. But they did not take the time to see if facilities would be available in which the group could perform. The day of the concert arrived and there was still no hall for the concert. While this is a flagrant example, other such examples of malfeasance are familiar to all of us.

It does not require much stretch of the imagination to determine what goes on in a group when the time comes to plan the details of a program. By the time a group has gone through the process of investigation and has finally hammered some kind of proposal together, they are so fatigued that they are normally not able to face the complicated steps of program planning. It is at this point that a systemized and rigid agenda is most useful, for it will indicate that the time for satisfaction is not at hand, there is still work to do. While this may generate some frustration, it materializes better solutions and thus is an imperative in the problem-solving process.

It is unfortunate that some groups are not aware of what they are after until they have accepted a solution. Often, when they have arrived at their solution it is not at all clear that they had solved the problem they set out to solve. Group members often become startled by the implications of their original commitments. For example, a self-organized committee of parents was concerned about "bullying" and "violence" that took place as children went to and from school. In an effort to "save their children" they organized themselves into a pressure group and made proposals to the school board for discipline and protection in the school district. Once they got into the problem, they discovered they were dealing with questions and issues that transcended their neighborhood and exceeded their personal knowledge and commitment. Eventually they arrived at a proposal which said simply that the school board should safeguard their children on the way to and from school. Such a proposal is not a solution at all. It is a method of getting the group "off the hook." Early in a discussion it is necessary for the members of a group to ask themselves what they are about and what they would like to see as the end product of their deliberations. They must determine whether their final solution will appear in the form of a recommendation to a decision-making body, in which case they must assume the responsibility of defending that decision, or whether their final outcome will be a planned program in which they will play some administrative role. Determining the nature of the output may spare them much unnecessary wandering and assure them that their efforts will be devoted to a legitimate end.

Thus, in summary, while it is impossible to train people to change their personality in order to become effective participants in small group activity, it is not impossible to inculcate in group members some basic attitudes that will improve both their personal contribution and the operation of the whole group. Suspending judgments, suppressing personal goals, taking sufficient time, and understanding the requirements of the group process might well be the responsibility of a good group leader. But high quality leadership cannot always be counted on, and, therefore, these matters are rightfully the business of all members.

Group members cannot afford to forget that, as they participate in a small group, they engage in a number of acts of individual and collective persuasion. Each verbal contribution made to a group lies in a persuasive context. To the extent that the contribution is logically based, interacts with the emotional predilections of the listeners, and comes from a person regarded as reliable and coherent, it will make its impact. Often skilled members find themselves exerting an inordinate influence as they develop the image of cogent participator. Others may have no impact at all because their remarks reveal excessive personal concern and are made without skill or concern for the sensitivities of the listeners. In analyzing effectiveness within a group, skill at oral communication must be taken into account, even though the pattern of group talk appears to be impersonal and social. The criteria normally applied to speaking are still relevant and germane.

Concern must be shown for the capability of the listener to understand, as well as for his personal biases and concerns. Remarks must be organized sufficiently to make sense, and be uttered in a voice loud enough to be heard, yet soft enough to remain conversational. Controversial points should be supported with proof. Statements should be inserted to catch and sustain attention. The main difference is that while the response to talk on the public platform is usually applause, in the small group it is an oral response from another member. Skill at speaking in the small group can be achieved by studying the kinds of remarks offered in rejoinder, as well as by obtaining a general understanding of the requirements of speaking well to an audience.

Through skilled participation in a small group, an individual can achieve a kind of status that lends credence to his remarks. Ineptitude makes his statements suspect by other members. It will be noted later on in this book that clearly established hierarchies of influence develop in groups. These are based on the experience that the group has with each individual as well as the personal reputation he carries into the group with him from the outside. While some pedagogical approaches attempt to differentiate small group communication from more formal types of oral communication, it is necessary for the participant to understand that his remarks are worthless unless they are accepted by other members of the group. Consequently, he is as much engaged in an act of rhetoric when he speaks to peers in a small group as if he stood on a platform in front of an audience of thousands. Recognition of this simple fact will help the participant to understand the reasons for his successes and failures in his interaction with others. Participation in small group activities is not a simple matter of saying words or enunciating facts. It is a pervasive exercise conducted in a microcosm of interaction, demanding from each participant his best qualities as a public persuader. Intelligent and coherent oral communication is important for personal success in the group and for the success of the whole group. A number of studies show that business executives and government leaders tend to evaluate the executive potential of their employees largely on a basis of speech skills. Since the bulk of interaction in business is done through small groups, it is the quality of this participation as perceived by executives that determines a man's advancement in the company. Success, in general, in the small group demands the same skills as success in life. A knowledge of how people behave, how a society behaves, and how to exert influence on both individuals and society are the basic tools of small group interaction and of survival in a complex world.

What the Individual Brings to the Group

Before we carry these general discussions of the small group
further, it will be well to introduce some knowledge that is
available on what an individual confronts when he joins a
group.

All of us are involved as new members of a group at one time
or another. In addition, as old members of established groups
we occasionally observe new members being admitted to the
group.

What is observed in these situations is that the larger the
proportion of new members introduced into a group at a single
time, the greater will be their problem of assimilation, that is,
the greater will be their disruption of the ongoing group process.
What seems to happen is that the established relations tend to
govern the new relations. Let us say that Jack and Jim have
been with the group long enough to know most of each others'
biases. They have established a *modus operandi* and accept
each others' positions on matters that concern the group actions.
If a new member enters the group and, for whatever reason,
gets along badly with Jack, Jim is more likely to relate to the
new member with the same sentiments as will Jack.

Now, of course, as the number of new members increases
Jack and Jim must have an increasing number of relationships,
and therefore it will be more difficult for them to use their old
relationship as a bond controlling the new relationships.

It should be remembered that relationships are based upon a
past history of experiences. These experiences often establish
unspoken but nevertheless real relationships among the actors.
Another dimension of the new member's reaction to these relationships is that he feels inferior. It is understandable that he
does not share all of the experiences and understandings that
have built and determined the relationships which occurred
among established members.

Morale, too, is one of those vague unspoken phenomenon
based upon sentiment. Again it should be noted that the fewer
the new members the higher morale is likely to be. This is a
case of fewer disruptions to the older and established patterns of
sentiment and therefore the old patterns are likely to be main-

tained. For "new" groups, that is, groups in which all the members are strangers to one another, all of these relationships must be developed. There are no standards, or there are few standards, upon which the members can base their relationships with one another.

There are some other aspects of morale that tell a good deal about normal group processes. Look for a moment at the degrees of liking that are established among members. Remember, the fewer the new members introduced into the group the higher will be the morale. This is partly the function of the fact that morale is related to the degree to which members like one another. And if there is liking among the members there also tends to be agreement among them.

But not only is there agreement or a tendency toward agreement but some very interesting perceptions of agreement. For example, people tend to *think* that people they like agree with them and, in contrast, that people they dislike do not agree with them. Sentiments such as these have significant implications for the way in which groups process information and arrive at solutions to problems. *People hear what they like to hear.*

Extending this same idea, the more favorably members regard one another the more uniformity there is likely to be in their attitudes and in their actions. So it is not only that people tend to think that other people agree with them, but that over a period of time there seems to be a uniformity in attitudes and actions among people who respect one another.

William H. Whyte in the book *The Organization Man* tells the story of a suburban housewife who liked to listen to the opera. When she first arrived in the community she discovered that the other women not only didn't care to listen to the opera but most often didn't even know what she meant when she said she was listening to *The Magic Flute*. She soon discovered that it was relatively easy to relate to these people if she did not mention her keen interest in highbrow music. Instead, she joined the discussions about diapers and washing machine service calls. She found that in order to be accepted by the group she had to join, at least to a minimal degree, in their attitudes and concerns.

This is another dimension of being liked. It suggests that the

more closely an individual conforms to the norms of the group
the more liked he will be.   In contrast, the more he ignores and
disregards the group's standards of behavior the more disliked
he will be.   There is then a strong and significant basis for
uniformity in attitudes and actions.

But how does a group influence this behavior?   If the individual conforms to the standards of the group, the members of the
group provide protection for the individual.   They provide
protection against loss of status, deflation of ego, and so forth.
And, in contrast, members of a group can punish by a variety of
symbols of dislike.

Group members also have an emotional attachment for one
another.   Within groups such as the family there is a high
degree of emotional attachment.   The purposes of the group are
various.   Over the years as the members have interacted with
one another they have undergone periods of strong emotional
and senitmental attachment or involvement.

In contrast, some ephemeral groups are so totally task
oriented that there is hardly any emotional involvement at all.
When a class meets to take an examination the members are
entirely focused on task and the emotional involvement between
members is minimal.

These two broad extremes are useful to remember because
some group processes vary with the degrees of emotional attachment.   For example, in long established groups that have very
diffuse functions and in which there is a high degree of emotional attachment, the quantity of interaction will decrease
sharply as dissension among the group members rises.   It's
understandable that when group members who are strongly
attached to one another with emotional ties face a situation of
disagreement, disliking, dissension, they are likely to put up
defenses to minimize it.   One of the best defenses is to avoid it
or reduce or even stop the interaction.

The contrasting situation is also true: as cohesiveness grows,
and as liking of members for one another increases, there is a
tendency to protect those relationships.   One means of protecting them is to increase the amount of interaction the members
have with one another.

But what of those groups in which there is little emotional

attachment. These groups probably have a relatively specific function to perform or a certain job to get done. The members may not have had a long period of sustained interaction with one another. In these cases where disagreement is perceived a curious thing happens. The interaction tends to increase. This is the opposite of what happens when disagreements and dissensions occur in a group that has already established a high degree of emotional involvement. Interaction can increase in this context because there are no sentimental relationships to protect. In fact, the increase in interaction and the increasing exchange of information that results may tend to build a degree of emotional involvement into the group process. This, in turn, tends to create a higher degree of cohesiveness. It is a curious process.

Another dimension of group sentiments is the effect that personal satisfaction and personal goals have upon the group goals. There are two important but distinct products. One is the goals and satisfactions of an individual member of the group. The second is the goals as they are advanced by the group itself. These need not be, and indeed seldom are, the same.

It is interesting, however, that the more similar an individual's goals and satisfactions are to those advanced to the group itself, the more effective the group becomes in meeting its goals. This is probably what is referred to when a group is described as "pulling together." But it also states explicitly the notion that individual sentiments can be related to the total group process.

The contrast is also meaningful. As individual members feel personally threatened, and as they become emotionally involved in the group atmosphere, their satisfaction is likely to decrease and in the more total sense the ability of the group to achieve its ends decreases. And though satisfaction probably varies by the nature of the group goals being achieved, it also seems true that as individual members find they are more compatible with one another in terms of their skills, their standards of behavior, and the prestige they give to one another, not only does their individual satisfaction increase but again the effectiveness of the total group increases.

There is a judgment of the effectiveness with which a group is able to achieve its goals. The nature of group goals can vary from the specific tasks to very generalized functions. For example, groups like a family or some friends meet regularly and may have no other purpose than to maintain a place of contact for their members. In groups with very generalized goals, the members are unlikely to permit much dissension. Let us call these general goals "social" goals.

In the process of interaction, one constant and consistent process is taking place in interpersonal relations—the ranking of each member to each other member. Ranking can be based on very specific kinds of evaluative criteria. A baseball team ranks its members on the basis of the degree of skill they have been able to achieve in specialized roles important to the team. Musical organizations require the coordination of specialized roles in a team fashion. Ranking in these instances is relatively easy because the criterion upon which people are rated is either singular or simple. (There are some important qualifications that have to be made to these statements when team members interact with one another over an extended period of time. Under these conditions the ranking process becomes much more complex.)

In friendship groups, on the other hand, ranking also takes place but on a much more generalized basis. A friend is a friend because he doesn't insult you. A friend is a friend because he keeps you company when you are lonely.

Putting these two ideas together, that there are "social" goals peculiar to some groups and that a ranking process takes place among the members of groups, we suggest that the more social the goals of a group, the more general will be the basis upon which ranking takes place.

Interaction and Communication

It has already been pointed out that interaction frequencies among group members are affected by the sentiments that members hold for one another. It was also suggested that this interaction rate varies by the degree of emotional attachment that group members feel for one another. There are other relationships between interaction and communication and group process.

Frequency of contact of members is one of these. In groups in which there is relatively little quantitative interaction among the members or in which those interactions take place on a short-term basis there are much less likely to be recognized standards of proper behavior agreed upon by the members. It is understandable since standards cannot develop except by way of exchange in symbolic processes. In groups in which there is little emotional contact, interaction will increase as there are signs of disagreement. Now to extend these ideas. The more interaction there is among group members the more tension there is likely to be until an agreed upon proper behavior is defined.

Interaction is an exchange of meanings or communications. Those groups that have particular tasks to perform undergo particular and peculiar processes as these communications are changed. For example, groups with tasks to perform tend to alternate their communications. Some communications are essentially emotional and are designed to reduce the tension, while others are directed toward the task of the group and tend to create tension. It is understandable that these task groups or special purpose groups have functions to perform, and in this context it is difficult to allow for all the feelings of all of the members. Thus, they are likely to create tensions as they try to perform the tasks. The groups can seldom stand this kind of emotional concentration for very long and so there is a specific attempt to reduce tension among group members. Thus even task groups tend to include both types of communication.

It might be helpful to give an illustration of one type of analysis of communication that classifies types of contributions and evaluates their tendency to help or harm discussion.

A related observation (one that is in many ways frightening) is that over a period of time groups tend to devote an increasing amount of time to personal relations and controls, to controlling sentiments and emotions, and to relieving tensions, than they do to the tasks they are supposed to perform. It is quite possible that there are some good, sufficient, and even necessary reasons for organizational transfer of personnel.

Bales' System of Categories

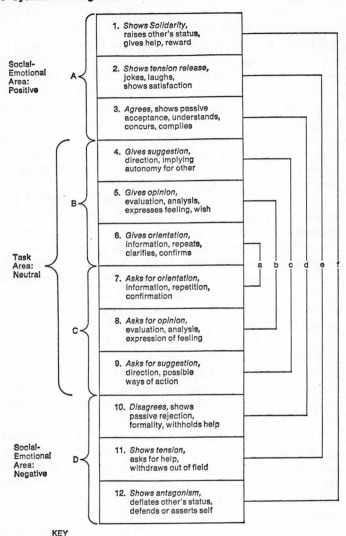

Social-
Emotional
Area:
Positive
A

1. *Shows Solidarity,*
raises other's status,
gives help, reward

2. *Shows tension release,*
jokes, laughs,
shows satisfaction

3. *Agrees,* shows passive
acceptance, understands,
concurs, complies

Task
Area:
Neutral

B

4. *Gives suggestion,*
direction, implying
autonomy for other

5. *Gives opinion,*
evaluation, analysis,
expresses feeling, wish

6. *Gives orientation,*
information, repeats,
clarifies, confirms

C

7. *Asks for orientation,*
information, repetition,
confirmation

8. *Asks for opinion,*
evaluation, analysis,
expression of feeling

9. *Asks for suggestion,*
direction, possible
ways of action

Social-
Emotional
Area:
Negative
D

10. *Disagrees,* shows
passive rejection,
formality, withholds help

11. *Shows tension,*
asks for help,
withdraws out of field

12. *Shows antagonism,*
deflates other's status,
defends or asserts self

a   b   c   d   e   f

KEY

a = Problems of Communication
b = Problems of Evaluation
c = Problems of Control
d = Problems of Decision
e = Problems of Tension Reduction
f = Problems of Reintegration

A = Positive Reactions
B = Attempted Answers
C = Questions
D = Negative Reactions

Training for Participation in the Small Group

We still have not provided a definition of the size of the small group. Experts disagree on a number, and it is, perhaps, best to avoid rigidity by asserting that if more than a specific number of people are in a room, it must be considered a crowd or a "large group." When we speak of the "small group" we are referring more to situation and purpose than to size. In addition, it is necessary to consider the small group in its context—a larger society. The lines are blurred between the small group and other kinds of entities like legislatures.

Generally, however, a small group can be identified by the fact that the people participating in it are gathered together because of a common sense of purpose and they are seated face-to-face and are trying to do something about achieving the purpose that brought them together. They do not rely on parliamentary procedure or rules of order to resolve their difficulties. Rather, they seek general agreement or reconciliation, called "consensus." They do not engage in face-to-face combat to decide whether or not a single alternative should be adopted. Instead, they attempt to explore several possible alternatives and synthesize a solution out of them. Their interaction is relatively devoid of formality, and there is considerable opportunity to lapse for periods of time into social, emotional, or integrative behavior. Indeed, it is often difficult to discover where social interaction leaves off and deliberation begins.

The small group is probably better defined by its characteristics and its goals than by its size. In subsequent sections we will attempt to examine some of the characteristics and goals of the small group and to assess its importance to the individual and to society. What we will not consider are parliamentary groups, legislatures, or purely social groupings, though we will concern ourselves with parliamentary tactics and socialization as they become relevant to our study of the small group aspects of human interaction.

Learning to participate in small groups raises many pedagogical problems. It is difficult to train someone in the classroom in techniques useful to him under real conditions. Much formal training in small group participation is fundamentally unrealistic. There is a gap between theoretical concepts and behavioral prescriptions. Only limited amounts of time can be devoted to participation; furthermore, discussion topics selected for the classroom more often than not are not relevant. Consequently, it is virtually impossible to predict how the learners might respond under real conditions. Assessments of quality represent only estimates of classroom behavior. It is equally difficult to evaluate the group as a whole. Normally, there is no output possible in classroom discussions. Evaluations must be made either on the instructor's estimate of the quality of the proposed solution, or a judgment must be applied to the individual behavior of panel members. In the former case, it is hard to avoid basing the assessment on the quality of writing in the solutions. In the latter case, there is often a tacit assumption that quantity of participation represents quality of contribution. To the extent that evaluation of classroom discussion is distorted, students will pursue unrealistic or useless goals.

Only when the learner is involved in problems in which he has a stake—problems from which he stands to gain or lose—is it possible to measure the quality of the group and then only after the group has generated a solution that can be activated and evaluated for success. Unfortunately, the quality of a solution cannot be estimated solely on the quality of the writing in which it is phrased. The best worded solution to a problem cannot even be considered a solution until it has been worked into a program, activated, allowed to operate for a period of time, and then assessed as to its efficacy in solving the problem. Classroom groups, however, cannot help getting preoccupied with words. Unfortunately, this also seems true of many "real" groups whose reports call for "bold new programs," "the advancement of quality education," or "betterment of human relationships." It is important to learn that the wording of a solution must lead directly to a program that can utilize time, money, personnel, or material. The words of a solution will not solve the problem.

At least in part, the tendency of groups to regard wording as a solution may be to avoid confronting the problem. It may also result from the impression given by training in small groups administered in the classroom. Group members may honestly feel that their responsibility ends with the presentation of the verbal report, exactly as it did in the classroom. Somehow classroom training must be reshaped to include the feeling of hard-headed realism that is essential if problems are to be solved.

Of course, it is entirely possible that the verbal report may be a conscious ploy used by a group who seeks to evade its responsibility for solution of the problem. At least a well-written verbal report will convince others that the group has been doing its job. But the usual reason that groups fail to complete their job is that the members are not fully aware of their responsibility for presenting a solution that can be activated and applied. Most groups are not fully aware of their responsibilities as problem solvers. It should be clear that a group asked to generate a solution for an observable problem must produce a proposal for some kind of observable activity. People must act, spend money, utilize material, and take time in order to eliminate the difficulty that the group confronted. Something must happen to the events or conditions that constitute the problem the group was supposed to solve.

This is an admittedly cold-blooded and hard-nosed approach to group problem solving. However, once we have accepted the premise that it is not the main purpose of problem solving to provide for the mental health of the participants and that the only legitimate outcome of a problem-solving group is a solution to a problem, our primary attention must be on outcomes. Our concern for the individual must be limited to those aspects which, if altered, would improve solutions.

However, the word "group" is a reification that presumes the existence of an entity. A group is an aggregate of behaving individuals. Our statements about norms or climates are inferences drawn from observed similarities. Somehow, we must reconcile our concern for group productivity with natural concern and interest in the behavior of the individual. Once we can differentiate purpose, we have little problem defining the individual role. The matter of using the small group to improve individual personality is properly the business of the clinic. The business of the way personality affects the group, and particularly its output, is our legitimate concern. We might also inquire about the effect group activity might have on individual personality. Throughout, our concern is with improvement of group productivity.

As far as training is concerned, once understanding of the requirements of problem solving has been achieved by the members of the group, it is possible to generate solutions efficiently and to avoid the frustration that comes from failing to resolve the problems of concern. An understanding of the difficulties of problem solving will prevent the group from confusing the desirable and the possible and thus avert neat common denominator verbalizations that will satisfy the group members without affecting the problem. Furthermore, rather than attempt to declare prescriptions about behavior, our search will be for general hypotheses about the behavior of groups and of people in groups. The goal of the learner is to discover something about his own behavior in groups and to develop his own program for improvement. He can do this only if he is familiar with what is likely to happen to himself and others when confronted with the stresses that attend the art of solving problems in groups.

The word "consensus" means "general agreement or harmony, concord." In most small groups this is taken to mean "decision, without voting." An expression of agreement among members is generally taken to mean a consensus exists. The concept of consensus, however, can be both overworked and overused. Consensus is desirable in a small group because it indicates the commitment of members to the solution. Consensus is preferable to decision by ballot because it does not polarize a hostile minority. Sometimes, however, groups spend their time seeking consensus without determining whether what they reach consensus on will have any effect on the problem. Consensus may reveal a spirit of goodwill, a desire to reach agreement without agreeing on something applicable. When consensus, rather than solution, becomes a group goal, members may feel better; the problem, however, remains unsolved.

By the same token, though, we will point out quite clearly and at great length later on in this book, that there is, indeed, a correlation between a spirit of goodwill in the group and the quality of output. But it does not appear that specific focus on training to achieve goodwill has a material effect on improvement of output. That is to say, goodwill generated in the group may well be a function of the quality of output at the same time as output may be a function of goodwill. Certainly members of a group can look back with considerably more favor upon their participation if the group output is successful. Incidents that may have been construed as hostile or threatening can easily disappear in the light of an effective and applicable solution. But those who can remember only the pleasure they got from participation and cannot seem to make sense out of the solution have probably misinterpreted the reason they were called together. Training in the responsibilities of members of problem-solving groups and the nature of output would help avoid spurious consensus. This would, perhaps, be preferable to sensitivity training or trying to make each small group member a personal psychotherapist to his fellow members of the group. Emphasis on personal development training often sacrifices training in techniques of problem solving and requirements of solutions. Furthermore, much sensitivity training is more directly relevant to normal socialization than it is to the purposive small group.

It might be said that if the group is successful in solving its problem then concentration on goodwill among the members may be irrelevant, but concentration on goodwill among the members can only be regarded as relevant when the group succeeds in solving its problem. Somewhere along the line this means that group members need basic training in the techniques of group problem solving. These techniques can be discovered not only within a discipline called "small groups" but in a variety of disciplines. For example, a first phase of problem solving must necessarily include an examination of the rules of evidence, an understanding of how to evaluate authority, and, indeed, in most cases these days, considerable knowledge in quantitative methodologies. Exercises in the simple logic of casual relationships could also be useful, for a group must decide somewhere along the line if they are going to apply symptomatic treatment of a problem or whether the problem must be solved at its root cause. In addition, groups need to understand that within the framework of group problem solving it is necessary for them to set some clear and specific goals so that they can establish a set of criteria against which to establish their solutions.   Furthermore, small group members must understand that selection of the first solution is not necessarily the most efficient method of procedure but actually it is wise to allow a number of solutions to emerge so that they may have the option of building an eclectic solution or choosing the individual solution that most closely approximates their criteria.   Finally, they must understand that the basic requirement of solutions includes the preparation of a specific plan of activities.

Training in goodwill may make members feel good about their output and about their fellow group members, but training in goodwill contributes nothing specific to the solving of small group problems.   It simply cannot be assumed that all group members understand what is required of them when they participate in the small group.   Consequently, simple training administered by a group leader, even to the use of a chart (see pp. 22–23) indicating the steps that must be gone through to achieve a solution, would be more effective in improving discussion than attempts to heighten the sensitivity of group members.

EXERCISES

GROUP PROJECTS

Divide the class into small groups and require as "output" a formal report in their topic area.   The class may engage in an exercise in decision making to determine the precise format for these reports.

1. List as many as possible of the small groups that exist on the campus.   State their aims and objectives, their composition, and as complete a record as possible of their effectiveness. What appears to differentiate an effective from an ineffective group?   Be sure to come to some agreement about the meaning of the word "effective."

2. Find several examples of group decision that have not worked.   Explain why they have not worked.   Isolate those

that failed because of a lack of administrative plan or program presented by the group.

3. How do the faculty and university administration use small group activities? What powers do the faculty members have and how effectively are they using them? How do faculty members feel about the "committee system?" Gathering material for this project would, no doubt, call upon the group to prepare a program for interviewing or questioning the faculty.

4. Examine the rhetorical function of some campus groups. Do a case study of three or four groups, explaining their scope of activity, the kinds of problems they solve, and who makes the final decisions about whether their ideas are put into operation. What is their responsibility in convincing those who make the decisions? How effectively have they fulfilled these responsibilities?

5. Prepare a handbook of rhetorical strategies that members of small groups in your campus student government can use to convince decision makers that their ideas ought to be adopted.

6. Prepare answers to the questions, "What is necessary for us to know about each other in order to do an effective job in working on our group project? How can we get to know these things?"

7. Examine some of the basic works in group discussion. Prepare a report on the personal qualities these books require of a discussion participant. Assess the realism of these demands. Come up with a program for training students in these qualities.

8. Prepare a role-playing demonstration of groups in which members have not learned to curb their verbalization of judgments. Now do one with people who attempt to curb personal motivations.

9. It might be interesting to check the amount of time each of the groups spent discussing its projects before it was necessary for the members to take a break. How long were the breaks and what did the members do during their break time? Did the quality of discussion improve after the break?

INDIVIDUAL PROJECTS

1. Prepare a personal group profile for yourself. What groups are you a member of? What demands do these groups place on you? Where do these demands come into conflict? When demands come into conflict, how do you go about deciding which demands are to be met?

2. Continue your profile by listing the decisions about your life and behavior that are made by groups over which you have no control. You might examine school rules, traffic laws, and so on. How would you get access to these groups in ways that might change their decisions?

3. Prepare and maintain a diary of your personal feelings as you participate in small group activities. What activities of others distress you? What form does this distress take? What activities of your own seem to annoy your group partners? How might alteration of these behaviors change the outcome of the group?

The Individual in the Small Group

Your personal behavior in a small group will be unlike that of any other person. You come to the group a unique person, and you adjust your uniqueness as far as you have to or care to in order to remain a member. The groups you choose to belong to will probably contain members who share your beliefs and behave much like you do. It is easy to feel comfortable in such a group and most of our socialization is carried on in groups of this type.

Sometimes, however, you may feel that membership in a particular group will elevate your status. In such a case it will be necessary for you to alter your behavior to fit the norms of the new group. This is particularly important in work groups, where your ability to conform to developed norms may well determine your progress in the organization.

But any small group you might belong to will have some effect on you personally. There is no question but that you will

change as a result of your participation, because it is necessary
to achieve a feeling of belonging. To feel a part of the group,
some of your behaviors and values must be changed. This does
not mean that groups tend to destroy the values of their members. Rather, groups will tend to strengthen and reinforce
those values that you hold most strongly and will tend to reduce
your commitment to values that are not so important to you. It
is virtually impossible for you to belong to a group whose values
conflict with your own. Even an occupational group in which
your livelihood is at stake cannot compel you to change deep-
seated values. It is not rare for a person to change jobs or even
to quit without promise of another because of a value conflict
between himself and the people with whom he works.

Apparently, people tend to seek membership in groups that
best reflect their values. In this sense, we have an empirical test
of our own values. To find out "who you are," an examination
of the groups in which you hold membership and the people
who belong to them, may well reflect back your own personality
more effectively than solitary contemplation. For example, any
number of people set out to pledge fraternities and sororities
with a great deal of eagerness, only to discover that there is a
fundamental difference in values between themselves and the
members of the organizations, as a result of which it becomes
necessary to withdraw. On the other hand there are those who
pledge half-heartedly, and then find themselves making deeper
and deeper commitments to the values of the group. A great
social psychologist, George Herbert Mead, contends that you
discover "yourself" by reflection from the people around you.

Joe Marks went off to the office anticipating another day
of anguish. The merchandise planning committee had been
meeting regularly all through the week and each meeting
had ended with a flare-up between Joe and Tom Smith. It
wasn't even clear what the issue was in these arguments.
There just seemed to be something about the men that made
it impossible for them to get along at all. There was no
question that the work of the committee was seriously
subverted by the hostility between the two men. Often
members of the committee couldn't see why they fought. It
seemed to these observers that Marks and Smith agreed on

most issues. They could see no reason for conflict and they had told the men to "cool it."

Joe thought about this as he rode to the office and decided that this day would be different. He thought he knew what it was he didn't like about Tom Smith. It was that patronizing attitude, that aura of Anglo-Saxonism, that consistent display of superiority. It seemed to Joe that Tom picked up every one of his ideas and swallowed them and then came out with a slight modification, acting as though he had presented something original. Joe felt threatened, as though while Tom was around it would be impossible for the rest of the group to discover his own worth and merit. Furthermore, he experienced in each of these conflicts a fundamental value clash. Being the only Jew in an advertising agency was a difficult task, even though there was no blatant anti-Semitism. It seemed to Joe that underlying each of the disputes he had with his colleagues, particularly his conflict with Tom Smith, was some patronizing attitude, some demeaning of his worth. But this day was going to be different! This day would not be marked by conflict. This day would end the discussions and the program would be reported out. Win, lose, or draw, Joe resolved to himself that he would not dispute again with Tom Smith.

About ten minutes into the conference Joe had occasion to support an idea that appeared to be accepted by the entire group. As a matter of fact, the idea had been presented originally by Tom Smith. Joe had shown some resistance to it earlier, but in contemplation it had come clear to him that the reason he had resisted it was not the quality of the idea but simply because it had been presented by Smith. In order to show his goodwill, he asserted strong approval. Smith's response was quick and decisive. He shifted ground and began to mount an attack on his own idea, to the great confusion of the entire group. Joe Marks sat quietly for as long as he could and then took the floor to point out to Tom Smith that the idea had originally been his. Smith replied that there had to be something wrong with an idea "if your kind of person approves of it." All of Joe's firm resolve was forgotten. He launched into a vicious tirade against Tom Smith. All of the suppressed hostility came to the surface and within five minutes the two men were at each others' throats. Once again the group got nowhere but the issue was even more critical for the general chairman felt that the decision making could no longer proceed as long as the two men were in the group. The issue of which of them would remain with the company would be passed on to a higher authority.

Incidents similar to this occur in virtually all small group activity. It is impossible to tell how strongly a value operates until it is tested. In the case of Tom Smith, his opposition to Jews or at least to non-Anglo-Saxons did not appear to be a major force in his life, but the confrontation with Joe Marks revealed that he held the value more strongly than he thought, for it was impossible for him to function without referring to the one "outlander" in the group.

Joe Marks was lukewarm in his religious commitments, even neutral or mildly hostile in his religious behaviors, yet he felt compelled to respond to the attacks on his ethnic ancestry with considerable vigor. Apparently his sensitivity on this issue was deeper than he thought. It was impossible to get either man to commit to the group goal, even though each knew that his economic future was at stake to the point where both their livelihoods would be in jeopardy if they continued their antagonism. Their personal values transcended their economic values. Neither would have predicted this would have been the case. Both would have declared with vehemence that they were primarily dedicated to their career advancement and that their "petty biases" would not be permitted to interfere.

Much behavior people carry on in small groups can be tested against a model of this kind. It is very difficult to separate support and hostility to ideas from support and hostility to people. It is difficult for anyone to know whether his opinions are motivated by logical analysis of facts or by some deep-seated commitment that distorts the facts to permit the attitude to emerge. In the case of Joe Marks and Tom Smith it was possible for their supervisor to work with each of them separately and then together to make it clear to both men that they were permitting social values to interfere with their effectiveness in the organization. Through a painstaking examination of those values, followed by a direct confrontation between the two men, it was possible to train them to curb some of their hostilities. While the two never became fast friends, the examination of their behavior and what it meant made it possible for them to work together in the same organization. Their self-awareness had been expanded and since they were now consciously aware of how deep their value commitments were, they were in a much better position to prevent them from interfering with their careers.

It might be added that a situation like that between Joe Marks and Tom Smith is a good example of where "sensitivity training" was useful. The whole group need not be exposed to the confrontation. Work could be done with the two men privately and only in the context of the vocational group. No one tried to psychoanalyze them to discover the reasons for their commitments. It was assumed that they were there and they were entitled to be there. The difficulty was approached as a legitimate problem. The supervisor dealt with the questions, "How can these values be prevented from interfering with the business of the group?" not with "How can these values be eliminated?"

Furthermore, even after making a commitment to a small group, you cannot predict that its values become your own values and supersede those that you brought with you. Most of us live in a situation of ambiguity, where our beliefs and behaviors are controlled, to some extent, by the groups we belong to. We do not act or verbalize the same way at home with the family as we do on the street with friends or on the job with colleagues. This multiplicity of behaviors is what the sociologist calls "roles." Most of the time we have little difficulty reconciling conflicts, for we recognize the differing demands of the situations. However, when some belief we hold deeply is challenged or threatened, we discover the strength of the belief as we find ourselves acting counter to the demands of the group, and counter to our own expectations. The small group affords a fine arena for testing what we really believe in, for our real values will emerge in action and, more often than we expect, they will run counter to what we have been verbalizing. The following example illustrates this point:

A recent study with small children indicated that children do not necessarily make choices in line with their verbalized values. The children in the study were asked to state whether they would prefer to use their free time to (1) watch a movie, (2) play a game on a playground, (3) play a "board" game with others, (4) do art or crafts alone. Each child made a choice. Then the children were put into groups to discuss the question, "Which of these activities will be the most fun?" After fifteen minutes of discussion, the children were moved back to their seats. They were then told that the next hour would be "free time" and were asked to go to the place where the movies were to be shown, or go out to the playground, or move to the tables where the games were, or go to the arts and crafts area. Very few children hesitated. Within three minutes all had made a choice. Interestingly enough, only about 50 percent of the children actually chose to do the thing they said they were going to do. The same results were obtained when the discussion step was omitted!

The implication here is that some values are suitable for verbalization because of understanding of social requirements about what can be said. Other values are designed for action because of what we, personally, hold to be important. Sometimes the two are in concord, but sometimes they are not, so that a man who wants to discover what he believes must test his belief against some active demand before he can be sure.

Entry Into the Group

It is not difficult for an individual, alone, to enter into the work and action of almost any group. While it would be moderately difficult for someone named Goldberg to participate well in the Sons of Italy or someone named O'Brien to become an officer of B'nai B'rith, for the most part task groups can accommodate individuals that come voluntarily or by assignment. On the other hand, entering a group with a block of others often stirs up considerable difficulty. An examination of some tendencies on college campuses might illustrate this point.

There appears to be, in the social interactions of college

professors, groupings of people of similar rank and academic interest. In the case of large universities, those people who came in the same year seem to cleave together. In any case, the college is a fluid institution and each influx of new personnel represents a potential threat to the calm and serenity of the institution. An individual newcomer can easily be absorbed because he does not have sufficient strength to subvert the establishment, or if he attempts to do so the organization has sufficient strength to bring him back into line or see to it that he is ejected from the organization. Furthermore, there is small chance that an individual would feel sufficient confidence to make threatening gestures and the social pressures his colleagues could bring to bear would, in most cases, be sufficient to whip him into line, to compel him to suppress his antagonism to practices of the institution.

When more than one person enters an organization, however, it is possible for them to unify in programs and policies hostile to the status quo. The act of working to implement their ideas brings them closer together and that closeness reinforces the pressure they are able to exert on behalf of their programs. Particularly if the decision-making authority is remote, newcomers may gain access to the administration more readily than those who have been in the institution for a long period of time. There is a myth, which may be rooted in fact on some campuses, that newcomers have about three years to accomplish all they can in effecting change. After that, they fade back into the pack. Consequently a unified body of newcomers threatens the security of the older members who seek to protect themselves by purging hostile or antagonistic ideas. Indeed it may very well be that some organizations select their newcomers on the basis of how closely their ideas accord with those already in force. Assimilating acquiescent new members into a group does little to improve the group, or help it become more fit to face new problems. Organizations that restrict themselves to admitting only a few compliant new members often find themselves facing extreme crises and pressures for change and may well have to generate solutions from within the group. The challenge of new members who disagree often stimulates activity on the part of older members and is generally helpful to the organization.

A model of this kind of vitalizing activity may be found by observing the role that minority groups play in American society. The Anglo-Saxon heritage for American society was forceful, vigorous, and viable during the days when it was necessary to cope with a great many problems. By the late nineteenth century, however, many sectors of society were growing smug and highly contented. New sources of labor were needed to staff the industrial machine. Open immigration was encouraged. The people who availed themselves of open immigration, however, were not fully immersed in the value structure of the American society. Some who advocated open immigration had hoped that the immigration would come from Northern European countries. They were surprised to find that it was the Southern and Central Europeans, who differed drastically from established norms, that entered into society. The huge influx of immigrants mounted a number of threats to the established residents, who not only felt their economic survival threatened by the newcomers, but also their value system and life style. They felt it necessary to defend their values by excluding the newcomers from the mainstream of society. This they did with considerable vigor and "know-nothingism." Anti-Semitism and discrimination against the Irish and Italians flourished. This pattern of social rejection exists to this day. There is little anti-Semitism, for example, in parts of the country where there are few Jews. It is possible for one or two Jews to assimilate themselves into a town very nicely, but when the minority is sizeable people in the town begin to show signs of rejection. Only after the newcomer shows outward signs of accepting the mainstream of the culture does he find acceptance. If he is unable or unwilling to accept the main values of the culture, he finds himself rejected in a number of areas. Rejection of minority groups most often involves a stereotype. That is, a relatively simplistic classification of the person suffices as the basis of evaluation.

As in most cases where a simplistic rejection (or acceptance) is involved, one must be careful to recognize that the entire group (especially if that group is a community or a society) will not reject the individual or person or group. But whether all the members reject or accept is not particularly significant. The point only needs a large number acting alike to be sustained.

The people who do not reject members of a minority group are the ones who serve to bridge the two systems. They introduce new ideas, new practices from food to clothing which, eventually, are likely to meld the contrasting and rejecting systems.

The Negro today faces much the same problem. Most of the dominant white society find themselves able to accept an individual, successful Negro, whose life style very closely approximates their own. They are willing to overlook his blackness, recognizing that this is a matter about which he can do nothing, not recognizing that it might be a matter about which he wishes to do nothing. While there is an air of patronization it is possible for the individual, successful Negro to survive and prosper in white society. But the thought of millions of black people pouring out of the central city into the mainstream of American life fills the hearts of most Americans with uneasiness. The different appearance and the obvious disparity in values and life styles represents something akin to a threat to the main society. Riots and violence are the results of this kind of conflict and this macrocosm neatly recapitulates the microcosm of threat when newcomers enter a small group.

For the most part, however, people tend to select and form their small groups in such a way that they will reflect their values and biases or reinforce them. Within a small group people tend to show preference for members with similar life styles. In any small group there is a strong likelihood that cliques will develop. A clique is a small group of people inside the framework of a group whose values and behaviors so closely approximate each other that they can be counted upon to behave as a unit. These smaller units characterized by highly intense human relations represent a prime support for an individual as he functions in juxtaposition with others he does not know as well and consequently with whom there is some possibility of antagonism and conflict. While cliques may be individually supportive, they are potentially disruptive to small group activity, for clique members will tend to make decisions more on a basis of personal affiliation than on the potential for the decision in implementing the group's goal. Although there is much concern about how to dissolve cliques and broaden contact among members, it appears that cliques are necessary, for each individual has only limited capacity for close contacts. The zoologist Desmond Morris, writing in *The Naked Ape,* said we tend to select friends about to the extent that we could handle them in small tribal or herd units. There appears to be, in his opinion, a limitation on the capability of the human to make close friendships and consequently as the size of the group increases we can expect more subgroups to be generated. Furthermore, as cliques develop the style of their members tends to diversify, thus increasing the possibility of conflict within the groups.

Strategically, the individual seeking to exert influence on a small group must show considerable care. First, it is necessary to display caution when speaking in the early stages of group membership. A new man can't say too much, for he holds no status within the group and excessive talk on his part may be considered by others to be presumptive. He may, however, display solidarity and support for the ideas of others and, in doing this, cement bonds with other members. He will soon discover the "power" in the group and play to it or he may find himself admitted to membership in a clique. Until he has some influential member willing to give support to his remarks or has gotten three or four other members to back him, it will not be possible for him to exert very much influence, regardless of how good his rhetoric or how good his words. Even his most effective ideas will be largely ignored. Many people, newcomers to groups, are dismayed to find that the ideas they expressed on Monday are presented by someone else on Friday and adopted by the group even though they were rejected when originally expressed. While there may be considerable frustration associated with this kind of ostensible rejection it must be recognized that the group cannot afford to concede too much deference to a newcomer, for once people concede that a newcomer has ability it must be conceded that they might have disabilities. If several members enter a group at once, however, it is possible for them to exert considerable pressure by presenting a united front.

The pledge period in the typical fraternity or sorority exem-

plifies this kind of behavior.   If a group of fifty or sixty members takes in ten or twelve new members all at one time there is
a considerable potential for threat to the values of the organization.   As a result, it is necessary to develop a format in which
the new members can be acculturated to the values of the larger
group.   Those that resist acculturation can be dropped from
potential membership or pressured to withdraw voluntarily.
Those that survive the acculturation or pledge period can be
moved into the group with confidence that they will not disrupt
the existing value system.   Furthermore, fraternities protect
themselves by assigning specific duties and activities to pledges
and new members to give them the feel of working for the order
in such a way that they can learn to accept the prevailing
values.

Similar kinds of "pledging" are often found operating infor-
mally in companies.   A new employee has considerable difficulty gaining acceptance in a group.   If the other employees
have been together for a long time they will have developed a
style of operation that accommodates their needs.   The newcomer will find that dissidents and nonconformists will make
the initial overtures to him.   Those with some position in the
social hierarchy will accept the new employee only to the extent
that they do not perceive him as a threat to their position.
Thus, he will have to demonstrate compliance and acceptance
of norms and will have to seek a position not yet held by anyone
else.

New entry is exceptionally difficult at the executive level.   A
new supervisor will often find himself threatened, particularly if
he is brought in from the outside.   The group he is to lead has
habituated a problem-solving style with which they are comfortable, and they will attempt to defend it against infringements
even if it is flagrantly ineffective.   The new executive from the
outside will take considerable time to understand the values and
characteristic behavior of his group.   Until he does, it is impossible for him to do much to change operations.

The situation may often be more difficult for the new leader
coming up from the ranks, for if he is not the choice of the
greater number of members, he will find himself leader in name
only and will be forced to ratify and implement decisions made

according to established procedures of the group.

It seems that the new member of a group must engage in a variety of self-effacing acts in order to demonstrate that he is willing to subordinate himself to the norms of the group.   Only after he makes this clear does he begin to win acceptance. Newcomers to small towns find this graphically illustrated to them for they may be regarded as newcomers or interlopers even after they have been residents for ten or fifteen years.   If, however, they move through accepted channels in the hierarchies of established organizations in the town they may achieve some status and aspire to positions of leadership.   For the most part, however, in college towns, the academic community separates from the town community and develops its own set of values and rewards so that newcomers need not be too frustrated by the social customs they find around them.

There is no reason to believe that a small group of five is much different from a large group of five hundred or five thousand, except in degree of complexity.   The essentials of interaction can be found in both.   The member who seeks to exert control over a small group will need to use political and social techniques similar to those employed for the same ends in society.   Unless he is willing to utilize strategies to achieve his goals, he will find himself being absorbed into the group, which will make of him an "ordinary" conforming member with little ability to alter the character of the group.

EXERCISES

GROUP PROJECTS

1. Prepare a list of the basic values of the various members of a group constructed from your class.   Try to find which values are "shared."   Deal with such values as general political orientation, religion and the church, economic values, the welfare state, values in sex and social interaction, and so on. Attempt to make an assessment of the extent to which the shared and dissonant values would help or hinder you if you were assigned (a) to prepare a fact-finding report on reli-

gious activities on campus, (b) to function as a pressure group for open housing in your town community, (c) to work together for a period of several years as fellow employees in a public relations consulting corporation, (d) to function as a civic betterment group interested in beautifying the community.

2. Ask your instructor to prepare a list of short books or articles about the small group and give you a paragraph describing the contents of each. Ask him to set as an assignment the writing of an abstract on one of these. Make sure he means to stick to his guns and will grade the assignment rigidly and strictly. After reading the descriptions, have each member of the group declare his preference for one of the readings. Then discuss the relative merits of reading the various articles. Be sure to consider the ease with which the article can be read and abstracted as well as its importance in understanding the small group. Then have each member declare his intention again. [Keep these declarations private for the moment. Let the instructor function as Price, Waterhouse and keep them in a sealed envelope.] Next, have each person read an article and submit his abstract. Then compare the two declarations of intent and the actual abstracts and attempt to determine the relative weight of the influences that account for discrepancies between the intended and the actual.

3. As an experiment in sensitivity training, try to make a judgment about which members of the class you would choose to work with you on the preparation of a final term project, the nature of which would be determined by you, but which would make up fifty percent of your final grade in the course. Have each person make a private list. Now suppose that the grade for your entire class would depend on one project to be developed by no more than five class members. The selections must be made today, and the project would be considered in competition with all the other projects produced by similar classes throughout the country. Furthermore, the grading will be "on the curve" and there will be no further explanation of what is meant by a "final project." Attempt to decide on the people your class will

select to do this job, the results of which will affect all of you. What reasons can be given for the choices you have made in each case?

4. Construct your group as an interview team and select a number of recent initiates into fraternities, sororities, college clubs, and so on, to interview. Be sure to select new members of organizations that have some kind of pledge period. Try to develop a composite picture of how these people felt about changes in their value structure and the difficulties they have making their entry into the group. Try to construct a short "information sheet" for prospective new members explaining to them the kinds of problems they might encounter as they seek membership in similar groups.

5. Prepare an information booklet for administrators of "Upward Bound" programs explaining what kinds of problems their students might have when they first appear on campus and how they might go about eliminating or alleviating them.

INDIVIDUAL PROJECTS

1. Try a little introspection. Think back on the various organizations you have joined since coming to college. Can you recall whether you had any ideas at the time of your joining that ran counter to ideas expressed by the group? What happened to these ideas? Do you still cling to them? Verbalize them? Fight for them? In a situation of maximum compulsion, which of your ideals and values do you think you would refuse to give up? For example, how much money would it take to "buy" your vote? What would someone have to do to induce you to change your religion? Would you change your religion to advance your position on a job? Would you change it because you were asked to do so by the woman or man you want to marry? If there were a group of people you wanted to be with very, very much, how many of your personal values would you be willing to recant in order to gain membership in this group?

2. Can you find a case in which you were involved similar to the case of Joe Marks and Tom Smith, where your antago-

nism to another person, or his to you, was so great that you could not respond coherently to what was said or think rationally about the ideas under discussion? What was the outcome of that clash? Did you win or lose and why?

3. If you feel motivated, without notifying the members of your group, why don't you try to force yourself into a position of leadership and keep a record of what happens as the other people respond to you. It would be more interesting if several other people in your group were trying to do the same thing, wouldn't it? How would you prevent them from achieving their goal? How would you conceal your own aspirations? At this point what is happening in your group? Are you sure that there is anyone who is not seeking a leadership position? Is it possible to get a "true" answer?

Leadership, Ranking, and Membership

The literature of group discussion contains the idea that to attain leadership it is necessary to conform to a specific model of personality traits, actions, and appearance. The traits of a leader listed in books read very much like the qualifications of the Ideal Boy Scout. Most of these traits are so nebulous that training in them is virtually impossible. Strength of character, quickness of wit, high intelligence, and so on, may occur separately or simultaneously in many people, but presumably they are the result of a long period of acculturation and development and not amenable to training in a classroom or workshop.

Qualifications of Leaders

But leaders do conform to a kind of model. In the typical American city the representative leader possesses the following characteristics: he is wealthy, educated, older than average, Anglo-Saxon (usually), white, middle-class, and Protestant. This should not be construed as a denigrative statement. The norms of our society are essentially middle-class, Anglo-Saxon and Protestant. To a large extent people born into this culture, or those with other characteristics who participate in it, have learned over the years to adjust their behavior so that they too conform to the model. It might be said that we have developed, since the closing of unlimited immigration, a uniform middle-class American model for leadership. For example, a leader is usually taller than any of his followers. A leader is neither too fat nor too thin. Nor does he have distinguishing peculiarities such as scars, beards, long hair, and so on. Cynically, the leader is the gray flannel man dressed according to the temper of the times—neat, handsome, not bald, smiling yet intense, aggressive but understanding. He is intelligent but not intellectual, and he is somewhat humble about his leadership aspirations, feeling more that the task has been pushed upon him than that he has sought it out. Even leaders that do not conform to this image tend in their behavior to approximate it once they have attained either a formal or informal position of leadership.

This probably sounds like a Madison Avenue description of the ideal man. But it is likely that as you "picture" a leader in your mind the image will be similar. Of course, as we observe specific groups of people, the people who emerge as the leaders have a different pattern. Television has done wonders to "help" us recognize not only the ideal leader described above but the typical Mafia leader, the typical Black Panther, or the typical minister of the First Presbyterian Church.

The recently televised political conventions have demonstrated how widespread this stereotype of leadership is. Without questioning the capabilities of men like Richard Nixon, Eugene McCarthy, Hubert Humphrey, or John Lindsay, it is clear that they do not physically resemble William Howard Taft or Abraham Lincoln. Since they are highly visible, it is necessary that they fit the image of leadership that most Americans have in their minds. Probably, in today's world, it would have been impossible for Einstein to become chairman of a physics department.

It has probably occurred to you that this sounds not so much a description of a "leader" as it is a description of the modal group member. As we will see a little later, there is not much difference.

Short of the question of how a group achieves its tasks most effectively and efficiently, there is probably no subject that is of greater interest than that of leadership within the group. Leadership is a general term that, though useful, tends to obscure some of the important elements which comprise it. Leadership is closely related to the ranking that takes place among group members, the authority that the occupant of a position of leadership chooses to wield, and numerous other qualities of personal style.

Seeking leadership positions normally does not pay off at all. Excessive aggressiveness in striving for leadership positions tends to alienate followers, for the image of, what shall we call it?—humility—must be retained. It is good to be aggressive but not to one's peers. The humble leader always conveys to the followers the notion that they, the followers, could have his job if only they aspired to it and that, furthermore, they, the followers, have the power to manufacture the leaders they choose. Only groups that are centered around a specific and formal organization permit the emergence of authoritarian leaders who have specifically sought the position. And in fact some extremist organizations seem to be led by men who founded the organizations so that they might have a group to lead.

The rank and file can sympathize with an aspiring leader who does not fit the image but generally they will not adopt him, regardless of his policies. In his two campaigns for the presidency of the United States, Adlai Stevenson succeeded in polarizing the emotional commitment of millions of people because he appeared to be more intellectual than they could accept. There is even a hierarchy of professions that are preferred by the rank and file. Physicians and businessmen, for example, are preferable to college professors and factory workers.

The generalization that can be made is that leadership style is determined by the expectations of the membership and the requirements of the situation rather than by the traits of the aspirant individual.   In those cases where leaders are imposed, as in a business or a governmental unit, the criteria for appointment appear to be essentially the same as those criteria that lead to the emergence of leaders in the group.   The operation of a complex industrial or governmental unit cannot be trusted to an individual whose qualities and personality are not acceptable to the people he must lead.   Most attempts at placing people in positions of leadership because of their professional qualities without reference to personality and appearance seem to go awry quite quickly.   Consequently, it is hard to see how people can be taught to become leaders, though it is clear that leaders can be taught.

If we were to ask, "What does a leader look like?" the answer would come back loud and clear, "Very much like the membership, only more so."   A leader may look somewhat more distinguished than his followers and perhaps be a little more forceful, though his force need not be expressed either in vigor of oratory or intensity of movement but rather in "quiet dedication" to the principles for which the group stands.   His capacity to lead is reinforced by his ability to do the things that group members do as well as any and better than most.   In a group of businessmen, for example, leadership usually comes from the middle ranks.   Neither the most committed capitalist nor the most dedicated liberal can lead the whole group.   In his attitudes and commitments the leader must be able to synthesize the widest possible range of beliefs on the part of the membership, and his ability to do this will determine the amount and the extent of loyalty that he receives from his members.   In a group of Negroes the leader has neither the darkest nor the lightest skin and can come from neither the upward mobility ranks nor from the completely déclassé.   In Jewish organizations, at least those that are ecumenical in nature, the leader is usually conservative rather than reformed or orthodox, and in Christian groups members of "the accepted" Protestant denominations are usually tapped for leadership.   On the other hand, as the nature of the group tends toward extremes, the leader may emerge as more extreme from the followers.   A leader of a group of orthodox Jews may appear as quite fanatic to those who do not adhere to the creed. The leader of a group of militant Negroes may appear to be a revolutionary to those who do not share commitment. In short, *the leader looks like the modality of the membership* or what the membership feels the majority should be. If he does not look this way at the outset he will tend to take on the coloration as he consolidates his position.

Leadership and Norms

Every group establishes proper standards of behavior. Some of these standards are simplistic agreements over the proper language to use, accepted mode of dress, and so on. For example, you don't curse in a Baptist church but it is permitted and acceptable in the army. Other standards are extremely complex and based upon acceptance of the modal values of society. In some groups it may be necessary to have agreement on complex religious commitments or on important political attitudes. The less interaction members of a group have with one another the less likely they are to have established a coherent set of standards. These agreements, however superficial, simple, complex, or pervasive they may be, have an effect on the roles of members, and they particularly affect positions of leadership.

There are degrees of agreement that the members of the group have concerning what are the proper standards of behavior within it. If this agreement is minimal, the group is less able to exercise control over its members. This is partly a result of the point that if standards are not agreed upon, the sanctions, that is, both the rewards for adherence and the punishments for departures, are less clear.

In sharp contrast, the more certain a group is that its standards are correct, the more likely it is that member behavior will be affected. In an extreme case, if there is unanimous group judgment, a single individual tends not to hold his contrary opinion even when he "knows" that the group is clearly in error. Fortunately, illustrations of this extreme case are not too common. However, mob action falls within this category. One reason for the infrequency of this extreme unanimity on group standards and objectives is that it is dependent upon thorough, constant interaction of members.

In general, smaller groups tend toward uniformity in the attitudes and actions of their members under a number of conditions. One condition or characteristic of the small group that affects the attitudes of members is the greater quantity of personal interaction. Uniformity will also be enhanced if the interaction occurs on a basis of greater equality, that is, if no individual is selected out and arbitrarily given a very high rank to which others defer. Uniformity will also be enhanced when there is no one exercising authority over other persons in the group. Finally, uniformity would be enhanced when there is less personal competition among group members.

To sustain his position, the leader must not only develop a style representative of the group which he leads, he must also avoid tampering with group goals. He may request and obtain a *specification* of goals. He may even suggest alternatives, but by and large his most effective strategy is to attempt to lead the group to a well-defined goal to which he and they are committed. The leader must be basically a pragmatic man. He is a craftsman; he may be a dreamer but he must temper his dreams with an ability to direct the efforts of others through the essentials and requirements planned and devised as goal seeking. He is more honored for successes at achieving small and well-defined goals than for glorious failures at achieving lofty and nebulous ones.

The concept of separation of powers, embodied in the American constitution with vast powers of legislation, adjudication and execution vested in three different bodies, is essentially characteristic of any democratically based group. The plan or program and, more particularly, the goals of the plan or program, emerge from the group itself and in most cases are the raison d'etre of the group. The specific techniques of achieving goals usually are devised by specialists under the direction of a leader often with some participation by members, but all activities are subject to ratification by the group, which is, in the final analysis, responsible for the work necessary to carry them out. Judgment about the effectiveness of the solutions most often generates from an external body, sometimes the same body that generated the goals. For example, in a corporation, the aims and objectives of the organization are determined by a board of trustees or directors who delegate to an individual called the president the responsibility of achieving the goals. The president assumes control over a membership selected for its skills and abilities and for its commitment to the aims and objectives. These people then proceed to generate ideas, and methods for implementing them, which are in turn passed to the executive and from him to the board of trustees who pass judgment on the prognosis for success. The execution is carried on by a wide variety of interacting and intersecting groups, each representing a microcosm of the main organization, and after a period of time the final judgment of the effectiveness of the whole operation is once again made by the board of trustees, usually after a careful look at the annual audit and particularly the profit-loss statement. Thus the first basic requirement of the leader, regardless of where he came from, how he achieved his power, or where he fits on the organization chart, is to reach the group goal.

Leadership Roles

The nature of the group tasks has an important effect upon the role of the leader in the group. The more specific the task the group has to perform the more important it is the leader possess the knowledge, information, and skill necessary to perform that task. This means that the leader must conform to the standards of the group because the standards are directly and significantly affected by the functions that the group must achieve.

A second major consideration for a leader emerges directly from the first. In order to achieve the group goal, the group must fail minimally or not at all and if the group is to avoid failure, the leader must avoid failure. For this reason leaders are often conservative and restrained about their programs of action. They are normally suspicious of bold programs and are not normally amenable to sweeping reforms and drastic changes in the organizational structure. Although leaders, as well as ordinary mortals, recognize the kind of praise the massive victory may earn, they are quite aware of the effect of devastating failure.   The effective leader concerns himself with doing the doable and to a very large extent his success depends on his ability to distinguish what can be done from what it would be nice to have done.   Effective leadership proceeds through a series of small successes.   Activities in which there is little risk of failure can be added up to represent sufficient success to maintain the forward movement of the organization.

This, of course, is not quite so true in those organizations that develop around the "charisma" of an inspirational leader. There, the followers commit themselves to follow the leader wherever he takes them.   The "revolutionary" leader, for example, retains his power as long as he sustains the struggle, although some followers may return to the establishment ranks. It is interesting to note, however, that when radical leaders bring their followers to victory, they tend to become preservers of a new establishment.   One of the most startling aspects of present-day communism is that the leaders are as conservative and "grey flannel" as those in the more staid and less radical capitalist lands.   The old adage, "reaction follows revolution," becomes meaningful in this light, for once a revolution succeeds, it becomes the establishment and must be conserved.   For this reason, leaders in general tend to discourage or disparage excessive dissent and deviation by the members.   Verbalized dissent, which might lead to the formation of groups hostile to the group goal, tends to threaten the leaders' position and must therefore be avoided.

Within systems, the conservative behavior of leaders is quite rational and results, normally, in limited but steady progress, providing about as much success as the organization is able to accommodate to.   At times of crisis, however, this kind of conservatism is probably not the most effective policy, but the problem is to distinguish between real and spurious crises. How, for example, were buggy manufacturers to know that the noisy, smoke-spewing horseless carriages would eventually destroy their business enterprises?   How were the importers of silk to understand the implications of the invention of synthetic fabrics?   Perhaps if we were looking for the ideal, though impossible, qualifications for leaders, we might include the ability to see the future and to take action to cope with it.   A modern novelist has asserted that sometimes great change is necessary in order to keep things the same. Certainly the buggy manufacturers could have shifted over to the manufacture of automobiles and thus preserved their organizations, and incidentally kept their leaders in power. Perhaps in the organization there were even men who foresaw the potential of the threat and called this to the leaders' attention. Even so, the natural conservatism of organizational leadership prevented the leaders from taking steps to meet the threat.

Retention of power by the leader is often a goal in itself. One other aspect of leadership that must be considered is the tendency that leaders have to enjoy the power conferred on them as leaders. Sometimes the capacity to wield power is so inviting that leaders operate to conserve that capacity rather than to use it to implement organizational goals. This results in a kind of conservatism that threatens organizational purpose, and its result is the proliferation of a complex bureaucracy. So complicated do some organizations become that the task of maintaining the existence of the organization is totally engaging and supersedes the task of utilizing the organization for the purposes for which it was intended. This topic is dealt with facetiously by C. Northcote Parkinson in his book, *Parkinson's Law*. For our purposes, it is necessary to know that there are people who prefer leadership for its own sake. That is, they enjoy the position and the power. They may utilize legitimate channels to obtain their power, but once it has been achieved, their goal becomes rhetorical, that is, to convince the membership that they, the leaders, ought to be retained. There are many students who allege that this is the problem that is causing the present state of unrest on college campuses.

The type of discussion characteristic of most policy planning appears to center around the meaning and implication of events. In the State Department, for example, experts meet in groups and attempt to foresee crises so that a course of action can be ready when they occur. Those who lead, however, have a vested interest in the problems they know how to cope with. New problems threaten their position. The man who heads the South American group would lose his position of power if he were to come up with the notion that relations with the Middle

East should be the cornerstone of American policy. Thus, the leader cannot avoid refracting the information he receives through the glasses of his power, and part of his effort at leadership will be to retain the kind of organization he knows how to lead, dealing with problems he knows how to handle, and utilizing methods at which he is expert.

When something goes wrong in an organization, it cannot necessarily be ascribed to failure of method. Some person must suffer, and it is usually a man in a position of leadership somewhere in the organization. The leader who takes over a failing organization will often play the "new broom" game and sweep the organization clean of its previous leadership, often uncritically. The fault, however, may not lie with the leadership. It may lie in methods of implementation, or in the attempt to pursue spurious goals set by the board of directors, but the fact of life is that the leader is normally penalized when the group fails. (There are those who would add that the group is rewarded when the leader succeeds.)

This leads to a third strategic requirement for leadership, the ability to implement. During organizational phases of group development, leaders are deeply concerned about achieving agreement on aims and goals as well as with setting norms of behavior so that future problems can be dealt with. But once a group has begun to function these kinds of responsibilities are not so important to the leader. Norms will change or remain the same depending on the membership, and this in turn will depend on both internal and external threats to the organization. An industrial organization that has a drop in sales may generate changes in goals throughout the organization, and a new group style might emerge. If the membership feels their economic survival is threatened they may set norms devised to protect their jobs. The leader cannot alter these norms without altering the conditions that led to them. He must, somehow, reconcile the organizational goal with personal goals. For the most part the requirement of leadership is to implement, to carry out, to accomplish, without doing damage to group goals and without thwarting group norms. It is interesting, for example, to note the role of rumor and scandal in complex organizations. For example, in an organization in which the various executives and junior executives largely keep mistresses, the man who is publicly discovered and divorced will be rejected by the other members even though they were also indulging, for the group norm includes the proposition that one not be caught.

A recent experience illustrates some of the problems of leadership within organizations. An affiliate of a major corporation, engaging in research and development work financed by government contract, experienced a crisis. With the change of administration, available research money became scarce. The company attempted to fill in some of its lost business by engaging in light manufacturing, but the parent company moved the manufacturing to some of its other plants that were better equipped to deal with it. Leadership, concerned more for its own survival than for the survival of the organization, began to tighten the reins, cutting costs by cutting employee privilege, and discharging those employees who were most vulnerable. Rumor took over and several key employees, in order to "protect themselves," took jobs elsewhere, thus making the company less able to compete. The leaders attempted to struggle for more business, but couldn't seem to get contracts because they had lost important personnel. The failures of leadership to obtain more business fanned the flame of rumor, and more personnel left. It was impossible to get replacement personnel because of rumors in the community about the impending failure of the company. Thus even the contracts the company had could not be completed. Throughout this entire operation leadership lost contact with the group. Employees were not consulted nor were they kept informed, but, throughout, leadership continued its formality, continued dispensing honors, even to the point of holding a testimonial dinner for one of the vice-presidents. Clearly, this was an instance where the accoutrements of leadership were more important than the objectives of the organization. Leadership could not think clearly for their personal power drives had superseded their concern for the group.

Leaders of organizations find themselves taking a great deal of care not to be caught; for example, not to be caught communicating excessively with some members of the organizations to the exclusion of others. Such activity may generate in the membership the notion that the leader has favorites or that some members have an inordinate amount of influence with him. The leader cannot afford to eschew drinking nor can he permit himself to drink too much. While he may have political opinions he must be careful about expressing these opinions, particularly if they run counter to those of the greater number of group members. In short, a leader's public and private lives are intrinsically bound up with the operation of the organization. To the extent that organizational values permeate his life, his survival as leader depends on the organization's success. It demands that more and more of his private behavior become public. This accounts for the natural conservatism of expression by leaders, and for the dean being the loneliest man on campus.

Groups in which members interact a great deal have a diversity of functions that the leader cannot ignore. Some groups are essentially organized for the purpose of promoting cohesiveness. A family is a group in which the goals are very diffuse or hard to specify and in which there is a protection of those activities that promote emotional and affective satisfaction. However, no matter how specific the task a group must perform, all groups have both of these elements. Similarly it is often the case that different individuals perform a leadership role in attempting to achieve these functions. Thus, a group is likely to generate a task leader and at the same time to develop a social leader or an individual who attempts to promote cohesion and to overcome potential disruption. Most group leaders will give up the instrumental or task role in favor of one which leads to popularity.

Leadership Styles

To achieve group cohesion the durability of the group must be insured and individual members' satisfaction must be maintained. The kind of leader that can best achieve these group and member goals is one who is not overly directive or authoritarian. These points are, of course, most applicable to the small group where most of the members interact constantly with one another. Sentiments are significant and important parts of group life. It follows that leaders will tend to choose those roles and actions that promote those affective member goals.

In small groups authoritarian leaders are less effective in maintaining group cohesion. The authoritarian leader in the small group tends also to be less effective in his ability to permit the group to achieve the tasks for which the group is formed. Thus, it also follows that democratic leadership in the small group is more effective in achieving productivity.

Overall, the leader who will be followed the most devotedly is one who is able to permit the individual members' goals, as well as the group goals, to be achieved.

In contrasting democratic and authoritarian leadership, it should be clear that we are not describing an active or passive person. The activity or passivity of the leadership seems to be quite independent from the style of that leadership. In fact, activity of the leadership is much greater when the group itself is allowed to set its goals. When the group goals are imposed on it, the group tends to be more passive. The leadership process does not take place in a static situation. Instead, it is eminently dynamic. Over time there are some interesting changes that are likely to occur in a leader's relationship to the group process.

First of all, it should be clear that the leader is directly and centrally involved in the ongoing interactions, therefore in the ongoing expression of attitudes and values and standards that characterize the group. The leader affects the means that the group uses to achieve its goals more than he does the goals themselves. The means are the activities that take place as the group attempts to achieve its objectives.

Since the leader is most involved in this process of affecting the ongoing activities of the group, he also tends to stress those activities that are most directly related to the competencies (skills) that he possesses.

Another somewhat disconcerting characteristic is that the longer a given individual possesses leadership within a group the less open and free will be the communications that are exchanged among the group members. And not only are the communications less open but the group also tends to become less efficient in its ability to solve new problems or achieve new goals. This follows from the fact that when groups have been established there have also been established the standards of behavior that are accepted within that group. And it is within the context of these standards that it is difficult for a leader to shift a group's activities. New leaders will have greatest difficulty when they enter groups that are very cohesive and in which there are clearly established standards of action.

Authoritarian and Democratic Leaders

Most discussions on the small group devote considerable space to consideration of leadership style, that is, disadvantages and advantages of the various leadership styles—democratic, authoritarian, and anarchic or laissez faire. Authoritarian leadership is classified as efficient and decisive; democratic leadership is described as slow and sometimes confused but generally most effective because of strong cooperation that generally emerges with decisions in which the members of the group have participated. One must be careful about a rigid categorization of types of leaders. A leader may have achieved his position through democratic action and become very high handed and authoritarian in his operation, while another, externally imposed and possessing considerable power, may choose to democratize his operation. In any case there will be a residue of democratic action in virtually every authoritarian leader and a tenor of authority in the style of virtually every democratic leader.

One of the hazards of authoritarian leadership is that the cooperation in the decisions that result from it may be perfunctory. People may do what they are supposed to do solely out of economic necessity and not because of any commitment to group goals. Such participation need not necessarily be decried for in many authoritarian units perfunctory cooperation is all that is necessary. By the same token, however, unsuccessful authoritarian leadership can generate factionalism, a decline in morale, and considerable behind the scenes jockeying and maneuvering for position among the members. The man who holds considerable power may dispense it at will. Consequently part of the agenda of individual members may very well be a quest for personal approval so that baksheesh can be obtained from the leader for activities peripheral or not even related to the group activity. Furthermore, the authoritarian leader who craves from subordinates only communications of approval may be surprised to find private grousing, back biting, and bickering to be common in the group. The authoritarian leader may move decisively, but if he fails he can expect little support from the members.

On the other hand the democratic exercise of leadership often appears to a superficial observer to be grossly inefficient, resulting in considerable muddle and confusion. Viewed objectively the democratic leader doesn't really appear to be doing his job, and it is for this reason that in industrial complexes many individuals whose natural personality would incline them towards democratic operations affect instead an authoritarian style, for it is necessary that they conform to the norms of executive behavior of the group to which they belong, which is led by another individual with power. The obvious hazard of democratic leadership is that the private complaining characteristic of the authoritarian situation becomes public conflict in a democratic milieu. The things that disturb and rankle the membership become manifest items on the group agenda. Interpersonal hostilities between members, antagonisms toward the leader, dissatisfactions, and concern for personal advancement all become necessary parts of the problem solving that the democratic group confronts. Viewed in these lights it appears, then, that the authoritarian leader will be the most effective leader, but the word "appear" is crucial, for the perception of success may drastically differ from the actuality of success. It doesn't take very long for superordinates to discover that the success that they had perceived resulted from inaction and verbal conformity rather than from problem solving. The potential for sabotage in an authoritarian framework is legion and therein lies the advantage of a democratic leadership style. Once the public conflict has been played out in a democratic group and a consensus of policy and action has been derived there is a strong personal commitment on the part of the members that motivates them to act legitimately to implement group decisions rather than to subvert them. Personal loyalties go to the group cause and the leader; thus the strain of resolving interpersonal conflict reflects itself in the relative satisfaction derived from mutual participation in achieving group goals.

The precise style of democratic leadership escapes description. It is found neither in verbal style nor problem-solving format but somewhere in the interpersonal relations that the leader maintains with members of his group. There are many examples of sham democracy. The use of the vote, for example, does not mean that the group is democratic, and in fact the use of the vote is very often employed by the authoritarian leader in order to obtain ostensible democratic ratification for his personal authoritarian decisions. Quantity of interaction is not a reflection of democratic leadership. For a supervisor to call in his subordinate and ask for his honest opinion does not mean that the opinion presented will necessarily be honest. In order to protect his economic concerns the subordinate will respond according to his notion of what his leader wants him to say. If the leader is a known authoritarian who punishes dissent, expression will be directed to the leader's prejudices. There may be considerable talk in groups run in an authoritarian fashion. Each member may attempt to prove through quantity of output that he is loyal to the leader. To the extent that the authoritarian leader has the power to reward, particularly in the pocketbook, members will attempt to affiliate themselves with his ideas and methods. The man who dissents does so when he has another job lined up. On the other hand, when the going gets rough and disagreement seems to offer the prospect of a new leader, the authoritarian may find himself betrayed by those who appeared quantitatively to be the most loyal.

The democratic leader, on the other hand, may have little actual contact with the members of his group. His leadership may be a leadership of respect—he permits the members to do their work; he listens and utilizes their comments and suggestions, and offers advice when it is either solicited or absolutely necessary. Furthermore, the democratic leader knows that some mistakes are inevitable, and that the group will necessarily suffer from them. He devotes his prime loyalty to achievement of the group goal and operation of the group norms; consequently, his rewards and punishments are designed to promote the group goal.

The dismal fact of democratic leadership is that it demands the ability to stand by and watch considerable human hurt without interference because interference might impede the progress of the group towards its goals and thus harm its general welfare.   A good subordinate who perhaps at one time was a good friend might have to be fired.   An individual with a most violent personality may have to be rewarded because of professional competency.   As long as the norms of the group permit and support this kind of operation the leader dare not intervene. The moment he appears to be a person whose loyalty to the individual is more important than loyalty to the group, he loses his effectiveness as a leader.   This does not mean that the leader must be inhuman.   Most leadership decisions are quite humane when considered in the light of their ramifications for the greatest number of members of the group.   Perhaps it means that the leader must be humane without being human.   For he is the prototype, the image, the embodied expression of the group membership.

Retaining Leadership

This general statement holds true: The more people associate with one another on the basis of essentially equal rank, the more they will share values and attitudes, standards of behavior and, in addition, the more they will like one another in an emotive or affective way.   The statement implies that interaction occurs over a period of time.   New members in small groups tend to feel inferior, that is, not equal in rank, to established members.

Equality, however, is seldom if ever totally achieved. Instead, people evaluate one another on the basis of the values and standards that they have learned to deem significant.   Thus, there are ranks or statuses that men occupy.

In what is one of the classic treatments of leadership in small groups, George Homans in *The Human Group* suggests the hypothesis that *the higher the rank of a person within a group, the more nearly his activities conform to the norms of the group.*   We have defined "norms" to be the standards of behavior that have been accepted by the group.   This suggests a form of centrality in which the persons who conform most closely to the norms or standards are also the persons who have the higher rank.

These persons who have higher rank are also the persons who are most involved in interactions within the group. And finally, and most significantly, they are the persons who are held to be the most influential. To say an individual is most influential suggests he is most capable of getting other persons to do the things he wishes done.

Once a leader has reached a position where his influence is firm he will emerge as an individual norm-setter. The group will acclimate itself to his problem-solving style and their communications will adapt themselves to his speech style. If the leader displays concern for personal feelings and expresses individual understanding in his communications, this pattern will be reflected down through the hierarchy. If, on the other hand, the leader is peremptory in his direction, this too will become characteristic of the communications of his subordinates. But as the leader retains his position there will be a tendency among group members to rely upon him more and more for routine decisions to the point where the leader becomes a director of activities according to plans previously developed and agreed on. While formal assignment of this responsibility may not take place there seems to develop a passive acceptance of the leader's authority to direct the behavior of group members, and often it is difficult for the group members to distinguish routine tasks to which the leader may appropriately devote directive efforts from goal setting that should legitimately involve the membership.

In any event, retaining a position of leadership depends on the support of the membership. The members may make or break a leader. There are numerous examples of executives placed in charge of industrial units whose tenure of office was exceedingly short because their employees would not tolerate their personalities or their problem-solving styles because they were not representative of their previously evolved norms. A leader remains a leader only as long as he succeeds and his success is measured from two vantage points. If he holds a position of leadership in a complex structure, there will be someone over him with higher authority who will evaluate his work. At the same time, his work is evaluated by those who constitute his group. It is evaluated by them in terms of personal payoff; that is, in the feelings of comfort and security they derive from group membership, the amount of satisfaction they derive from participation and the tangible reward that comes from successful problem solving. Furthermore, very few people are leaders without being members of some other group. The supervisor or foreman may lead groups and at the same time be part of another group made up of his peers and supervised by another person higher up in the hierarchy. His position as leader in one milieu may depend on his ability to conform to the norms of the group to which he belongs.

Retaining leadership is thus a tenuous activity at best. It is for this reason that there is considerable shuffling of personnel between jobs in industrial units. Those who succeed are moved into positions higher in the hierarchy and given harder tasks to do. Those who fail may be frozen at a specific level in the hierarchy. It is perhaps for this reason that the "Peter Principle" of administrative leadership reads, "each man rises to his first level of incompetency." Once a leader has been clearly defined as incompetent there is considerable striving among the members of his group to displace him or bypass him regardless of the rules of seniority and tenure that may prevail in the organization. Leadership must then be characterized by sensitivity of communications in two directions. Communications upward to superiors in the hierarchy must demonstrate accomplishment while communications to the followers must reflect concern for their welfare and that tangible rewards have accrued from the leader.

Supervisory leadership is somewhat easier to examine than the leadership of more amorphous group structures such as action groups, pressure groups, and social groups. In supervisory leadership there is a clear appointment of the leader and clear assignation of the responsibilities and duties both upward and downward. In groups that function independent of an organization leaders are more easily replaced, and, as a matter of fact, in such groups there is considerable fluctuation in leadership and frequently no crystallization of a formal leader. Various members may assume different types of leadership. In a formal sense the group may be leaderless. The formalization of leadership through a vote represents the initial stages of institutionalization. But it is the rare organization that endows a leader with permanence. Virtually all have built into their basic rules of procedure a method of naming new leaders periodically as well as a method of removal of leaders whose activities have not been satisfactory to the group.

In a supervisory capacity, the leader's task, that is, the problems he is to solve, are externally imposed. For this reason it is not so necessary for him to extend his activities into the social arena nor is it mandatory that he develop a style of individual interaction with the people who constitute his group. It is in these groups that a "social leader" most often emerges to care for interpersonal needs. The imposed leader cannot afford to be too warm and friendly, for he has authority to interfere with the economic goals of those designated as subordinates. Thus, he has a formal weapon for enforcing his will. Although he may be bypassed or replaced because his solutions were not satisfactory, he has considerable leeway to act on his own without consultation. Such authority as the members of the group possess to decide on matters of consequence to them is granted to them from the reservoir of authority that the leader possesses.

The leader of a group that determines its own activities may find it necessary to democratize the decision making if he hopes to retain his position of leadership, for his membership has sufficient authority and power to remove or replace him if they are unsatisfied with either the decision making or with his style of leadership; and it is not uncommon to have members of such groups point out, while the organization is going nicely, that they can no longer tolerate the high-handedness of the leader. It is understandable that leaders of voluntary groups that determine their own activities are considerably more active in interpersonal communications than in groups where tasks are designated and the leader appointed.

Specialized Leadership Roles

Within any type of group, regardless of how a formal leader is designated, various members will and must assume leadership roles and these are needed by the group. The democratic kind of leadership is perhaps best characterized by the fact that it permits special purpose leaders to function. The authoritarian may hold in his hands all the power and all the responsibility—and he will usually end up doing all the work. The democratic leader is sensible enough to permit and often encourage the development of people with special skills who can emerge from time to time and lead the group through a problem that calls for his special talents.

The various types of leaders that might emerge, and this is only a partial list, are the front man, the expediter, the game leader, the wisdom purveyor, the idea man, the inspirational figure, and the master of technique.

The front man is the individual who possesses singular skills at dealing with external bodies and individuals outside the group. He is usually quite loyal to the group's goals and embodies within him most of the group norms. He also possesses the skill of being able to adapt and adjust himself to the norms of other groups at least temporarily so that it is possible for him to develop a channel of communication to others on matters of common concern.

The expediter, the efficiency expert, is an individual who can perceive that the group is going astray—either spending too much time on recreation and enjoyment, or wasting time, or pursuing false leads. The expediter will assume the position of demanding that the group return to its agenda of problem solving and devote its attention to the task at hand.

The game leader is the counterpart of the expediter. He recognizes that the process of group problem solving is complicated and often boring. From time to time he plays the role of lifting the spirits of the group, leading them out of the morass in which they might find themselves into a sort of temporary game interaction—perhaps telling jokes, perhaps inserting digressions. This is a role that cannot be consciously played. Formal attempts to get the group to digress or relax may meet with failure. But a person with particular skill can temporarily command the attention of the group and lead them into a more relaxed demeanor.

Most groups profit from having a man of wisdom among them who has had considerable experience in a followership role or perhaps an old, deposed leader who has confronted a problem many times over even though in other contexts. Such a person can intrude into the group and provide essential history both of the particular group and the ways that the problem has been approached by others in the past. While excessive power in the hands of the giver of wisdom may make the group excessively conservative and reactionary it is imperative that a group understand where failures have taken place both within it and elsewhere, and unless someone is present who can provide a historical record it is quite likely that the group will recapitulate the errors of those who came before.

Every group seeks ideas and unfortunately not all members are capable of giving an original cast to their problem solving. For this reason, those group members who are capable of a bit of imagination and who are willing to assert boldly new and unique ways of approaching a problem are quite useful. The more alternatives that a group of problem solvers has to explore, the wider the range from which they can make their choices. There is no substitute for an idea man. Although techniques have been devised to force an output of ideas (brainstorming), there is still no substitute for the original thinker, and, as a matter of fact, brainstorming proceeds best when the people who participate in it are original and spirited. It is not a substitute for originality, it is a cultivator of originality.

Sometimes an inspirational leader is necessary, a veritable Billy Graham of discussion, to admonish the group to continue. Group interaction is very likely to get boring and frustrating at periodic intervals. Often, groups will follow the path of least resistance, and when they encounter periods of boredom, they will seize upon the nearest available solution and adapt it to provide surcease to their ennui. A pep-talker can keep them moving, get them over the hump. Perhaps after the game leader has eased the tension, the inspirational man can take over, whip the group back into a state of interest and permit the idea man to move in with an original path for the group to follow.

A master of technique, a systems man, is often vital to group progress. If a group is moving too rapidly it may be that they have omitted some very necessary steps in their thinking. Someone is needed to keep the group on a track, to follow some kind of system or agenda so that their final solution will not be "half-baked." A systems man in charge of a group often becomes a pedant and routine fellow, but if he exists in juxtaposition with idea men, wisdom-givers, game leaders, and a group led by a democratic leader willing to allow these men to function freely, he may provide necessary frameworks around which the apparent anarchy of problem solving can be systematized.

Most groups could also use a personal advice-giver, a "Dear Abby," whose job is to provide personal guidance and counseling to the frustrated and defeated. Factual experts are often necessary, specialists who emerge to help the group through complicated matters by sharing their expertise. Public relations men are sometimes helpful, particularly when a group has found a solution that does not appear to be popular with those outside who may have to ratify it. In a democratic framework all of these leadership types and more may emerge. It is unreasonable to expect the designated leader to perform all of these functions, but it is not unwarranted to expect that he will encourage their emergence, or at least permit them to operate when they do emerge. Therein lies the real strength of democratic type leadership, for the autocrat presumes to combine all these talents, but usually does not.

Robert Bales once studied problem-solving groups and found the roles in small groups could be classified into a number of neat types. The types were based on three behavioral variables: attempts by individuals to stand out and achieve personal goals, attempts to assist the group in achieving group goals, and efforts to assure satisfactory (not tension filled) relations among the group members. Rarely are all these activity types found in the same individual. When they are, the group has in its midst the embodiment of the traditional concept of the "great leader." Other combinations yield types such as the task specialist, the social specialist, and the over- and under-active deviants.

The task of leading a group is arduous and unpleasant. It is, as some say, an ulcer business. The pressure to succeed in an organizational structure combined with the pressure for satisfactory interpersonal relationships with fellow workers, supervisors, and subordinates, generates much personal tension, yet there seems to be quite a competition to attain positions of leadership. Few of us, for example, do not, in our daydreams, see ourselves in positions of great responsibility and authority. It is easy to romanticize the life of the leader. Outwardly leaders do have the power of control, but it is rare that laymen, even close followers, can appreciate the kinds of pressures and tensions the leader feels. As a result, contention for positions of leadership runs high, but only a few attain it and even fewer are successful at exercising it.

The task of leadership would, perhaps, be easier, if leaders did not have to defend themselves constantly against power plays of aspiring leaders. On the other hand, if people did not aspire to leadership, control of groups would be frozen in a few hands and leadership would become co-opting or oligarchic—the group would lose its vitality and power to motivate the best talents from the membership.

Some Dilemmas of Leadership

Perhaps the foregoing has been simple to read and simple to understand. If so, we have not done a satisfactory job of detailing the complexities of leadership of groups. To be absolutely sure that there is no misunderstanding of the complexities of leadership, we offer, for your consideration, some problems which are unresolved and which confront most participants in group activity.

1. It is hard to isolate group activity within complex organization structures. We have, thus far, in this chapter, talked about both large and small groups. We did so because we had to. In every case, members of one group may be leaders of another, and leaders of groups are members of still other groups. The complex motives that are generated because of multiple membership exert considerable influence on the behavior of both leaders and followers. The democratic leader of a

task group may be a member of another group, higher in the hierarchy of the organization run by an autocratic leader. How do the demands placed on him by his autocratic leader reflect themselves in his leadership of his own group? What of the lieutenant who wishes to be a "friend to his men," but whose captain is an authoritarian of the old school?

2. The problem of multiple membership confronts us with the problem of conformity. To what norms do we conform when we act? When a leader is functioning as leader on one hand, and as member of another group on the other, how does he reconcile the problem of being required to represent the norms of both groups to which he belongs? If the norms are not vastly different, there is no real problem, but if the norms differ considerably, real dissonance can result. An engineer who supervises men in the field in a casual, democratic way has considerable difficulty when he reports to the home office for a year-end meeting and he is required to adapt himself to the internal norms of the main organization.

3. In a task group, how are followers motivated to do the task imposed by an outside authority when they can see no particular relevance to the task? In what sense must the leader also be a rhetorician functioning on behalf of his authorities to motivate his followers to take an interest in their activities? It is fairly simple to pay men to follow routines and perform simple tasks, but it is quite difficult to get them so involved in what they are doing that they will devote talent and energy to improving the process or activity. Furthermore, what if the goals implied in the task assigned run counter to personal or group goals of the men who have to do the work? Can a group of men plan for the integration of a computer operation into a company when they know that the new operation will mean that many of their friends or even they will lose their jobs?

4. How is it possible for an organizational leader operating in a remote position of supervision to get information from the people who are performing the tasks? The very nature of the position demands an authoritarian air. How is he to assess the accuracy or the lack thereof of the reports that reach him from his subordinates or group members, who in turn are supervising aspects of the operation? Can he be guaranteed that each man

will report honestly or will each of the subleaders try to make his own operation look good in order to earn rewards for himself and his men?

The problem of individual input into the determination of group standards and methods becomes more and more complex as the size of the organization increases. As size increases, the number of interactions and, in turn, the number of communications necessary to achieve optimum contact increases. The larger the group the more certain active and highly motivated individuals are to dominate the communication process within the group, yet it cannot be assumed that the people who talk the most also make the most sense or possess the most accurate and important information. It is almost impossible for a leader operating remotely to discover reliable sources of information, and when he discovers sources that are clearly unreliable it is sometimes too late to save the organization.

Followership and Ranking

We have talked, at length, about leaders, where they come from, and what they have to do. The work is really done by the followers, however, and it is specious to assume that followership confers equality. There are degrees of followership and degrees of quality in participation. For this reason, hierarchies, or ranks, develop in groups, which in turn may result in disruptive factions, or in the emergence of highly talented new leaders.

The act of participation in group activity is dynamic and challenging, if the individual wishes it to be, or it is dull and routine, a legitimate escape from challenge. Some followers are eager and aggressive about asserting their ideas and they affiliate themselves strongly with implementation of the group goals. Other followers seek a kind of nurturance from the group and use it as a refuge from personal responsibility. One of the problems of leadership is to distinguish among the various types of followers, for as the leader is able to discriminate quality from a lack thereof, he can improve the function and operation of his group.

The concept of "ranking" is closely associated with the con-

cepts of "role" and "status." Taken together, these three ideas
provide the substance for the development of norms of behavior
to which members must conform if they are to remain participating members of the group. Failure to play an appropriate
role, excessive challenge to accepted roles played by others,
threats posed to the hierarchy, challenging to the values which
permit one member to hold a rank over another, spell lack of
conformity. Conformity is the imperative for survival as a
group member. It is not a bad word!

Conformity of members to group norms provides the cohesiveness that permits a group to remain a group. Acceptance of
conferred role and status, adoption of the system of communications approved by the group, deference to the leader, association with group goals, and in some cases, behaving in a fashion
similar to that of the other members are essentials in conformity. While the word "nonconformity" has taken on connotations, of late, of being a sort of virtue, there really can be no
such thing for any person who remains within the confines of
some sort of social system. A person, through an act of not
conforming to the norms of one group, may find himself conforming specifically to the norms of another.

Thus, understanding of how members develop their relationships in a sort of conformity hierarchy is essential to understanding the group process, and appreciation of this aspect of group
behavior is imperative to survival in a group context.

During our stay in the elementary school we are exposed to a
kind of training known as "learning social skills." Presumably
this is to prepare us for social situations we will face in life.
The success or failure of our training in social skills pays off in
our ability to participate in groups. Virtually every group,
regardless of size, develops a ranking of members. Sometimes,
as in formal organizations, this is expressed in the organization
structure, so that professors outrank the associate professors
who outrank assistant professors and so on or, in the fraternity,
seniors have considerably more prestige than freshmen. There
is an informal ranking system too. There may be no clearly
stated set of rules, yet virtually every member can point out
people in the group to whom they accord high or low status.
Presumably these decisions are based on how well the members

conform to the accepted norms of the group. The closer the conformity, the higher the social rank as measured by accepted group norms. In formal organizations there will probably be two independent ranking systems: one formal and one informal.

The individual who does not conform to group norms and values is generally not highly regarded by the members. While there may be some interaction with him during the time the group is transacting its business, he may be effectively barred from social or recreational activities outside the group. As a nonconforming member he stands as a challenge to whatever mores and norms the group has developed. However, a threat to norms from outside the group is not particularly dangerous to morale and in fact it tends to solidify the group. For example, the most effective way to build a strong fraternity system is to have it vigorously challenged by a vigorous group of independents or by a college administration. When the challenge comes from within the group, however, it develops a seed of doubt in the minds of the members who may find it singularly uncomfortable to reexamine their belief structures. The easiest way to resolve dissonance caused by the nonconforming member is to reject him and deny him the benefits the group has to confer.

Interaction Networks

Within each group, regardless of size, a series of interaction networks will tend to evolve. These networks are made up of people similar in communication styles, social choices, and attitudes toward legitimate questions confronting the group. But there are few gross differences between separate interaction networks in the same group and each of them will maintain lines of contact with others so that they do not develop into cliques or factions. Some members, in fact, will function in several networks. Once again an examination of the fraternity is useful. In any house there will be a group of men committed to card playing, another to dating, another to athletic events, and perhaps even one devoted to academic pursuits. Members of these networks will spend the greater part of their social interaction time with each other. But each will tend to reserve some time to make contact with participants in other networks and even to participate occasionally in their preferred activities. If, however, the social interaction networks are permitted to solidify, then there is a severe threat posed to the structure of the entire group.

What this really means is that as long as there is tight conformity and commitment to the stipulated goals of the organization, a degree of diversity can be permitted in secondary or peripheral interests. It is possible to reject the marginal interests of various members or networks of the group without losing influence or position in the hierarchy. In fact, often the strongest leadership develops from individuals classified as social loners whose commitments to the group's aims and objectives transcend the marginal social commitments. The individual who rejects the main goals and norms of the group, however, will be barred from significant influence within the group structure as well as from social interaction.

As groups tend to solidify and crystallize—to institutionalize —norms it becomes less possible to change them. At the early stages of group development, dissenting members may have a strong influence on decision-making methods depending on the reputation and skill that they bring to the group. But once norms have emerged and are clearly accepted by the greater number of group members, change in style becomes less and less possible.

To the extent that a group's objectives are vague and not directed towards a specific goal or are purely social, the hierarchy of the membership will be developed around social skills. Once a group has confronted a number of problems, however, it becomes necessary for them to develop techniques of problem solving. They will tend to orient themselves around fact finding techniques, verbal formulae, inspirational discovery, or they will seek what Eric Berne refers to as "euhemerus," that is, a charismatic figure who embodies the aims, objectives, and goals of the group. Once style has crystallized, the member who rejects it is regarded as a deviant by the greater number of members and loses his ability to exert influence. The group may not be able to expel him, but they can regard him as irrelevant and accord him low rank.

Assignment of Rankings

Not all groups are thoroughly rational about their problem solving. Some groups, the John Birch Society for example, base their decisions on words of wisdom by accepted authorities. The leadership determines which authorities are acceptable and which are not. The accepted authorities are exemplary of the norms and goals of the group. Consequently, the possibility of bringing about change in goals or methods of achieving them is sharply reduced. The group will then decide on hierarchical positions by determining how faithful the member is to the revealed dogma. The man who challenges an accepted authority, or offers as an authority someone not accepted by the leadership, will find his status lowered and his capability of finding nurturance from the group materially reduced.

Social groups also may not choose to use formal problem-solving techniques, and may rely on high status members for inspirational ideas. Many campus organizations, for example, will embark on projects doomed to failure because they have not been satisfactorily planned. Failure, however, will not be ascribed to the members who proposed the idea, but will rather be blamed on the "system" or some external force. The value of members in these groups is determined by wit and sparkle rather than by solid performance. In fact, the member who insists on careful planning may find himself reduced to low status and ignored.

Often, in social groups, high rank is accorded the individual who conforms most rigidly to the obvious norms of appearance and behavior. The good drinker, the fashionable dresser, or the effective lover may hold high rank in a collegiate social group, regardless of his other qualities or lack of them. Capacity to influence decision making will depend, then, on social popularity measured by conformity to norms of social behavior and appearance.

Some groups, whose goals are nebulous and vague, as community service groups—Kiwanis, Rotary and the like—may utilize verbal formulae in their problem solving and will attempt to phrase statements in response to problems which are they themselves phrased so loosely that they can be accepted by the greater number of members. In such cases, the member who demands a planned course of action will appear to be the deviant in the group and will have small chance to exert his influence. For example, one such organization, responding to the assassination of Martin Luther King, Jr., came up with a report that said all members should "search their hearts and attempt to take whatever action they deem necessary to satisfy their conscience at this dark hour." A member who suggested that a collection of funds be made for the Southern Christian Leadership Council was summarily rejected and his further attempts to achieve a specific course of action were ignored by the bulk of the members.

Still another way of achieving a higher position in the group hierarchy would be the achievement of a record of success. In organizations such as the PTA, the rewards conferred on successful committee chairmen are other committees to chair. A secondary leadership structure becomes definitively established, and the bulk of the decision making is vested in the hands of a few high status members who are willing to do the work. The organizational structure is sufficiently loose and the goals of the organization sufficiently cloudy so that individual members feel no sense of loss when programs are carried on that they find uninteresting or dull. The higher status members who decide on the programs can be honored for their willingness to work and privately the rank and file of the membership can assert that they could have done better if they had had the time to devote to it. But since they did not they are perfectly willing to give public approval to the program and confer high status on those responsible.

In an industrial organization proven success receives significant payoff in dollars. Both promotion and economic advancement are very closely associated with demonstrated skill in confronting problem assignments. When these kinds of rewards are at stake there is considerable scrambling for opportunities to display skills and more than a little effort exerted to subvert those people who are succeeding. The successful problem solver in an industrial organization may find himself rewarded by a higher formal status position and more money in the paycheck but he may find that each move upward brings him the hostility of those individuals who remain in a lower position in the hierarchy.

Still another way of achieving status within the group is through what the rhetorician calls "ethos." The reputation a man brings into the group may confer on him high status and considerable ability to influence others. This reputation may be based on solid achievement or it may result from a number of public relations techniques, but if he can pose as an expert in a group in which there are no experts, his ability to control is almost limitless. For example, a university committee on "disadvantagement" had on it one member who had a reputation for contact with highly placed government officials, whose names he dropped with great frequency. Because of his presumed expertise, he was permitted to generate several programs, which he turned over to others to administer. When they failed, he was not penalized; the blame was placed on the subadministrators and he was permitted to generate more and more ideas and achieve more and more power. Apparently it occurred to no one that he actually lacked ability as an administrator. In fact, this was not even at issue. He had a reputation and this was sufficient!

People with high reputations in one grouping tend to attempt to extend their influence into other groups. Actors turned politicians, athletes turned social actionists and endorsers of razor blades and deodorants are examples of this tendency. More important is the apparent tendency of school boards to select successful athletic coaches for positions of administrative responsibility.

A long record of ineptitude on the part of a group member with a high reputation may motivate opposition after a time, but in some cases, reputation can be so strong as to make the possessor immune to attacks from the membership. Belief in the high reputation member becomes a group norm.

Status in the group does not necessarily correlate with affect. People in a group may enjoy high status and may retain it against opposition but this does not necessarily mean that they will be accepted as social companions. Even those who achieve their status through exercise of social skills do not necessarily retain their social acceptability once they have had an opportunity to utilize their status in decision making. At the point where a social group becomes a task group, or at the point when goals and norms crystallize, new criteria of evaluation may be employed by group members in order to determine status. For this reason, in most groups, position is tenuous. Today's hero may be tomorrow's bum and yesterday's bum may be today's prophet. A few groups attempt to protect themselves through the use of a euhumerus concept and limiting the kinds of outcomes of problem solving, particularly where the problem solving involves some kind of stake or reward system for them. They will alter their evaluations of others depending on the contribution made to their personal gain.

Status and Conformity: Dissent

On college campuses all over the country there has been, in recent years, a great deal of concern with "conformity." This is an elusive word and hard to pin down. It is not clear at any moment whether conformity refers to the accepting of norms of belief or whether it means outward behavior similar to the behavior of the norm. Some cynics view conformity as the ability of a man to alter his beliefs and behavior in order to remain in the largest and strongest group. In any event, the person who rejects the norms and the behaviors of the group and shows either through actions or words that he does not accept standards of belief and behavior held by the others around him can become a pariah, a "reject" to be laughed at or scorned. Since rejection is quite intolerable, the irony is that those people who dissent soon find each other and develop their own group with their own norms of behavior and beliefs to which they can then conform. Individual dissenters in a dissenting group may not conform to the norms of the majority around them but they will conform to the norms of their fellow dissenters. It is necessary for them to do this in order to maintain a feeling of homeostasis and to avoid the feeling of alienation that comes from total rejection.

The dissent characteristic of the college peace groups in 1967–1970 was unsettling to those who conformed to institutional norms. While the spokesmen for the majority of society gave lip service to the doctrine that dissent was important, it was clear that in most cases the dissenters were watched with a beady eye and were either opposed vigorously or not taken seriously by those who had influence over the decisions of the majority. Thus even a collectivity of dissent may make little headway in adjusting the norms of belief and behavior of a larger group. However, it is possible for groups of dissenters to pull members from the majority group by offering to members warmth and toleration, thus making themselves stronger.

Unfortunately, the less influence the dissenting group exerts on the majority, the more likely it is that the minority will become solidified in their own beliefs and behaviors to the point where they find it equally difficult to accept newcomers into the group. Their norms force them into a kind of doctrinal purity characteristic of radical groups of both the right and the left and despite their verbalized concern for the welfare of the majority, to maintain their structure they find it necessary to cleave together so tightly that the very people that they seek to act on behalf of are effectively barred from participation with them.

Communication Skills in the Group

Most groups, however, recognize that some divergence of opinion is necessary to sensible problem solving. Accepting only one view is a policy fraught with peril, though it is difficult to recognize that out of diversity can come the kind of intelligent and ordered program best suited to the solution of a problem. It is virtually impossible, however, to introduce contradictory information or ideas into a group without evoking some kind of hostile response. As a result, many participants in small groups resist responsibility for introducing such material even when they are capable of doing so. Some leaders and members even find it useful to adopt a position of devil's advocacy, hoping to persuade people who advocate ideas to put themselves in a position of risk by considering opposing ideas. Such activity is jarring, however, and, on occasion, instead of motivating new ideas, hostility polarizes against the devil's advocate. His recourse may be to admit that he was merely presenting an idea to the group for their consideration, but sometimes it is possible for such an advocate to begin to believe what he says and to find himself forced into a position of defense in which each attack on him by group members only strengthens his commitment to the view he started out with in fun.

One of the chief concerns of training in small groups is to inculcate into the learner the proposition that he has a responsibility to share ideas with the group, even though they may be contradicted or objected to by others. The extent to which an individual member can overcome his awkwardness or embarrassment about doing this, and the extent to which he does not go situationally reticent, will determine much of his influence. The individual who seeks power blatantly may relish the chance to present his ideas, but the group can usually distinguish sincere advocacy from a power play. Status is usually conferred on the man who tries sincerely to persuade others that his information is at least worth listening to and, if possible, that it should be believed and incorporated into the group decision.

To this end formal training in communication skills is quite useful. Unfortunately, most groups have unbalanced participation, with a few people who are skillful as speakers and others who, because of low self confidence or lack of experience, evade the responsibility to speak out. They become passive, low status members.

The action in groups centers around the more vocal members. They tend to dominate the deliberations and, to the extent that they do this, they also dominate the decision making. A recent study of young, unemployed males in the ghetto indicated that the most powerful person in the street-corner community is not the one who is most powerful physically but rather the most effective talker. This should not be surprising for there is a tendency throughout our society to confuse glibness with intelligence. There is no necessary correlation between the two. Although a glib and facile person may be intelligent, he may also possess only a superficial knowledge of the subject on which he speaks, and, consequently, the group may be led astray by according high status to those with high verbal skills. Some kind of arrangement is needed for those who are somewhat reticent so that they will have an opportunity to speak out.

The critical dissenting member of the group can be exceedingly valuable in raising the quality of group decision making. He may sacrifice some of his popularity in the group, though he may achieve high status because of his contribution to the group goal. Each time he uses his skill at persuasion to compel the group to accept a new idea, he may store up a reservoir of hostility. No matter how a member may focus on the goal, it takes considerable strength of character to admit error, even when it is obvious. Once the admission is made, one cannot help but feel some hostility directed toward the person who evoked the confession.

As groups work through the initial stages of organization, attempting to crystallize their objectives and develop norms of behavior, the dissenter may emerge as a leading and dominant figure. There are usually many dissenters representing a variety of positions in groups that are just getting started and, indeed, it is even possible initially to obtain in a group a norm of dissent. Sometimes, however, the norm of dissent leads only to a consensus of "agreement to disagree" and consequently does not assist the group's efforts in developing tangible programs designed to meet its problems. These groups, however, which have built into their norms a policy of acceptance for dissent, generally can develop the most effective solutions to problems. Furthermore, groups in flux normally do not have rigidly developed norms and so there is considerable opportunity for members to adopt a variety of roles within the group and experiment with them until they find the role that is most comfortable for them. Once most of the members reach this stage, the norms of the group crystallize and protocols are established between members so that it is clearly understood that one will take notes, one will state facts, one will question the facts, one will prod the group ahead, one will attempt to amuse the group and dispel boredom, and so on. Hierarchies and ranks will tacitly emerge—no formal agreement is necessary. Adoption of roles will solidify in the individual minds, and once a role has been adopted the other group members will continue to perceive the individual as playing that role. He will be almost obligated to sustain it, in order to hold his position in the group, for if he alters it he appears to be a dissenter and his status begins to diminish.

If a strong leader has emerged and set a style, the rest of the group conforms.   Or a leader may emerge to represent the group style.   At the outset of group organization, when members are seeking their appropriate roles, it is easier for them to reject ideas than it is to approve them.   It is for this reason that organizational phases of groups are often attenuated.

Once norms have been established, however, agreement is an easier course of action than dissent, and it is at this point that the group begins to institutionalize.   Once the institutional phase has been reached in group organization the quality of group decision making and its ability to respond to external challenges is severely weakened.   Institutional phases of organizations are usually concerned with the establishment of records, buildings, and the formalities of interaction.   Activity directed toward group problem solving often then becomes perfunctory and routine.   Those decisions that have been made in the past will be made over and over again.   The perceptions of the group will be drastically altered so that decision-makers tend to alter conditions in their own mind to make them fit the solutions they have available, rather than attempting to devise a solution for conditions as they are.   In the institutionalized phase of group activity the man who communicates dissent must be ejected because he represents a severe threat to the structure of the group.

Those with considerable ethos, however, may continue to object.   A man of considerable reputation with a long record of participation in the group may take it upon himself to change his mind and introduce new ideas into the group norm.   This may be illustrated by looking at the career of the late Arthur Vandenberg.   Prior to World War II, Senator Vandenberg, a confirmed isolationist highly regarded by his senatorial colleagues, altered his view of world affairs and demanded that the United States begin a stronger participation in the world community.   Because of his strong ethos he was capable of persuading many others of the correctness of his position and thus brought about a change in his political party which has continued to this day.   A person of lesser ethos, however, in a similar situation, can easily be regarded as a troublemaker, while the high ethos person may be classified as an "objective man," "a clear thinker," "a seeker after truth."

What is important in confronting the small group then, is that there is generally considerable activity among members as they seek a position within the group. They may seek their position because of deep feelings about the group goal, or merely because it is satisfying to them, but hardly any group member will remain static in his ideas or his behavior. Consequently, it might be asserted that the small group has considerable influence over the behavior of its members.

The Influence of Small Groups on Their Members

Once you've committed yourself to membership in a small group there is no way to escape pressure to conform to whatever norms the group has established. The word "conformity" has received considerable attention in recent years and it has taken on some very unpleasant connotations. "Conformity," however, is not an evaluation. It is a description. Totally idiosyncratic behavior is normally handled by incarceration in either a prison or a mental hospital. Regardless of how individualistic we might think we are, our survival in society demands that we conform to some set of norms for behavior. Though there is no requirement that we feel in conformity with others, our public acts of conformity tend to push our beliefs into line with those of the people around us. The intensity of your commitment to a group will tend to determine the degree to which you conform with the standards of behavior of the group. That is to say, a group that satisfies a great number of your personal needs will very likely influence many of your personal behaviors. On the other hand, a group to which you have made limited commitment will have minimal effect on your behavior. The various groups to which you belong may contend with each other for your commitments, and, as we have noted in the previous section, the stronger you feel about the importance of the group, the more likely you are to conform to that group's demands. Or, viewed from another perspective, if you have a choice, you are likely to elect membership in a group that reflects your basic values.

The fraternity–sorority system is a good case in point. Normally fraternities and sororities attract individuals who have been acculturated, prior to their arrival on a college campus, with the notion that fraternity and sorority membership is of very great importance and necessary to their success in a college environment. Others may be attracted to fraternities and sororities who haven't had sufficient social interaction prior to coming to college and who have built in their minds an image of a fraternity and sorority satisfying their individual and personal needs. There may be others who, because of their skills, qualifications, intelligence, athletic capability, or personal appearance are desired as members by the fraternities and sororities, but who are neutral in their own commitment. Once these various individuals have been pledged to the organization an acculturation process begins. The fraternity is essentially a social group. Its problem solving consists mainly of finding recreation and amusement on one hand and solving the nittygritty problems of managing a residence house on the other. These problems can and do occupy the major amount of decision-making time among the fraternity members charged with their responsibility. But since fraternities and sororities represent "microcultures," that is, small groups of people living, working, and interacting together over extended periods of time, the influence of the organization will spill over into other areas. Norms of behavior become so deeply rooted that on every campus there is a folk wisdom about the behavior patterns of the respective Greek letter organizations. One may be identified as an "athletic house," another as a "brain house," a third as a "social house," a fourth a "drinking house" and so on. The image of the organization is a reflection of its norms, which in turn pressures the members to conform to the image and provides a criterion for selection of new members as well as a standard against which personal behavior can be evaluated and adjusted.

But not every member of a Greek letter organization adjusts his behavior. Those who have been sought after and have no deep commitment often find themselves believing and acting against the organization norms. Each Greek letter organization has had considerable experience with members either disaffiliating from the organization entirely or moving to the fringes and taking little part in the business or social interactions of the group. Those who are committed to the norms of the fraternity and whose basic needs are satisfied by its activities are perfectly willing, however, to commit themselves to make adjustments in their behavior and so become conforming members of the Greek letter house. This may mean that they submit themselves to advice about how to dress, who to date, and who to associate with outside the fraternity although none of these matters is crucial to the main business of the organization. To the extent that the preponderance of members commit themselves to the aims and goals, values and behaviors of the organization, cohesiveness results.

Cohesiveness in Groups

Cohesiveness may be regarded as a synonym for conformity. An organization may be considered "tight" when there are a great number of values and behaviors on which the membership agrees. Those may be relevant to or peripheral to the aims and objectives of the organization. To the extent that an organization is cohesive the member who will have the most influence and decision making is usually the member who best represents the values and behaviors prized by the group. Members who express deviant opinions or who engage in activities that are not group-approved will lose their influence. Members may find themselves moving toward the fringes of influence because they took part in political activity, if political activity is not part of the commitment made by the group. While the political activist members may attempt to persuade their "brothers" to take part in political activities, the likelihood is very great that the majority of members would seek to persuade the deviant to cease his activity and to dissuade others from joining him. The likelihood is rather that the deviant member will either be persuaded to return to activity in line with organizational norms, or that he will be impelled to separate from the group and seek an affiliation more representative of his personal values.

When external pressures are applied, however, fringe members may find themselves becoming modal. For example, in the agitation and concern over civil rights a number of fraternal organizations were confronted with a "shape up or ship out" order from the college administration. This meant that the fraternity had to demonstrate that it did not discriminate because of race or religion in the selection of its members. On many campuses those fraternities that were unable to do so had their privilege of campus organization revoked. In these cases individual members who had long been advocating integration but who had been ignored by the group became leaders in devising ways and means for integrating nonwhite members.

In short, it is clear that your participation in any small group to which you belong will be successful to the extent to which you have assimilated the values and behaviors of the group and can act them out. Your best efforts to represent a minority opinion against the group norms generally result in pressure to change and reduction of your value as a member.

For the most part, a nonconforming member must either content himself with ineffectuality or seek out a group that more accurately reflects his attitudes and opinions. If he remains marginal, the likelihood is that the group will eventually try to bring about conformity on his part or will find a way to separate him from the group, for no group can tolerate consistent threats to its prevailing norms.

Groups, like society, are more responsive to pressures from without and are more likely to develop changes because of outside events than they are to respond to persuasion by nonconforming members. American society–1970 shows considerable change in norms and values in response to pressures applied by groups of black men pressuring from outside the mainstream.

The emergence of new groups is characterized by a great deal of interaction designed to develop group norms. Groups that come together once for a specific purpose need not go through this, but on-going groups cannot really get on with their business until they have established norms and adjusted the members to them. Early organizational behavior is characterized by a good deal of awkwardness and overreaction. There is much testing and questioning of belief and behavior until some "traditions" have been developed. One relatively new university, for example, went so far as to establish a "committee on new traditions." It was a most ineffectual committee but it was evidence of the need for some kind of cohesion for the members.

Vocational groups of employees charged with the task of problem solving are often characterized at the outset by a variety of social interactions as the members test the limits of group cohesion. As groups of employees come together for the first time there will be a great deal of interaction around water coolers and coffee cups, extending to meals together and even to occasional socialization after hours. In some cases a sufficient number of commonalities will exist among enough members of the group so that social cohesion will be added to the requirements for group membership. For the most part, however, the attempts at social interaction will materialize a few cliques and a few interpersonal hostilities, both of which may impede the group's decision-making ability as it deals with its real task.

There is really no way to avoid the necessity of testing group norms. Doubts about norms are natural and questions about them must be answered before the group can go on about its business. In some cases it is useful to obviate the necessity for external interactions by developing a social climate within the legitimate problem-solving milieu of the group. For example, if a group of fellow workers meets regularly in austere surroundings and is formal about its conduct of business, there will be a need to experiment with social interaction among the members. If, however, group problem solving is carried on in a climate in which social interaction is permitted under comfortable conditions, with coffee, ashtrays, and frequent breaks, the participants will have an opportunity to test each other out and discover the limits of development of group norms without the awkward tests that would otherwise be necessary.

Most groups have a limited scope of behavior with only a few matters on which the members are initially cohesive. Workers assigned to problem-solving activity can easily agree on the fact that they have been assigned but they may not necessarily agree on their task or the way they ought to go about it. To the extent that there is agreement about the control the group may exert over the behavior of its members, the more conformity will be demanded. If there is less agreement, fewer demands will be made on the members. The extent to which the group control extends beyond that for which it was originally constituted may depend on the fortunate accident of having people come together who have values in common. Or, the problem-solving activity may be so satisfying that an aura of goodwill develops that extends into the social activities. The necessity of regularly coming together might facilitate additional interaction. Finally, the development of agreements among members may lead to an extension of the amount of control the group can extend.

Dogma and "Party Line"

All groups appear to develop a desire for some sort of "party line." Basically it is about the business of the group, but it may extend to other activities. Political activist groups, for example, may come together because of a shared creed but somewhere in the group history attempts will be made to gain commitment to other types of values. For example, in the case of the civil rights movements of 1967–1968 efforts were made to gain commitment to peace activities and finally a creed emerged that demanded that belief in one proposition required acceptance of the other. By the same token, right-wing political activists combined hostility to integration with belligerence in foreign affairs and extended these commitments to a demand for acceptance of a conspiratorial view of the behavior of national figures.

To the extent that a group can make its own standards perfectly clear to the members, they will be able to demand conformity. If, however, members are permitted to derive their judgments from other standards like scientific evidence, objective reality, norms of other communities, religious revelations, or moral codes, members will tend to resist the development of dogma. Another possibility is that a member who strongly needs the kind of support that membership will confer may tend to distort his view of scientific evidence, objective reality, cast off the norms of the larger community, and regard the wisdom of the group as total creed. Groups that demand this sort of conformity, the John Birch Society for example, are xenophobic in their behaviors. One element of their problem-solving technique is rejection of the admissibility of any kind of information that is not specifically generated by approved group members. Such groups develop a hierarchy of acceptable authority in order to maintain adherence to group norms and to block the possibility of an external influence leading the member astray. Thus, scientific evidence, objective reality, community norms, religious revelation, and moral codes become the legitimate business of the group, and it is necessary for the group to control these members' beliefs on those matters in order to survive as a group. To the extent that they succeed in ensuring doctrinal purity, they reduce their capability to attract new members and utilize new ideas.

Groups that become excessively dogmatic and extend their control widely beyond their assigned domain often enforce a kind of brainwashing to insure conformity. This procedure may be exceedingly subtle, consisting of withdrawing association from members who do not openly subscribe to the beliefs and practices of the group. It may become an intensive effort in the form of persuasion to compel conformity. The group will first persuade, then punish, then expel nonconforming members. Consequently, we might say that brainwashing exists in many forms in the groups in our society. The deviant member is often not even aware he is being brainwashed, for the interactions that result in adjustment of nonconforming behavior are quite subtle. However, they only work when membership in the group is deeply prized. The initial withdrawal of affect usually so reduces the value the deviant member places on the group that he makes voluntary withdrawal, or perhaps joins an opposition group.

Groups that come together infrequently can exert less of this sort of control. Intensity of control is magnified when there is regularity in the association. The more widely you participate with fellow members, the more likely it is that you will be able to perceive what the group desires and, for that matter, the more likely it is for you to be a pacesetter rather than a fringe member.   Among industrial and government groups there is limited association, so problem solving is relatively formal.   As a result there is some degree of tolerance for deviant behavior in matters external to the concerns of the group.   On the other hand, as in some business contexts, if a group is seriously concerned about maintaining an image, the amount of control it can exert may extend beyond the vocational setting and may well direct the kind of home to be purchased, the kind of clothes to be worn and the nature of the member's recreation.

This kind of control can be exerted over anyone, depending on the extent to which he finds support within the group for his own life-style and beliefs.   It is necessary, for example, to conform to what is demanded by a vocational group since one's economic survival is at stake.   Leaving a job, in most cases, is inconvenient and financially disabling.   Consequently, an employee, even in the executive ranks, will make a certain number of sacrifices of personal idiosyncracy in order to remain in the mainstream of the group and not jeopardize his economic position.   On the other hand, in the executive ranks, sale of personal skills represents the sole advancement potential and the individual who is more committed to professional advancement than he is to social nurturing will not long withstand extraneous pressures but will seek to sell his skills to the kind of organization over which he can exert the control.   Consequently, his vocational career may be marked by considerable movement from company to company until he finds one whose goals and norms are sufficiently compatible with his own so that he can assume the kind of leadership or membership he seeks.   This kind of personality seeks a group that will support his demand for control or executive advancement.   This may sometimes come about through close conformity with group norms for most groups tend to cathect into positions of leadership those men who best represent the norm.   On the other hand, there is considerable opportunity for competitiveness in this kind of advancement, and it is possible to find a group that demands no change.   A man with saleable skills is more secure in doing a bit of seeking so that he can move steadily upward in the hierarchy and thus assert more control over the beliefs and behaviors of his followers, enhancing his own security forever.

But it is not only money and power that people seek from small groups. There are those who seek groups that will support their behavior. For example, if an individual has already hit upon a course of action as a solution to a problem, he may also recognize that it is impossible for him to act alone and will seek out a group whose members would support the activity. Others may seek small groups because of a desire for reinforcement or security; to find other individuals who believe the same way or find security in some unusual position is interdicted by groups in which he presently holds membership. This kind of group affiliation is characteristic of extremist political groups of both the left and right wings or in nudist groups. Members seek strength in numbers or protection from onslaught of hostile opponents. Some members may seek a rationale for opinions by rooting them in the group code, and some may fear personal failure and want others to share the blame with them. Groups may nurture all of these.

Since groups both support and sanction personal behavior, there may be confusion in the mind of a member about why he believes what he does or acts as he does. In many cases, individual behavior may be group motivated because of social affiliation. That is, because individuals perceived as influential hold an opinion, you may express the same opinion in order to strengthen the personal affiliations. In a case of this sort, challenges from outside the group cannot be met for one group's hero may be a villain to the opposing group on the outside. The confrontation that is currently going on between groups of ghetto residents and the white power structure is illustrative of this. In the ghetto, hierarchies of power are established. The white power structure, however, may not "see" as leaders those who are respected by ghetto residents. Whites seek as leaders people the white community can control easily, and so the white community has little influence on the people with real power.

In intergroup relations, the only viable interactions must be between individuals who are willing to develop new norms and new relationships that permit the relevant matters of both groups to be considered.

It is hard for individual group members to defend their beliefs, or even find reasons for them, for often they are so much a part of their daily behavior that they are not even aware that they have come from a desire to remain affiliated with the group. One student, for example, could not discover why he found it so difficult to interact with members of a certain religious group until, after careful examination, he discovered that one of the tenets of belief of his main social group was hostility to that religion.

The talk that goes on in a small group cannot be analyzed solely in terms of its logical content or the extent to which it is germane to the solution of problems. It must also be considered in terms of the psychological reasons for saying what is said, how much support is conferred by saying, how much desire there is to "belong," and so forth. People do modify their beliefs in order to retain membership in prized groups, and they are quite willing and able to rationalize their shifts of attitude and behavior. Rarely will they admit that they have changed because of the group; and even more rarely will they be aware that this was the reason for change. Furthermore, private antagonism will not frequently be translated into public talk. It is easy to grouse about the pressures of the group in private, and thus release some of the tension felt about conforming to norms.

The participant in small group activities (apparently that means everyone) must recognize that a good part of his behavior is controlled by the group, and that he has sacrificed a part of his personal choice-making ability in order to remain a conforming member of the group. While there is no way to avoid this bind, a conscious awareness of this fact of membership life might result in more sensible choosing of groups and the development of a policy of test and trial before making a total commitment to a set of group norms. While the group may need the individual commitment to survive as a group, the individual needs to retain some of his personal integrity to survive as an individual.

EXERCISES

1. Go into some formal organization with about twenty to forty-five members and draw a formal organization chart. Sketch all the offices, committee chairman, and committee members. Remember, one individual may have more than one office. What you want here is the formal positions as prescribed by the organization. In the military they call these T.O.&E., "Table of Organization and Equipment." A fraternity, a platoon, a Rotary Club, or any similar group may be used. Be sure to make your observations on an organization that meets rather frequently.

   Next, make some observations as to who is awarded deference in the group. If possible, observe them as they actually go through a decision-making sequence. Observe which individuals speak and what effect their comments have on group outcomes. As you make these observations, try to develop an informal system of interaction and ranking. Compare this system to the formal organization chart.

2. Watch a series of television programs; it shouldn't make much difference which ones. Try to characterize the "good" guy and the "bad" guy. What characteristics do they have? Are they consistent from program to program? Do your observations compare with those of others? How similar are these characterizations to those of our political and business leaders?

3. Go through one of the compendia on small group research and choose an article which reports a research experiment. In your small group, try and verify the research results. In some experiments it may be necessary to appoint one of your members as an observer. When you have finished the experiment, discuss the results, how they compare with the findings of the researcher, and what other forces were at play as you went through the task.

4. Read Rocky Graziano's *Somebody Up There Likes Me* and detail the different influences of Rocky's life. Note particularly how the groups with which he associated had distinct and direct influence on his life.

5. Explore the meaning of task and social leaders. To facilitate the study, have a small group of about five members assigned a fairly specific task to complete. They should be given about an hour to get a job done. (The time is significant only in that they must function together long enough so that the trial periods that hold back group action initially can be passed. It is quite conceivable that one hour is not sufficient time.) Choose a task like writing a letter to the student paper on some current campus issues, working out the design for a newspaper ad protesting the food in the dormitory, and so forth. The task should be specific enough to be realistic, yet difficult enough so it cannot easily be completed in the time allowed.

   Assign one person the job of "task leader." This should be someone who has a keen interest in the topic itself. He should feel that it is a significant task. Let someone volunteer for this job. The other role to be "played" is that of social leader. This task consists of keeping everyone "happy." Someone might volunteer for this role too. But whoever does should be careful that controversy is averted wherever possible.

   The observers, who are to remain as conspicuous as possible, should watch for the extent to which the two persons playing roles succeeded in doing so. They should also watch for roles that other persons who are not role playing have assumed.

6. Try a little role playing! Write out, on cards, the following roles:
   (a) You want to lead this group because Sally Anne loves a leader.
   (b) You don't want to lead the group, but you are the only one who knows anything about the problem.
   (c) Find out who likes Sally Anne and don't let him be the leader, because it will beat your time with Sally Anne.
   (d) As far as you are concerned, you were appointed leader.
   (e) You've been chairman of everything else; why not this group?

Your topic: "A criticism of the course!" The leader will read it aloud to your professor. See if you can get yourself a leader within fifteen minutes while sticking to your roles and without voting.

7. Working together, list all of the things you can find that people in this class conform to. Show similarities in dress, speech style, manner of seeking attention, response to volunteering in class, interests, values, and so on. Have each class member write on a slip of paper what would be, to him, the most offensive type of nonconformity that anyone could carry on in the class. Now divide up into groups and see if you can predict what the norm will be as to the most offensive nonconformity.

8. What is a hippie? If you have some people in class who label themselves "hippies" have them get into a group and list those aspects of behavior and belief that distinguish their norms from those of "squares." Get the squares into a group and ask them to do the same thing. Compare the two lists. Are perceived norms identical with felt norms?

The Human Interpersonal Transaction

This chapter will offer a "philosophical" point of view about what happens when people interact. We will examine interaction primarily as it takes place in the dyad, the smallest unit of interaction. From this, we may be able to generalize to somewhat larger groups.

Psychiatrists and clinical psychologists have been utilizing the dyad as a mode of treatment for many years, and they appear to understand a good deal about the therapeutic nature of dyadic interaction. Whether their discoveries about the ways in which disturbed persons interact are applicable to normal persons is questionable. Furthermore, therapy offers little hard data, for each therapist has his unique mode of behavior, and there has been little opportunity for controlled experimentation in the clinical situation. Furthermore, even to attempt such experimentation with humans would be questionable ethically. However, from the experiences of the therapists it is possible to derive understanding and, hopefully, empathy for the behavior of people in small groups.

Through an examination of dyadic transactions, it is possible for students to discover something about themselves and their behavior that might assist them in understanding the behavior of others as they observe or participate with them. The understanding of self in relation to others is crucial in improving quality of behavior in small groups, and may be the key to a more scientific understanding of the possibilities for behavior when people interact.

We offer an "almost existential" view of interaction. We assert here that it is possible to discover self through interaction with people one at a time, and, eventually, the understandings can be applied to other forms of interaction. Knowing your own behavior when confronting one other person may help to understand what happens when a speaker faces an audience or when a board of directors sits down to transact business.

In examining human interaction on a highly personal level, we are looking for two outcomes. The first is information, which might contribute to the study and lead to a general theory of small group behavior. The second is personal insight and awareness, which might contribute to improvement of participation behavior.

When we approach the measurement of human behavior as a mass phenomenon, we are capable of great precision. It is possible, for example, for pollsters to predict with great accuracy the voting habits of a population and even to declare a man a winner in an election before five percent of the total vote is in. It is not possible for them, however, to predict the voting behavior of any single individual in the mass. The pollsters know that there is a possibility of a great many events and attitudes, and they calculate the probability of each and their potential incidence in the whole group. They cannot foresee, however, to whom these events will occur, and so they are unable to predict individual preferences. So it is with interaction in general. The probability curves we generate about groups tell the individual participant very little about what his behavior will be or ought to be. Conscious control over his own behavior can come about only after an analysis by him of his behavior in a variety of situations. We must, of course, continue to measure mass phenomena, but we also need some set of methods or insights that might be useful to the man who wishes to improve his participation with others in society.

What we are concerned with here is finding a useful method for examining the small group from two perspectives—that of observer and that of participant. It would be useful to have a way of assessing the quality of interaction in a group, and it would be equally useful to find a way to estimate our own contribution as members so that we could improve it in subsequent efforts. The understandings we seek are similar to those demanded of a public speaker, for our attempts to communicate in the small group have a rhetorical significance. Yet, we cannot use techniques identical to those of the public speaker, since we do not have the system of probabilities operating that prevails in the context of a large audience, which cannot make specific responses to the speaker's remarks.

The number of generalizations about what constitutes effective group behavior are materially reduced by the fact that the capability of response of the listeners is increased over that of passive audiences. There is not so much cohortative advice that can be given to participants, for the situations that might emerge are almost limitless. The small group is a microcosmic unit, removed from a general system about which generalizations can and have been made.

The problem of the participant in the small group is similar to that of the pollster. He may know some useful information about the use of rhetoric with people in general, but applying it in the given case to a particular small group is more than moderately risky. The compactness of the group and the nature of the participant's immersion in it make the generalizations available less useful.

There seems to be no shortage of people to give directive advice about how to behave effectively in a group. They do very little damage. Most of their advice falls into the category of "folk wisdom." If you know "how to get along with people," you may be able to get the group to "go along with you." What it is not possible to give is an infallible system to get individual goals synthesized with group goals so that the outcomes will invariably satisfy the requirements of the group as well as the needs of the various members. It is interesting that earlier sections of this book have relied on generalizations based on a variety of experimental methods to describe the nature of the small group. This information should be understood in context. When we describe "groups" we do not describe the group that you are presently in. That group is but one dot on the probability curve from which the generalization was made, and precisely where it falls we do not know, and you may be unable to find out.

The propositions we have offered about the small group refer to an aggregate or collectivity. Your group will behave to some extent like that "fictional" or prototype group we have described. It will have goals, it will be subject to the same requirements of problem solving, it will make similar demands on you, the participant. Even the types of people participating will coincide with the abstract description. The roles cathected in your group will be similar to those roles predicted for groups in general. But it must be understood that we have offered ad hoc data about groups as they have been. The information is DEScriptive rather than PREscriptive since it has been gleaned in relatively scientific fashion *after* events have occurred. It is easy to define what *has* happened, but quite difficult to explain what *is* happening. Our information adds up to what groups *are* up to the point when you begin participating. After you have participated, the events of your groups may be added to our pool of information. It will become part of the scientific–historic record of what has been done, but it may not be useful in determining how it can be done. We cannot predict, nor can you, what kinds of events will take place in a given interaction. Your facility to deal with what happens depends on your understanding of the possibilities gained from study of what has happened. But even this does not equip you to handle the unexpected, which cannot be planned for, of course, until we have learned to expect it. Furthermore, what has been concealed from all investigators of the small group is information about what participants feel and what their feelings do to their behavior. We see the behavior, but you, as a participant, must account for it and handle the results of it. You must do this in the context of your own emotional parameters, and often without reference to the feelings of anyone else except as you can project them emphatically from your experience. In short, as a participant you are involved in a very complex rhetorical situation, one which permits people to answer back, and one which demands synthesis of goals rather than victory of one set over another.

Understanding the Small Group as Audience

Thus, consideration of the small group as a kind of "audience" is one useful way to gain information that might be helpful to you as a participant. Whatever the record of formal audience analysis in an audience situation, there is no question about the fact that some planning and preparation are essential to even moderate success in speaking formally to others. Perhaps one of the reasons for failure of small groups is that most participants are not aware of the rhetorical requirements that face them as they confront their peers in direct interaction.

Generalizations drawn from formal audience speaking such as "feedback," "self-image," and "motivation," are useful concepts with which to examine the interaction of one person directly with another, probably to the same extent as they are useful in analyzing and predicting mass phenomena. What we must consider are the differences between the one-to-one relationship characteristic of the small group and the one-to-many relationship that prevails in audience speaking.

For example, in any communication situation, a speaker will respond to feedback. In an audience situation he may be responding to a general pattern of response that he interprets, and in a small group he may be responding to direct statements made to him by others. Whatever his behavior, it is built on input of feedback and the inferences he draws about it. To the extent that his inferences are consistent with events, he succeeds. To the extent that events are predictable, his inferences can be consistent with events. To the extent that the number of possible events are limited, his inferences about them can be predictable. This Thomistic chain adds up to the concept that there are a limited number of ways in which a responding audience can react. They can support, they can remain neutral, or they can reject. They can act as if they are listening, they can display restlessness or boredom. They cannot, normally, interrupt for questions, nor can they answer back. Thus, in a speaker-to-audience situation, the speaker moves ahead and attempts to adjust himself to what he sees and what he thinks about it, and once he has drawn a conclusion, he acts as if it were true. He goes from the start to the finish of his speech and then has the privilege of interpreting whether or not he did well. If he keeps at it long enough, he interlaces some propositions about what the audience does, and he develops a consistent style that works for him enough of the time that he can count on it, and thus he emerges as a professional platform speaker. His role is consistent and predictable, his image clear and unambiguous and the people who respond best are specifically identified in his mind. He can call his shots and "fatten his batting average." In short, he seeks consistency and skill in the role that brings the maximum success.

The problem with developing this kind of consistency in small group interactions, however, is that the perceivable response possibilities in the small group are considerably greater than in a speaker-to-audience situation. While there may be more "attitudes" in a formal audience, merely because there are more people, in the small group there are more ways in which people can express the attitudes they have. Thus the possibility of one person influencing another is considerably greater. Someone who responds to a speaker's remarks may generate a totally unexpected response from someone else in the group, which in turn may provoke a digression from the point the speaker was trying to make. The initiating speaker may try to get the conversation back to his ideas, but he is competing for attention with three or four, or more, practicing rhetoricians, each of whom has a cause he is defending. Skill at communication and random chance will determine the direction of the talk, and even though a speaker may understand what is happening, he is relatively powerless to control it without resorting to authoritarian methods, which will further reduce his effectiveness.

Furthermore, consistency in a role is dependent upon consistency in a situation. This cannot be guaranteed in small group interaction. A man who has become skillful as an effecter of compromise has no function in a group that comes to rapid agreement. Attempting to play the role will only attenuate the proceedings and annoy the members. The man who enjoys an argumentative role defeats himself when he tries to play it against passive people eager for consensus. Apparently, in the small group, success is not only dependent on a repertoire of roles but also on knowing which roles to cathect when.

The small group is made up of several people interacting on a one-to-one basis. To gain substantial understanding of some of the possibilities for this interaction, it may be wise to examine the one-to-one communication relation, the dyad.

The Dyad: Smallest Unit of Transaction

The smallest unit of interpersonal transaction is the dyad, one person interacting with a single other. We have, up to this point, considered interaction in groups of various size, including the interaction between groups in the larger society. The concept "small group," as we have already indicated, is exceedingly hard to specify. It is for this reason that we have found it necessary to refer some of our remarks to large and complicated organizations and sometimes even to a whole culture. Our American society is characterized by intricate networks of interaction between people and their groups. Each man involved in his own task is still locked to others because he is required to play many roles in the society. Groups and organizations may be concerned primarily with their own goals, but it is often necessary for people to work for the achievement of the goals of others in order to get what they want. People form alliances and cooperate when common concerns become apparent. Yet, it is impossible to achieve total consensus, and there is, therefore, considerable conflict between individuals and the groups to which they belong. The simple matter of getting through the day in our complex society cannot be accomplished without virtually perpetual interaction with others. Consequently, the business of trying to understand the behavior of groups, per se, or individual behavior in a group, is confounded by the incalculable number and variety of relationships that people can form with each other.

In many ways, it is less confusing to examine broad social movements than it is to understand the interplay of behavior characteristic of dyadic interaction. The social concepts used in the study of society can be manipulated by scholars in the manner of Humpty Dumpty. They can create words and make them mean whatever they wish. The concepts are abstractions and are amenable to verbal analysis. They can be juggled so that the theory comes out right. But people cannot be so manipulated. The *adjectives* used about other persons can be manipulated, but the person remains and must be dealt with no matter what he is called or how he is classified. As long as he is in plain sight, he is the reality, and the abstract concepts about him do not seem to be relevant. Once he leaves, then he can be subjected to a piercing and scholarly analysis. The immediacy of dyadic interaction removes it from the arena of scholarly introspection and places it in the realm of personal awareness and understanding.

The lover and the salesman, for example, understand the complex behavior of which the human is capable. We are able to avoid confronting this complexity when we consider society or culture in the abstract. The prediction of social movements calls for an understanding of scientific method and statistical procedure. Predicting the behavior of the individual person calls for more knowledge than it is possible to get. The problem of discovering what it is that motivates the person in front of us is often more difficult than discovering what might move the majority in the neighborhood or region. Much of what causes an individual to behave is locked up in his mind, bound up in his symbols, hinged on the memory of the experiences he has had, and based on the values which he has generated through his entire life.

The "Figure-Ground" Concept

A model which has proven useful in examining human behavior in face-to-face situations is provided by the psychologists

Combs and Snygg (*Individual Behavior*). Their "figure-ground" concept holds that we can pay attention to, or hold in clear figure, only one object, event, or person at a time. Presumably, when two people interact with each other, the chances of their "paying attention" are increased over what might happen with a speaker in a formal audience relationship.

The concept "holding a person in figure" may call for some explanation. There is a limit to the attention span of an individual. Whatever is perceived can only be attended to for a limited period of time, for it exists in a background (ground) of events and things that seek attention from the consciousness. There is, consequently, considerable shifting of attention as we go about our daily business. While we do not know, specifically, what happens when two people hold each other in figure, we would assume that the more they do this, the more likely that they will exert an influence on each other.

There is no firm data about the length of a "normal attention span." There are some people who can concentrate intensely for a long period of time; others whose attention shifts rapidly from thing to thing. We all give off cues that provide information about what we are paying attention to and how strongly and for how long. Veteran audience performers have learned to pick up these cues and use them to direct the style of their speaking. The problem for novices is accepting the premise that people vary widely in the way they signal their attention. Some people in the audience will sit rigidly because they are straining to see and listen, while others will sit rigidly because they are paying attention to something unrelated to the speaker inside their own head. Some will move about in their seats because they are stimulated by what they see and hear, and others will move about in their seats because they are bored, and uncomfortable, and concerned about something else. The performer has learned to estimate modalities and draw inferences about the probabilities of attention in a whole audience. He knows that he will be unable to get them all to pay attention at the same time, but he plays for the highest probability activity, that is, his estimate of what will get the greatest number to listen to him at a given moment. To learn to do this demands considerable experience with audiences. To do this with an individual demands considerable experience with *that* person. In fact, it almost seems simpler to generalize about attention in the case of a large audience than it is to make specific judgments about attentiveness of a single person, for virtually any guess has some chance of being partly right when it is applied to a great number of people.

The figure-ground concept is, therefore, of critical importance to the public speaker. He may consciously control his attention, and perceive what he decides is encouraging, and thus give himself reinforcement to go on. He may also block out discouraging cues. By the same token, a not-so-effective speaker may focus excessively on negative cues and thus convince himself that he is an inadequate performer. In either case, the imperatives in training are clearly indicated, even though the methods of administering the training are not so clear. Ineffective platform speakers must be equipped with methods to increase the probability that they will receive reinforcement from a greater proportion of the audience, and they must be taught how to distinguish between support and hostility. It is clear that focus on the nonrelevant can be disheartening and lead to ineffective behavior. But, then again, not everyone has to be a public performer.

Everyone does have to interact with someone else, however. The figure-ground model applies just as much to two-person or small group interaction as it does to perception of audience in a public situation. In a two-person interaction, each party gets an image of behavior, draws inferences about it, evaluates the inferences, and then proceeds to react. Once again, attention to the irrelevant, incorrect interpretation of meaning, or application of the wrong evaluative adjectives can distort the transaction, and interpersonal communication can go awry in the same way as audience performance can.

All of this, incidentally, is of particular concern to those school teachers who have long held to the myth that movement indicates lack of attention and sitting quietly means high interest. There are several authorities who attribute bad teaching to lack of precision in understanding feedback cues. This problem pervades our human relationships. When we try to describe what happens when one person responds to another, we are confronted with an empirical bind, for we are rarely sure what the meaning is of what we see. Each adult carries with him to any relationship a history of previous interactions; knowledge, beliefs, values, norms and words about them, which will control his interpretation of what he sees and hears. He has "learned" what others expect from him—his role—and he has made some estimate of his capability to satisfy these expectations. From his previous efforts at interaction, both successful and unsuccessful, he has built up in his mind a reification of what a relationship should consist of. There are certain behaviors that he is familiar with and that he can interpret as signaling success. If he does not receive these cues, he will alter his output to try to get them; or, he may stop trying to interact and write the relationship off as a waste. He might understand that not all people react the same way, but he is still controlled by his generalizations, and he expects, or hopes, that people will act the way he anticipates. Life is easier for him when this happens.

What he possesses in his mind is an abstraction built from his memory of what he has experienced before. Depending on how successful he has been with other people, he may have considerable skill in estimating his own success. But as he encounters unfamiliar situations and people whose style of response he is not familiar with, he may experience some difficulty interpreting his feedback. This accounts for the awkwardness he may display when he enters into an unfamiliar social relationship.

The important point is that we rarely respond to reality. We rarely make the effort to discover the meaning of feedbacks we see through our experience or to test them against our generalized criteria. It is only after we have experienced an unfamiliar feedback style for a considerable period of time that we permit it to alter the form of our criteria. In short, we do not know what is going on in the mind of the other. *We respond to what goes on in our mind as a result of our perceiving the result of what has gone on in the mind of the other.* It is filtered through and shaped by our memories and values. If that filtering process distorts the reality of the situation, then it is very likely to lead to unproductive and awkward interpersonal behavior. In a formal speech, the speaker can finish and leave, chalk the event off, and profit from the experience.   In a small group transaction, however, the response to awkwardness is immediate and productive or unproductive; it contributes to the "history" of interaction that will be influential as long as the group is together.

Perceiving and Interpreting Feedback

To improve interaction in small groups, in face-to-face encounters, it is necessary to be able to adjust individual roles to the demands of the situation.

The problem is how to interpret data situationally.   The generalizations that can be made about groups are moderately useful in determining a general course of action.   We know, or soon learn, for example, that it is not effective to demand compliance on the part of a small group, or to avoid interaction, or to engage in digressive levity.

It is our specific actions that are of concern here, however. In our interactive behavior we tend to look for propositions about "feedback" behavior that would enable us to develop a policy toward the people we meet.   We can examine the formal audience situation for principles of effective behavior to govern our actions in interpersonal situations, although the differences between the events are quite clear to us.

The most drastic difference between communicating with a dyad-mate and with an audience is the capacity that the other person has to take over the transaction.   The roles of communicator and listener are rapidly interchanged in the small group, while in more formal situations the listener remains in that role until the speaker signals, at his pleasure, that it is possible to talk back.   The sheer size of the audience, however, militates against participation, even in a directed question period, and so the speaker retains his control over the situation as socially defined.   In the small group, however, a speaker is required to play to many "audiences," each of whom has the privilege of sharing or preempting the speaker role and putting the present speaker into an audience role.   In addition to this capacity for rapid change, a consistent set of behaviors presented to each member of the group maximizes the chance of interpersonal failure.   Each individual member of the group will have his own ideas about the kind of talk and the kind of person he is willing to respond to positively.

The optimum interaction, perhaps, can be achieved with each participant seeking to maximize his rhetorical effect on each other participant.   This, however, presumes that only the speaker's goals are relevant.   The group situation, however, confronts all the participants with the necessity of affiliating with the group goals, accepting the group style, approving the group norms, and in short, understanding whatever the group "game" is and playing it well.   Thus, rhetorical control potential for the individual is influenced by the necessity of sacrificing some control in order to demonstrate affiliation with the group as a whole.

The Win-Lose Transaction

Examining the relationships that emerge from the dyad indicates that a direct interpersonal transaction can be examined as a competition in which there may be a winner and a loser, or in which both may win or both may lose.   The speaker-to-audience relationship is characterized by the speaker seeking victory over the audience.

Lately, however, it seems that audiences are seeking their own victories.   The pressure placed on public speakers, particularly on college campuses, illustrates the imperative that most people feel to participate, rather than to sit passively and experience the words of the speaker.   The large audience situation, however, is uneconomical for this kind of interaction, for only the most forceful or brash in the audience will be able to encounter the speaker directly.   The audience, as a mass, has only the capacity to heckle and annoy.   Thus, the small group encounter seems to offer the only outlet for the kind of interchange that people seek.

In an audience experience, the speaker has goals which he seeks to accomplish, and he has the capacity to prepare his words so that they will serve to help him toward those goals.   In the small group, however, the individual is asked to subordinate some of his own needs and goals to those of the group.   He must do a job of self-persuasion to get his goals in line with those of the group as best he can, and then he must apply rhetoric to the other members of the group to get the group goal into harmony with his own. To insist on a specific course of action because it is personally satisfying defeats the purpose of small group activity, and usually results in development of hostilities. To the extent that the individual confuses this aspect of the operation of the speaker in a small group with that of a platform speaker, he tends to become an impediment to group process and suffers the hostility of the other participants for his trouble.

There is little opportunity in small group interaction to develop a thread of argument. What is communicated must be directly relevant to what came before, and each speaker must adjust his remarks to those of the other members. Discourse in the small group, as in the dyad, is characterized by give-and-take between the participants until an idea emerges that is mutually satisfying. The tacit objective, then, is mutual victory. The relevant question is: What do two people have as options in common from which a choice can be made that is satisfying to both? As more people are added to the transaction the commonality must be extended, until the number becomes so great that there is no longer a possibility of direct interaction among them.

Observation and Measurement of the Small Group

Each unit of social organization is made up of smaller structures, each of which may have clearly defined goals and norms, and each of which is individually unpredictable. It is virtually impossible to find for study a natural isolation, a small group concerned with only one specific problem and having no distracting relationships or external responsibilities elsewhere. This represents the most difficult problem for those who seek to study the small group, and, as a result, much of what we know about small groups comes from controlled experimentation. We are, however, constantly confronted with the problem of gleaning specific wisdom from the generalizations that have been developed about small groups.

The physicist Werner Heisenberg pointed out that even in the "purest" of sciences, when an investigator attempts to measure a specific phenomenon it is necessary for him to control it sufficiently to make it amenable to measurement. The examination must be made without reference to possible influences from unpredictable forces. In his experiments with electrons, Heisenberg discovered that in order to measure the path taken by an electron, it was necessary for him to control its velocity so that movements could be picked up by his available instruments. In order to measure velocity, he had to get the electron to move in a straight line, so that the devices that measured speed could work accurately. From this he generalized the indeterminacy principle, which suggests that a viewer cannot see a phenomenon in its natural state: All observation is necessarily influenced by the observer and the instruments he employs.

While there is considerable argument about whether Heisenberg's ideas can be applied to research in the social sciences, it is clear that attempts to study the small group are necessarily complicated by the immense complexity of the interaction, the elements of which are difficult to separate for independent, controlled study.

It seems almost impossible to control the many variables involved in small group study. The simple presence of an observer taking notes seems to remove the group from its natural state. If attempts are made to measure specific attitudes and values, they must be taken in isolation, and they cannot keep pace wtih the rapid changes that result from the interchanges of rhetoric in the group process. Trying to combine the measurement of many variables results in statistical "interactions" that can only be interpreted intuitively, thus sacrificing part of the "scientific" context. Like most attempts to study human behavior, research in the small group presents the investigator with a seemingly hopeless dilemma. If he attempts to study the group as a participant, his observations are clouded by the stake he has in the group decision. If he attempts to study as a nonpartisan observer, he is not party to the internal tension felt by the members who have a stake in the outcome. If he attempts to isolate single behaviors for investigation, then he loses their context and can find out little about their relationship with other variables.

The situation, however, is not quite so hopeless. As we have suggested in earlier chapters, the careful investigation and measurement of small group activity has led to a number of generalizations that offer sound guidance to small group operations. The conclusions we have offered about norms, role, status, and so on, have come from the work of investigators over the years and result in a relatively good picture of what happens in groups in general. The problem, of course, lies in ascertaining what is happening in a particular group, and for the participant who wishes to improve his ability to contribute to the group's activity, the generalizations are sometimes not useful, for he must develop his own technique of perceiving and responding. The generalizations must be made active, and they must be related to what is happening at the moment.

There is always a possibility of distortion when laboratory results are applied under real conditions. The information derived is usually correct, but it is derived from an *experimental situation,* and the results must be tempered by live perceptions. For example, one of the most significant experiments conducted in small groups was done by Solomon Asch. Asch asked subjects to judge which of two lines was longer. In each group there were three trained subjects and one naïve subject. The trained subjects were told to report the shorter line as longer. In most cases the naïve subject, who answered last, would go along with the majority view, whatever his own perception. In fact, it is not clear whether he actually saw the shorter line as longer, or whether he perceived correctly but reported inaccurately so that he could remain affiliated with the rest of the group. From this experiment, it was generalized that in small groups the majority will tend to pull the minority toward their point of view.

In a subsequent study, however, Ted Grove obtained different results. The Grove study, also contrived and run under "laboratory" conditions, dealt with issues rather than perceptions. He noted that in an unusual number of cases, a committed minority member could actually move a relatively passive majority toward the minority position.   This does not refute Asch's findings, but merely adds depth, indicating, perhaps, that when there is little or nothing at stake, the minority will go along with the majority, but when deep feelings are involved, the minority members will work for their position and will have some capability of getting others to move to their point of view.

For this reason, the study of behavior of individuals in groups must have a "philosophical" as well as a scientific perspective; scientific in that any generalization that seems warranted after careful experimentation can probably be applied, and therefore should be learned; philosophical in that the specific nature of the application will depend on the peculiarities of the specific group to which it is being applied.   We are still some distance from the time when we can make "scientific measurements" on live groups solving real problems.   This does not mean that the scientific data about groups is not applicable.   By attempting to apply it, in fact, we can generate new hypotheses to help in further experimentation.   To the extent that we can apply scientific propositions to the group, the amount of confusion in observation is reduced.   What we are saying here is that the study of small groups is not an exact science.   Participation in the small group requires artistic endeavor as well as skillful manipulation.

A scientist does not *generate* rules and regulations for behavior.   He discovers relationships that appear to exist consistently and generalizes from them.   To the extent that his generalizations ring true when applied in various situations, he can develop "scientific" law—propositions of such high probability that we can count on them happening over and over again, and when they do not happen we can account for the peculiar situation by discovering some unforeseen events.   Such certainty is not possible with prediction of the behavior of human beings, but prediction of the behavior of human beings is possible to an extent that will enable the intelligent student–observer to increase his capability in dealing with them and working with them.

Some depth can be given to the preceding conjectures by examining the differences between findings from animal studies conducted in laboratories or of animals in captivity and those conducted of animals in their natural state. While it is possible to get more information in detailed fashion from the study of animals in isolation, sometimes the meaning of the information is not clear until we observe the animal in its natural state. For example, the basic principles of ethology assert that all animals in the natural state strive for (1) survival, (2) territory, (3) homeostasis, and (4) stimulation. In looking at the behavior of people in small groups we might connect "norms" with survival. The group will not stay together or survive unless some norms of behavior are established. Status represents a territorial drive, a grasping for position in the group. Role could be associated with homeostasis; selection and retention of role explains the nature of expected behavior. Finally, conflict resulting from clash of attitude or personality provides the spice of interaction and thus stimulates behavior.

This kind of analysis, of course, is loose and almost "poetic." We are dealing with a variety of abstractions, and as long as we know this, we can use them as a framework for our expectations and plans for behavior. If, however, we develop some constancies as a result of our abstractions, we may find ourselves in difficulty when we must examine specific cases. If our abstractions come to us from statistical generalizations, for example, we may forget that they came as a result of study of many situations resulting in a "curve." We cannot expect each specific case to conform to the curve, for the curve is made of a wide variety of different situations. Sören Kierkegaard might have been referring to this very problem when he said:

. . . a group in its very concept is the untruth. . . . The falsehood first of all is the notion that the group does what in fact only the individual in the group does, though it be every individual. For group is an abstraction and has no hands, but each individual ordinarily has two hands. . . . The group is untruth. Hence none has more contempt for what it is to be a man than they who make it their profession to lead the crowd. . . . The witness to the truth is to engage himself if possible with all, but always individually, talking to everyone severally on the streets and lanes . . . in order to disintegrate the crowd, though not with the intent of educating the crowd as such, but rather with the hope that one or another individual might return from this assemblage and become a single individual.

Thus the problem we confront when we examine small groups is to develop *two* methods: one for the general study and observation of small groups, hoping to arrive at generalizations about their behavior and the behavior of individuals in them; the second, to find specific modes of behavior that will assist our personal behavior when we are involved in small group activity. The two modes are not compatible. Individual understanding and perception is essential if we are to arrive at sound generalizations. Understanding of the generalizations is essential so that we have a system with which to classify our individual understandings. Our focus in this chapter is on the latter. Our unit of study is the human dyad, the smallest unit of transaction. Our goal is to obtain a perspective useful for you in *participating* in small group activity.

The Clinical Orientation

In order to gain some understanding of human response in the dyad it is useful to turn to the studies carried on by those whose professional careers make it their basic unit of study—clinicians. In a clinical transaction "mutual victory" is the goal. The clinician knows that he cannot impose his will on his client, for progress in change can only come about through personal volition. The clinician can gain little satisfaction from the transaction unless his client makes progress. The client cannot make progress (in the eyes of the therapist) unless and until he defines his goal as analogous to that of the therapist. The clinical transaction, furthermore, is both didactic and rhetorical. The patient must supply information about his condition; the therapist must provide information about the range of possibilities for change and the methods that can be used to effect them. The patient must persuade the clinician that his misfortunes are real and his goals legitimate. The clinician must persuade the patient that selection of a mode of improvement can effect a change and will help accomplish the patient's goals. In no case can the patient be forced to change against his will, nor can the clinician operate a mode of treatment without the acceptance of the patient. The patient seeks to persuade the clinician to perceive him as a unique individual with specific problems; the clinician seeks to persuade the patient to discover that he is not unusual and what has worked before can work again.

There is more than a simple interchange of talk in the clinical transaction. The clinician cannot order the patient to improve. For the most part, the successful clinician seeks an empathic understanding of his client. He must understand that the situation transcends generalization, for the patient brings his whole life with him into the clinic, though he plays out only a portion of it before the therapist's eyes. The clinician, too, brings his record of success and failure into the transaction, and some generalizations about behavior which he wishes to purvey. The patient has a personal obligation to understand the generalizations, and the clinician has the obligation to understand the specifics. Throughout this transaction, however, the two relate both in professional and nonprofessional ways, for in addition to patient and therapist, they are also human beings.

The patient will respond both to the man-clinician who sits before him, and to his image of the behavior of similar men and men in general. The clinician will respond to the man-patient who sits before him, and to his image of the behavior of similar men and men in general. Thus, both will respond to "fictions" rooted in phenomenal worlds and both will, to greater or lesser degrees, adjust the "fictions" to fit the situation. The ideas we have about what constitutes success and how people ought to behave will be highly influential in determining our behavior with others, and so it is in the clinical transaction. If one, patient or therapist, roots himself too heavily in the assumptions that underlie the fictions, he will not respond satisfactorily to the individual. If, on the other hand, they focus too intently on the specific individual, the relation may deepen and become so "sticky" that progress toward the goal of emotional health will not be made. In short, when we deal with others we try to determine what is expected; we test it against our capabilities of performance; and determine whether or not we will act to satisfy expectations, avoid the situation, or fight it. The whole

concept of "other-directedness" is built on the supposition that
we have the capacity to sort through our general awareness of
situations and discover a behavior that is effective in a single
situation.   Our success is dependent on our ability to make a
"situational" audience analysis, based in part on the specifics of
the interaction and in part on what we "know" about people in
general.

The Phenomenological Orientation

We must reiterate here that it is impossible to respond to "real"
data exclusively.   What we get in our heads is never the reality
outside, but is reality reshaped by our perception and our
inference process.   What we are able to perceive and the range
of choices available to us will shape the images to which we
respond and will provide the alternatives from which we can
choose.   We act in the world we have in our head, not the
world outside it.   Solipsism is singularly important in gaining
an understanding of personal behavior, for to recognize that we
do not perceive what is real affords us the opportunity to
become more realistically aware of nonreality.   That is, to
know that we act in our phenomenal world gives us somewhat
better control of what goes into that world and how it is
processed, and makes us more aware of what goes on outside.
Recognition of this process enables us to develop a "phenomenological" approach to data, which consists both of an awareness of the event *and* its impact inside our mind.

Phenomenological constructs make it possible to examine the
internal images to what we respond.   While the concept "phenomenal world" is another loose abstraction, it is useful in
understanding face-to-face human behavior because we are less
likely when using it to oversimplify the transaction through the
application of formal generalizations.   Use of the technique demands a holistic approach to the simple units of transaction.
There appears to be potential in this perceptual and nonscientific
kind of examination, to extract data that might be useful, and, in
turn, to develop more viable generalizations about the communicative process.

The basic premise is that we tend to respond to other humans as we are capable of doing (not in the sense of an ideal mode of response) because of the perceptions (stored in memory), symbols (words), and evaluations we have in our heads. Each of us has had a unique set of experiences that alter somewhat for us the meaning of generalizations we share in common. Because of our shared generalizations, our experiences appear to be sufficiently like those of others so that our gross behavior is amenable to measurement. It *is* possible to say something sensible about the behavior of people in general. Our response to a particular situation, however, cannot be predicted with any degree of certainty unless our generalizations are tempered by our own experience.

It is possible for those who know us well to develop a set of expectancies about our behavior. Couples that have been happily married for a long time seem to have a sense about each other that enables them to know when the other party is happy or sad, confident or threatened, and they act "empathically" according to these awarenesses. The knowledge comes from close (though not necessarily controlled) observation of the other in a variety of contexts, and is perhaps as "scientific" as more formal measurement of large numbers of people. In the small group transaction, however, there is neither the close contact nor the opportunity to make scientific measurement that would permit predictability. Somehow a blend must be made of general and particular knowledge if we are to improve our own response patterns when functioning in a group.

As a starting premise, we might infer a sort of rationality about all human behavior. We do not use the word "rational" here as an evaluation, but as a description meaning that behavior occurs for a reason at the time it occurs. At the moment of behavior there is some reason operating which leads the behaving person to select a particular kind of response from all the responses available to him. Consequently, his behavior could be classified as "rational" to himself at the time he does it, though later on he may decide that his response was not appropriate or right or useful, and to an objective person it might appear even at the moment to be "irrational," not productive of success in achieving perceived goals.

Behavior of individuals in large groups, such as audiences,

tends to be controlled by social exigency. People will, for example, suppress boredom (perhaps irrationally), because the social context demands that they appear to be involved. The person whose boredom transcends his feelings of social obligations may yawn in the face of the speaker. The speaker, seeing one yawn and many "attentive" people, will probably not be disconcerted. He will ascribe motivation to the yawn—perhaps the listener was tired before he came—and so it can be ignored as nonmodal. He may decide at this point that while he does not have the capacity to change the yawner, he can achieve success with the other people who are still listening to him.

The whole concept of an aggregate of listeners called "audience" is a fiction. It is hard to know whether "audience" is singular or plural. We do not really know when we employ the word whether we are talking about a collectivity which responds as one, or a number of ones which add up to a collectivity. Still, it is very useful fiction to the professional communicator and researcher in communication.

Audience Analysis in the Dyad

The tacit assumption in the concept "audience" is that, somehow, an aggregate of people attending to the same stimulus tends to make the individuals lose their uniqueness and become a collectivity, something which can be responded to by a speaker as a single unit. This assumption is supported by the doctrine of probabilities, which tends to show that there are some behaviors that occur more than others each time people are involved in such an activity. The behavior that is modal can be inferred to be the behavior of the audience and is what the speaker responds to. No critic worth his salt will declare that a speaker can succeed with every *person* in the audience, yet he can succeed with the *audience* by discovering and making his appeal to the modality in the situation.

Unfortunately, however, it is not possible for a functioning speaker to do the kind of study necessary to determine the specific behaviors characteristic of a given group. Whatever advance knowledge he has about belief and behavior patterns of the people who comprise the audience loses much of its relevance when the people come together at a particular time and place for a purpose. Once the individuals have entered the hall and have become an audience, the modalities will result in their reacting in a fashion unique to the situation, although their prior commitments will exert some influence over their behavior. Situational elements, including those imposed by the discourse of the speaker, tend to be reflected in overt behavior more grossly than the more subtle behaviors inculcated by prior conditioning and development. Thus, the speaker is obligated to modify somewhat his original speaking plan from his first moment of contact to take into account the modalities that develop from the situation. Each expression by the speaker, in turn, evokes more behavior from the "audience," which in turn may alter the speaker's plan of procedure. Thus, the speaker becomes part of the collectivity to the extent that he is capable of influencing components of it. The whole business becomes so complex that it cannot be handled exclusively through scientific propositions. The speaker must be aware of the nature of audiences in general, but his performance is also controlled by the nature of *this* audience in particular.

The speaker, like the clinician, is responding to a reification in his mind. To the extent that the reification is made up of general propositions about audiences he may commit various awkward and unproductive behaviors, and to the extent that it is made up *only* of immediate perceptions he may appeal to the overt and trivial. The most useful reification of audience is composed of at least six basic elements:

1. Any speaker in contact with listeners will have perceptions beamed back at him. He can hardly escape seeing his audience. What he sees, however, is influenced by his expectancies about the audience, built from what he knew in advance about the potential behavior of the "types" of people he assumed would be present in this particular situation.
2. Past observations of listening individuals and memory about their behavior will also shape his perceptions of the specific audience. These generalized observations provide a set of categories into which the behavior of the present audience

can be fitted.   There will be, in the mind of the speaker, a concept of attentiveness, for example, generalized from behaviors that he observed in the past and which he classified as "attentive."

3. There will be some conception in the mind of the speaker, however cloudy, about what constitutes "effectiveness."   He will have, consciously or unconsciously, developed a notion of how people are to respond when he is performing effectively.   If he is sophisticated he may adjust these standards to fit his immediate audience, but there is no escape from his generalizations.   Thus, in part at least, his success may be a function of random concordance between his criteria for effectiveness and the behaviors on the part of his audience.

4. He will have in his mind a data processing method which enables him to sort out feedback from his audience, which leads him to a classification and evaluation about their behavior.   He will make a variety of inferences about the *meaning* of what he sees the audience doing, which, in turn, will lead to more generalizations about them, which will affect his own behavior, which will lead him to give different emphases to the parts of his discourse.   His selection of what to emphasize and what to suppress will in turn influence the audience to behave—which starts the process all over again.

5. Whether he is experienced or not, he will have in his possession a set of symbols about speaking and audiences that provides limits for the operation of his inference process. These symbols will locate "storage bins" into which he can fit the information he receives from the audience and which will become the substance of his inference process.

6. Finally, he will have in his mind some causal connections about his behavior and the response of the audience, as well as an image of his behavior and the response of people, in general, to him.   The notions he has about the use of humor, hyperbole, metaphor, and so on, and their influence on human behavior, will determine for him the range of behaviors from which he may select as he confronts a particular audience.

These six elements interact to guide the speaker to a conception of audience which functions as a unity and becomes a manageable concept for him. He is thus spared the necessity of making an individual transaction with each person who sits before him. The abstraction process has helped him to work both his data and his data processing system down to a level of expediency, so he can work with it consistently.

This concept of audience has proven effective both descriptively and analytically. Because it is based on the natural tendency to pay heed to the functioning of probabilities, speakers with considerable experience are able to predict behaviors with reasonable accuracy, and they are also aware that their predictions work only for a part of the audience (albeit the greater part), and that there are exceptions to their generalizations. With great care and planning, the kinds of generalizations that can be drawn from "audience" can be used to predict voting patterns, for example, of large blocks of citizens, or to anticipate the demand for new products. Unfortunately, the type of speaking characteristic of the process of small group interaction does not afford the opportunity to contemplate response sufficiently to arrive at trustworthy generalizations. The need to act and respond is much too immediate. Even if a speaker has correctly anticipated what might "move" his audience, his ability to perform it is directly controlled by his capacity to perform and the immediate willingness of the audience to receive. A single gaffe, disorder in the last row, distraction outside, or an unexpected event in the community, could so severely distort his analysis that acting according to his original plan might result in failure.

The pollster who deals in trends in a large community has a decided advantage in predicting outcomes. He can select and stratify the sample he wishes to poll, and he has the benefit of the analysis of previous predictions so that he can perfect his sample. The speaker would confront only a small segment of that community, with no knowledge of where the segment fit in the stratification. Consequently, he cannot tell whether the "sample" to which he speaks is typical of the community norms. His actions are necessarily governed by the old adage, "What is true of the group as a whole is not necessarily true of any single part of it; and what is true of the individual parts is not necessarily true of the group as a whole." An average derived from statistical analysis is also an abstraction. There is no average man, Kiwanian, college student, or Catholic. Consequently, the speaker who responds to a rigid reification in his phenomenal world runs a greater risk of failure than the speaker who is capable of adjusting his reification to fit better with the perceived sample.

A public speaker does not, normally, speak for personal pleasure, although such pleasure may be a concomitant of his success. In addressing a formal audience, he has an idea he wishes to implant in the minds of his listeners, or perhaps some action he wants them to carry out. When he speaks to a small group he may wish to assist in achieving the group goal, or he may have some personal goal that he wants to achieve regardless of the group goal. In any case, talk to an audience (even of one person) is purposive and its effectiveness is measured by the extent to which the speaker achieves his purpose.

Goals can be worked toward effectively to the extent that behavior can be anticipated. But the behavior of individuals in groups may be very much like the behavior of Heisenberg's electrons. To the general student of behavior similarity can be regarded as statistical identity, since analysis might show that the chances of difference were entirely random. But what appears to be a minuscule difference from this point of view can represent a crucial difference to persons involved in the interaction.

In any case of measurement, there is always some deviation from established norms, and the more precise the measurement, the more deviation is possible. In the scientific study of human behavior, for example, scales are normally used to describe attitudes, and even among apparently similar individuals a range of scores can result. When huge numbers of individuals are included in the measurement, the difference in scores does not appear significant, but when members of a small aggregate of individuals are separated only slightly in their attitudes, the minimal deviations can appear to be quite large when displayed on a curve. While a good deal may be known, for example, about the social and political attitudes of the "Methodist

Church," the speaker who confronts a single Methodist congregation will have to consider what has happened to these generalizations in the light of the local community. He will also need to know what other issues exist, irrelevant to Methodism, that might separate members of the community one from the other in their attitudes. Thus, in any case, any speaker will find himself in a unique situation each time he speaks. Any general propositions he has and acts on will have to be adjusted and interpreted in light of what he sees in the group before him.

The man who addresses a small group cannot afford to assume identity or linearity among his listeners. The response of each person to the message is variable and in context. The group will develop its own norms and behaviors and will conform to or deviate from them in a way characteristic of the group. Thus, when the individual listener in a small group perceives the speaker he may respond to his image of the man, his interpretation of his ideas, his past experiences with the man, his past attitudes toward the ideas, his memory about the reputation of the speaker, or any or all of these in combination with a number of possible other (and unpredictable) elements. Furthermore, his ability to hold the speaker in clear figure, to attend him, will vary. Sometimes he will focus on the speaker, sometimes on the words, sometimes on preparation of his own response. Though there is little the speaker can do to control this, the response he receives will depend on it. In addition, at any given time, a listener may appear to have the speaker in figure but may be responding to a peripheral stimulus, an occurrence outside the room, a remark from another person nearby, the physical state of his own body, or, once again, the preparation of his own remarks.

The concept of audience thus affords a speaker only a probability to which he can respond. To be effective, he may need something more definite. He may find that he has to direct his activity toward the modal behavior of the audience at hand, and adjust some of his more general concepts about audiences. The very probabilities which exist in audience analysis give him a good chance of success regardless of what he chooses to do, for, in any case, he is not predicting success with a specific person, and there is usually enough diversity in an audience so that he will succeed with someone.

Speaker Requirements in the Small Group

The situation is quite different, however, for the speaker in the small group. The cohesiveness of the situation and the limited range of possible responses that permit a speaker to make a general analysis of a large audience does not exist in the small group, where members tend to retain their personal identity. In a sense, as he talks to a small group, the speaker is actually addressing audiences. Furthermore, since each participant has the opportunity to interchange the roles of speaker and listener, each may legitimately feel that he is capable of influencing the outcome of the discussion. This control is exerted by influencing, individually, various members of the group. In a sense, a small group may well be a competitive situation where each "victory" for a speaker represents a "loss for a listener." This is particularly true where personal goals are in conflict with group goals. The doctrine of consensus seems to indicate that either individual goals must be subordinated to the group goal, or the group goal must be adjusted so that it fits the individual goals. In this process there is bound to be some necessary sacrifice on the part of members, usually as a result of the urging of the rest of the group. An effective persuader can, for example, gain his personal goal by showing others how it helps accomplish the group goal. To the extent that the others have adjusted their goals to those of the group, they may be inclined to go along.

Furthermore, responsibility for communication is diffused throughout the group. When a speaker feels he has scored, he may stop and await response, thus permitting others to carry his cause for him. When he feels that he is not doing well, he may gracefully retire, courteously permitting someone else to take a turn and wait for a more opportune moment to attempt to assert his control. He may further serve his own ends by discovering members of the group who exert influence and associating with them. There are a number of strategies that must be employed to be successful in the small group, largely because feedback response is immediate and apparent. The response to reification is not possible; it is, rather, a response to several reifications of individuals.

Additional responsibilities are placed on the speaker in a small group because of the expectancies of each participant. In a small group, each person demands to have his influence catered to and his uniqueness recognized. Failure to observe strictures about status, role, and norms renders the speaker ineffective. The obvious struggle in the small group is to gain agreement about a *verbal* formula first, and then work through the implications of the agreement to a plan of action. There is little chance to leave the arena with the matter to be resolved in an obscure state. The public speaker may, if he chooses, deliberately obfuscate by phrasing his remarks so generally that anyone can affiliate themselves with them. This is not possible in the small group because sooner or later there is a necessity to act, and if the agreement has been spurious, this fact will be brought to light at that time.

The public speaker seeks to measure his success by interpreting feedback, and eventually his success is measured by the number of people who modify their behavior in line with his goals. Small group success, however, is measured by the extent to which the group solves the problem confronting it. Sometimes it is necessary for an individual to achieve influence by showing how much he has given up in order to achieve the group goal, for to attempt to win a persuasive success over the rest of the group may result in polarization which in turn defeats the group process. Thus, reification of audience is not so useful. Skill at rhetorical control in a small group is skill at interpersonal interaction. The people in a large lecture hall may be able to surrender their identity in part because the demands of the situation prevent them from trying to exert their own controls. They may daydream, fall asleep, or become otherwise distracted, for social necessity denies them the luxury of interruption. On the other hand, they need not, at any time, do anything explicit to indicate agreement or disagreement, nor will they normally make decisions that will affect their own lives or those of others as a direct result of the act of listening.

Consequently, their involvement is potentially minimal; they get involved to the extent that they care to, and to the extent that the speaker persuades them to.

The Interpersonal Transaction

To deal with flesh-and-blood people effectively, it is necessary to come as close as possible to interacting with the reality of the person.   Interaction with a projection of reality tends to cloud and distort the cues emitted, thus reducing the chance of controlling success.   Each misinterpretation made about the meaning of the behavior of the other person will evoke a kind of cue that must be negatively interpreted, and thus the speaker will be penalized.   Or, a behavior may evoke a counter-behavior that is interpreted as positive reinforcement, but which really may signal displeasure on the part of the other.   We tend, often, to view individuals in much the same way as we view an audience, we get an impression of the person and store it as a reification to which we respond.   The live person, however, is in a constant state of change, and it is necessary to get both a total impression of him and provide a means for adjusting that impression as new behaviors make it necessary to do so.

Inferences that are accidentally correct may evoke reinforcing behavior, but this behavior may be interpreted so wrongly as to cloud future interactions.   The simple inference, for example, that a man's moods remain consistent, or that he will oppose or support ideas consistently, often results in considerable surprise, for we may prepare our remarks to generate support only to find hostility.   The problem here is that any person may project to us an image very different from the one he has of himself.   It is to the image he has of himself that he wants us to respond, but our only choice is to respond to what we see of him. Consequently, if on Tuesday John Smith supports our ideas, we cannot count on his support for Wednesday, for on that day John Smith may feel that we are using him and trying to use his support to gain our own selfish ends.   The support given graciously on one day turns to opposition on the next.

Success we have in communicating with others may be a function of a variety of causes.   There is, of course, always a mathematical probability of doing the right thing in a sufficient number of cases to implant in ourselves a successful mode of operation.   Each successful transaction extends our image of possibility of success that serves as a kind of feedforward and helps us to generate our goals in communication.   Some students, for example, have habituated a kind of listening stance that, they have learned, reinforces their image in the eye of the instructor who gives the grade.   When they encounter an instructor who clearly rewards another kind of attention, they are often confused and unable to cope with the new rule. Furthermore, any formal learning of communication behavior extended beyond the specific context in which it was learned may be ineffective and penalizing.   The formalities of speaking learned in the classroom often do not apply to the life situations in which you find yourself speaking.   Only through an effort to structure situations to simulate reality can some modicum of carry-over be insured.

Success in Communication

Furthermore, it is not so easy to define the word "success" as it applies to the communication act.   There is no general description of what constitutes success at interaction.   The descriptions available are filled with high order abstractions.   They do not specify cues that might indicate that you are doing well.   We might define ourselves as effective, of course, if we have told someone to "jump in the lake," and he does so.   But such gross behavior is not normally found.   When a school teacher tells her class to "be quiet and pay attention," their compliance with her outward behavioral directive indicates nothing about their internal state.   She may perceive the students not moving or speaking, but she does not know whether they are listening. Further, she does not know what has happened to them inside, how hostile she may have made them, and the extent to which her authoritarian demand will impede the possibilities of future relationships with the students.

If "success" can be defined as "an ostensibly courteous hearing," some observations are useful in determining whether this is going on.   When an individual is speaking to a group, for example, he may observe individuals fidgeting, looking out the window, writing letters home, reading the newspaper, and so on, and say to himself that to the extent that he can reduce the incidence of such behavior he will do a successful job of communicating. But it should be understood that ostensibly courteous hearing does not mean that the speaker has been listened to. It is possible for a person to appear courteous and avoid activities that would annoy the speaker and still not hear a word he has said.

In most communication situations, a listener comes and goes without giving any hard information to the speaker about how well he has spoken. Part of the task of training effective speakers is to help them to develop some standards by which they can estimate success. More often than not, these standards are "fictions" which have a reasonable probability of according with fact, but they are rarely universal enough to guarantee success. Real evaluation can only come about when the speaker becomes thoroughly familiar with the behavior of listeners and has had an opportunity to test his inferences against some behavioral data. The successful school teacher understands this, for many are able to detect the presence of a class "mind" and work with it, without sacrificing their understanding and acceptance of the individual child.

Children are also experts at this sort of analysis. The "successful" child, the one who gets what he wants from his parents, has discovered the meaning of various tones of voice, facial movements, gestures, and understands when other concerns make it unwise for him to ask for something, and he can also detect when a manifest good mood will result in virtually any request being granted. He learns to time his requests for major concessions to catch the parents in their good moods. Happy marriages are also marked by the ability of husband and wife to sense the mood of the other through careful attention and precise interpretation of response patterns.

It is rare that we come to know our group mates so well, though. In most cases, the standards we use for our inferences there are the result of previous experience in a limited context. We may know something about groups and about the people with whom we are working, but we have established limited skill at interaction in general, and have achieved a level of intimacy with none or few of those with whom we must interact. Even if we have worked with a group of people over a period of years, we may still not have enough knowledge to do a consistently good job of interpreting their feedbacks, and, consequently, it is still possible to make egregious errors in interaction and thus motivate sulking instead of approval. We have so many listeners, so many people with whom we interact, that we can get really close to only a few. With our close friends, and sometimes our family, we can reach some precision in interpretation and evaluation of responses, but for the rest, we tend to act on generalizations we have made about human behavior.

Even if it were possible to obtain enough feedback information to determine how well you were doing in an interaction, it would be exceedingly difficult to decide how to respond to the information you have. What should a speaker do if he decides that the audience approves of both him and his message? Should he continue to make the kind of remarks he has been making, or should he use this acceptance to move on to new, and perhaps controversial material? If he senses disapproval, does this mean he should change the subject, change his opinion, or change the way he is presenting his material? Questions like these are at the root of the method known to most public speakers as "audience analysis." It is an activity engaged in almost as a ritual, for there are no answers to the questions. All we know is that adaptation is apparently essential to "success."

There are some speakers who are quite successful in finding behaviors that evoke what appears to be the maximum response. If we could examine the processes of such speakers, we might derive an insight about how behaviors in small groups could be made more productive. But unfortunately, attempts to determine what is at the root of such decision making are based on hindsight. Often the process is so deeply rooted in the activity of the speaker that he is not fully aware that he has made adjustments and consequently cannot discuss with you the reasons he made them.

One problem that arises consistently in small group activities is that some members begin speaking to the group as though it were a formal audience. They do not recognize the substantial difference between the act of speaking to a group of people who are required to listen and speaking to those who are entitled to talk back whenever they choose. We tend to follow the path of least resistance, however, and sometimes get carried away with our power to use the spoken word; we try to sway the group as though it were an audience of true believers. At this point we lose the capacity to respond to the individuals in the group as separate persons. If a public speaker were to address his remarks to only one person in his audience, he would run the risk of alienating the rest of the group, particularly if that person was not typical of the group. He must convey to *every* member of the audience the notion that he is the exclusive recipient of the oratory, and this calls for a general kind of performance behavior. In the small group this structure is even more important. When we participate in small group activities, we do not anticipate being lectured to or preached at. We demand a more direct sort of interaction. We are willing to listen only as we are accorded the right to respond. We expect that those who speak will give us an opportunity to respond and will take our responses into account when they talk with us again. Treating a small group as an audience disrupts this process.

Direct interaction, however, demands a kind of confrontation of which most of us are fearful. The kind of personal exposure we make to close friends and family is crucial in our interaction with them, but this kind of personal exposure to "strangers" is threatening to most of us. If we give away too much information, we assume that the other person does not approve of us. Consequently, we seek to maintain some kind of protective screen over our communication to impede the establishment of close interaction. Operating as though the group is an audience is one example of such protection.

In those groups classified as "successful," that is, groups which succeed in doing what they set out to do and in which the members are content with their production, there are clashes of contact between people. There are some who assume that the more direct and intense the interactions in a group can become, the more successful the group will become at its task. There are others who assume that success at doing the task will result in more intense and healthy interactions. Regardless of which view you choose to take, it is clear that there is some relationship between the nature of the interpersonal transaction and the success achieved by the group at reaching its goal.

Seeking Authenticity

A speaker to a large audience tries to appear sincere and genuine as he speaks his words. If he is perceived as fraudulent or "phony" the listeners will have the option of rejecting him and his ideas. Whatever contact he achieves, however, cannot be considered "authentic" in an existential sense, since there is no real responsiveness permitted on the part of the listener. If the speaker is authentic at all, he is authentic to his self-image and his image of the audience, once again a phenomenal concept.

In closer interactions, however, it is necessary to achieve authenticity in response. Stylization normally doesn't work, because the interactive situations do not demand formalized response. In the small group, each member will want the others to respond to him as a man of worth and convey the impression that his words are sensible and coherent (even if the other party chooses not to agree with them). Authenticity, as a concept, transcends both empathy and understanding. It presumes that the parties to a transaction will express their thoughts to the extent that they can, without controlling them to achieve some concealed goal. It is presumed that the group goal will evoke both support and hostility to the extent that each individual can give them. The hostilities must be expressed if consensus is to be achieved and the support is necessary if the group is to continue working toward the goal. The individual persuader can afford to avoid ambivalence, for he has a specific goal at which he knows he will only partially succeed, and revelations of confusion are not designed to help him meet the goal. In the small group, however, there is a latent expectancy that the communication will be open. Members are "supposed" to reveal their personal goals and attempt to find some group solutions that will help achieve as many as possible, if not all of them. Neither a problem-solving system nor authenticity alone will solve a small group's problems. There must be a genuine human transaction around a solid method in order to achieve group goals without jeopardizing individual goals.

The ingredients of "authenticity" or "genuineness" in this kind of transaction are:

1. A feeling of contact between phenomenal worlds.
2. A perception of commonality between two or more people.
3. A perception of the speaker as a unique self and the listener as equally sovereign.
4. A feeling of nontemporary involvement.

These ingredients are not amenable to statistical measurement, but they may serve as criterion points for examining personal participation in small group activity, as well as in structuring activities designed to teach participation in the small group.

Contact of phenomenal worlds comes from shared experience, common movements, synchronous common reactions, mannerisms. It may be summed up in the feeling of comfort and ease that we may develop with only a few people in our lives. It is with those people that we would feel free to bare our innermost thoughts and conceal nothing. This should not be construed to mean that it is good to expose one's deepest thoughts. Such exposure, without a feeling of contact, can be socially dangerous and damaging to all parties involved. But, if it is necessary to live and work with a person over a long period of time, such a feeling usually is more supportive than a feeling of suspicion, guardedness, or mistrust.

Commonality can be identified when two or more parties seem to be advocating the same goals and methods, even though for different reasons. Each of us has a person or two that we don't want on our side. When they express opinions similar to our own, we tend to reexamine our position since we do not want to be on the same side they are. Still, in consistent interaction, advocacy of common goals can assist in developing personal compatibility. From a common cause can come the feeling of contact of phenomenal worlds, as each person seeks to understand the reasons for the other person's advocacy.

Perceptions of uniqueness come when it is possible to begin thinking of a person outside of some classification. The protagonist is no longer "boss" or "colleague," but Irving, with his own unique set of responses. He is a boss unlike other bosses or a colleague unlike other colleagues. In fact, his personal behaviors and beliefs transcend any categories. As a person with whom you interact becomes more and more difficult to fit into a category, you are coming closer to perceiving him as a unique human. Presumably, it is this sort of attitude that we seek from others. Each of us wants to be known for ourselves and evaluated for ourselves and not made to carry the onus of belonging in some classification with ascribed characteristics. It is not easy, however, to overcome the tendency to fit people into categories and develop expectancies in their behavior to fit the expectancies of the class.

The final feeling characteristic of authentic transaction comes when you begin to care what happens to another person outside of the formal interaction in which you are involved. Concern for beliefs, activities, ideas, hobbies, family, all blend to enhance the image of the other. It is at this point that you may begin to understand his goals and reach out for common cause to achieve a consensus satisfying to you and him.

All of these notions, of course, sound quite "poetic," or "philosophical." There may be other epithets even more appropriate. They, too, are "abstractions . . . that have no hands." But if it is necessary to work with abstractions at all, it seems most appropriate to work with the kinds of abstractions that may have relevance to the situation. The search for authenticity has considerable practical value in the small group interaction, for it helps to breed sensitivity without engaging in spurious activities designed to inculcate it.

Influence in Interpersonal Transaction

It is rare when we can observe the influence we have on another person. Parents are sometimes too quick to take credit for their children's accomplishments and too quick to cast blame for their failures. Still, only contact over a long period of time can ever reveal the type of influence we may have. The teacher certainly does not know what kind of influence she has exerted over her students. She may give examinations and revel in her influence over the high scorers, or she may examine College Board scores and accept the high ones as a tribute to her teachings. This, however, is spurious. There is no guarantee that only she could have brought about the salubrious effect, or even that she had very much to do with it. As a matter of fact, the real influence of a teacher more often than not is felt later in life, probably long after the teacher has died, so that the notes of appreciation written by middle-aged successes never get to the teachers who regarded them as failures.

The public speaker, also, cannot really know what influence he has exerted over a particular audience. It would be presumptuous to assume that a single speech could have a major effect. Speakers can be easily humbled when they feel the flush of success merely by pointing out that the reason for their success was that "the audience was in the right frame of mind." The debate that went on over the relative effects of the Kennedy-Nixon debates of the campaign of 1960 has no real resolution, for with all our sophisticated measurement, it is not possible to assess influence.

Yet, the major tool that the participant in small group activity has at his disposal is just such intimate knowledge. The only real substance of audience analysis is awareness of how to influence others and how they respond; what to say and how to say it so that the audience will feel comfortable and accepting. If a speaker cannot get a perception of his hostility-evoking mannerisms, he will continue with ineffectual performance regardless of how much theoretical knowledge he may acquire about the workings of groups. While some groups only come together for a short time, there are many that continue meeting over long periods of time. Particularly in those, the individual who wishes to avoid being relegated to an irrelevant role must seek an awareness of his impact on the others. He must understand why he is assigned the role he has, and he must devise effective ways of changing his role and his image so that he will be satisfied by his interactive participation in the group. What we have here is an isomorphism of audience analysis, in which the reifications which underlie the concept of authenticity seem to be more relevant than those that underlie more scientific and more rhetorical concepts.

A Proposal for Study of the Dyad

There has really been very little done in the study of the interpersonal dyad. All of the preceding could be construed as an argument for extending this kind of study, but hopefully it will not be cybernated and will be devoted to intelligent case history reports which detail feelings of both parties to a transaction. There are some fertile areas to explore:

1. How does a clinician "bring about" a change in his subject? Does the clinician bring anything about or does he create an atmosphere in which the subject can elect to change? What devices does the patient use to assist and resist the therapy offered and why does he use them? How effective are clinical personality and clinical methodology in bringing about change? What happens to the clinician as a result of his participation in the process?

2. How do people choose the persons they prefer to interact with? How are allies and enemies selected when a small group of people comes together face-to-face? How influential are physical cues, past memories, instantaneous responses to behavior in determining who might be worthy of support and who must be opposed? To what extent do "first impressions" set the tone for subsequent encounters? How can the effects of first impressions be overcome?

3. What does a given listener perceive as influential when he listens and how can the speaker find this out? What criteria are used to evaluate people as significant or trivial? How does a person know when he is supporting another and how does he know when he does injury? Does he care? What satisfaction does he gain from both supportive and injurious behavior?

4. What does a speaker look for in his listener? Are there behaviors that are considered, modally, to be supportive? How can supportiveness be discovered in an individual case?

5. What is the effect of changing role? When one person changes role, what happens to the role played by the other? Is there some way that roles can be changed consistently and effectively? What happens to the listening behavior of a speaker when he becomes a listener, and vice versa?

6. What happens to people when they are required to communicate with each other at close quarters over a long period of time? Do we tend to become more sensitive or insensitive to the people with whom we are familiar? How do people control their hostilities and mask their emotions during unpleasant transactions? What cues give them away and what happens to the people who perceive them? What happens in a transaction when one party begins to perceive the other as a friend, enemy, father substitute, surrogate brother, and so forth? What role does sex play in the purposive communication of males and females in small group activity? Is it possible to be unaware of sex in such transactions, and if not, how can it be dealt with in such a way that it will not disrupt the transaction? What happens to an old relationship when a third party enters and evokes an interest on the part of one of the parties? How do groups of people who are very familiar with each other tend to resist and accept newcomers into the group?

7. Is it possible, by studying dyadic communication closely, to perceive the possibilities of influence one person may exert over another? Can one person talking to another exert any influence? Do the assumptions we make about the influence of speech on behavior stand up?

There are many other questions that could be asked. Many of you may be asking them now. Certainly, our past methods of investigation of small group activity have not been terribly productive. We have either been considering the small group as a small and limited audience transaction, or we have regarded it as a unique phenomenon, another kind of abstraction. We have not attempted to understand it through its smallest unit, the interpersonal dyad. Such study may prove to be fruitless, but we are not so certain of our present data to ignore its possibilities.

EXERCISES

We have ended this chapter with a series of questions, any of which would serve as an excellent group project. Check them out and select some of them. Be sure to compare the various answers given by the groups. If you choose to tackle one of these questions, the authors of this book would be very interested in seeing your results.

GROUP ACTIVITIES

1. Conduct a series of discussions on the following ideas or concepts and see if you can write a brief (one or two page) statement summarizing the ideas of your group. Then select a spokesman and report your ideas to the whole class. Have the spokesmen organize themselves into a group and see if they can come up with a summary statement synthesizing the ideas of the group. Have them do this while the entire class watches. As an individual project, have each observer identify and report on the following: Who was leader? What were the characteristics of his leadership (stated behaviorally)? (Avoid such statements as, "he was enthusiastic!") Who was the expediter? The game leader? The information giver? The devil's advocate? The sage? The authority-oriented (trying to find out what teacher wants)? What other roles could be identified and who played them? Was there a development of a clear hierarchy of status? Rank the members according to the amount of power they exercised in the group. Who was most influential in bringing about the group decision? Were there norms developed in the group? Describe them, identifying procedural norms, communication norms, topic norms. Now organize another group to go over the individual reports and come up with a general report covering the entire group. Ask them to make recommendations for improving the process of improvement and evaluation. Finally, using their report as a basis, set up several groups to grade the members of the group you observed. Set yourself some limits, like you can only give one "A", and you must give two "C's". Compare the reports

from each group. Next, ask each group to defend, by citing empirical information, the grades assigned to each of the participating members of the group observed.

Here are some topics for discussion:

(a) In every human transaction there is something up for grabs. What do people have at stake when they participate with others? How does this differ in a task group? A social group? An attempt to influence an authority? An attempt to get a teacher to change a grade? What general conclusions can you draw about "investment," socially and psychologically, in group activity?

(b) Examine the Kierkegaard quote on pp. 130–131. What does this statement mean? Does Kierkegaard mean that attempts to persuade others in groups are essentially dishonest? Does he mean that use of the spoken word impedes human psychological growth? What are the implications of this quotation for the seeker of political office? For the man seeking a date? For the student activist? For the professor lecturing to his class? For American society in general?

(c) Develop a "grading system" for a course in small groups. Prepare it in such a way that a department head could hand it to a young instructor and demand that he conform to it. Make your system develop a "curve." See to it that there is a way to flunk at least one person in every class regardless of quality. Fit your grading system into the prevailing system at your university. Be sure to state explicitly what must be done to earn each grade, and how to identify its quality.

(d) Now develop a grading system for participation in small group activity. How would you like to be graded? What would you want an evaluator to look for? To what extent would the criteria you agree on be advantageous or disadvantageous to you?

(e) Define "success in small group interaction." What are the behavioral components of success? How would you know a successful discussant if you saw one? What advice could you give not-so-successful discussants about how to become more successful? Perhaps you can expand this into a little handbook called, "How to succeed in group discussion without really trying."

(f) Generate a description of an average student. An average freshman. An average fraternity man. An average teacher. Use the prevailing norms on your campus. Now go out and see if you can find one. Identify individuals who come closest to your definition of average. See if you can get those people to visit with your group. Ask them some questions about their beliefs and behaviors and then reevaluate both your criteria for "average" and your selection of a prototype. How reliable are such judgments? How essential is it that you make them? How would you go about making decisions about the extent to which you could rely on another person without making such judgments?

(g) If there is some sort of election campaign going on during the time you take this course, why not take a poll? See if you can predict the outcome of the election. Set up a poll-taking operation, go out and ask the questions, interpret the data, and make predictions. Be sure you do this in plenty of time to get the election returns so you can discuss the reasons for your accuracy or lack of it. By way of hindsight (if you predicted the outcome wrong), what questions would you now ask and of whom—if you could do it all over again?

DYADIC ACTIVITY

1. Using a random technique, pair yourself off with another person and interview each other. Allow plenty of time for the interview. Find out all you can about each other in the following categories:

(a) Educational and social development—schools attended, subjects taken, past activities, recreation and avocational.

(b) Family—father's age and occupation, mother's age and occupation, siblings' ages, sex and personality. Extended family relations. Attitude toward family members and their attitude toward subject, etc.

(c) Current activities—educational, social, political, religious, vocational preparation. Evaluation of the school.

(d) Future goals.

(e) Immediate future plans.

(f) Attitudes on religion, politics, sex education, the arts, campus protest, drugs, sex, friendship, alienation, conformity (any other topics you think relevant).

(g) General philosophy of life.

Next write a report for your dyad-mate in which you report accurately on what he told you *and* present your evaluation of him as a human being. Present him with this report (he will hand you one about you) and indicate that he can now prepare a rebuttal statement called "the real me." It might also be useful if you could meet with a group and discuss what happened to you during the course of this project.

INDIVIDUAL PROJECTS

1. Assume that you are going to have to talk to the following audiences. For each, list the information that you think you would have to have before you talked to them, and what expectations you might have of their behavior in response to you.

   (a) Your professor in this class—to get him to change your grade.

   (b) Your minister—explaining to him why you were caught drunk on Main Street last Saturday night.

   (c) Your parents—on why some students take drugs and practice premarital sex.

   (d) Your fellow "inmates" of wherever you live—on why they should support a protest movement against bad food on campus.

(*e*) This class, to which you will give a "lecture" on the contribution to discussion theory by George Herbert Mead (or some other authority).

(*f*) (Males only.) Your draft board on why you should be deferred.

It might be a good idea here, too, to gather once again in your groups and compare your statements to see if there are consistencies in your analyses. Note that you are not asked to *do* the analysis. Just think out the question you would want answered.

2. Cicero once said, "A good speaker is a good man who also speaks well." In your own head, what are the things you might observe that would lead you to the conclusion that a man is a good man? Don't talk about abstract qualities, just about things you could see or experience. Now try to find the same sort of characteristics that would lead you to conclude someone is "speaking well." How well do you conform to your own criteria in your own speaking? Are you a "good man" by your own definition? What do you suppose this attitude of yours toward yourself might have to do with your "success" in interaction?

3. What are the "consistent inferences" you draw that lead you to choice making? For example, how do you go about selecting what to order in a restaurant? How do you identify someone you would like to date? How do you go about choosing courses? How do you decide whose ideas to support in a discussion? How do you select a political candidate to support? What effect do you think these consistent inferences might have on your interpersonal "success"?

You might be interested in playing out some situations in class and analyzing them according to the information presented in the chapter. Have students act out the following situations:

(*a*) A student who has been accused of cheating trying to convince the professor that he did not cheat.

(*b*) A smoker of marijuana trying to convince a nonsmoker of the virtues of "pot."

(*c*) A regular church-goer trying to get someone to go with him on Sunday morning.

(*d*) A son or daughter informing a parent of a desire to shift his or her major from education to philosophy.

(*e*) A young man trying to get a very uninterested young woman interested.

(*f*) (Females only.)   Two of you planning a surprise shower for Sally Anne who is getting married two weeks from now.

(*g*) A student trying to convince an English professor that *How to Talk Dirty and Influence People* by Lenny Bruce ought to be on the required reading list for freshmen.

(*h*) Two people who don't know each other very well forced to share a booth in the coffee shop.

(*i*) A conversation in which you try to convince a man who believes that black men are communist of the error of his ways.

(*j*) Any other dyadic situation you might be able to dream up.   In fact, your groups might be useful here.   Each one could dream up five or ten situations to act out.

In talking about these role-plays afterwards, try to find out what each party had at stake and how he acted to achieve his personal goals.   See if you can make some recommendations to either party about how he might have been more "successful," whatever that means to you.

The Impact of Communication On Human Behavior

The act of speaking to a large audience has at its base a specific purpose. The speaker specifies in his own mind some goals, some responses to be gained from the listeners. He then attempts to control his verbal output as best he can to ensure the achievement of that response. In the small group, speech is used to gain both personal and group goals. Someone addressing a large audience can work to his own goals exclusively, but he tends to fail if he does not take into account the goals of his listeners. The transaction is more direct in the small group, which is organized specifically to achieve collective goals by synthesizing personal goals.

The act of speaking with another person cannot be treated as an act separate from the effects it has on the listener. That act is part of an interaction and every interaction has its effects. The speaker may have a relatively singular purpose in mind when he speaks. It may be to release his tensions, to convince himself of his argument, to intensify his commitment, or merely to cathart. But included in that purpose is a response from the person to whom it is directed. And the listener cannot avoid being influenced by the speaker.

Learning Speech

In order to understand the kinds of responses that can be offered to speech, and the kinds of effects speech can have on listeners, the role of communication in the development of personality must be considered. The potential for speech can be represented as an interaction of biological endowment and environment. Speech is not a natural endowment. It is a complicated process which must be learned.

The parts of the body that are used to produce speech all have other primary functions. The lungs, which provide the power for speech, are, of course, designed to put oxygen into the bloodstream and to eliminate carbon dioxide. Their function must be synchronized into the speech process. The larynx, which vibrates to create the sounds of speech, is mainly a valve to prevent food from entering the windpipe. The tongue, lips, and teeth, which differentiate speech sounds, are specifically used for chewing and swallowing. The tongue, incidentally, is one of the most complex of all muscles. The operation of these complex parts of the body must be coordinated with the brain in order that sensible sound can be made.

The initiation of sound is almost a random accident. Noises are made while the child breathes, swallows, and protests. It is not until the child makes some association between the sounds he produces and the perceptions he makes of the external environment that he gets the notion of symbolization, and he becomes aware that he can control the kind of noises he makes so that they can represent a thing, an action, or a feeling. The awareness of the symbolic process is the first step in developing the personality. Furthermore, there is no guarantee that speech will automatically develop. The rare cases of wild children, abandoned and raised by the animals, indicate that they do not develop speech and cannot learn it once they have been brought back into the society of men. In fact, there appears to be a critical period in the development of the child when he must be exposed to speech or lose his chance to be initiated into humanity.

The Swiss psychologist Jean Piaget offers a developmental sequence of speech in the child. Up to about eighteen months, he contends, much of learning is random. The child creates sounds, the environment endows them with meaning. The infant may learn that mother can be obtained by producing sound. Mother, however, endows the sounds with meaning and can differentiate, after the infant has trained her, between a cry for food and a cry for cuddling. Once this point is passed, the child's developing personality will be largely dependent on his use of language and the responses others make to it.

Up to about five years of age, the child experiments with controls, but he does not have a subtle and flexible repertoire of responses. He engages in gross behavior, he demands, he orders, he does not seek to adjust to the needs of others, and, consequently, he does not persuade. His behavior is primarily egocentric as he seeks some understanding of where he fits in the universe around him. He lacks the capability to adjust his behavior even when it is failing, and once he embarks on a course of action, he is unable to cut it off and shift goals and strategies. His frustrations, however, will lead him to attempt more sophisticated controls. He begins, after the age of five, to learn something about human interaction, and he gradually comes to realize that everyone around him seeks the same goals —some control over the environment through the use of speech. He begins to emulate what he sees. He attempts play behavior to try out various roles. He will try "daddy" and "mommy," and, if his father offers a strong image, he will settle on the father role and learn how to become a man. He attempts "fireman" and "cops and robbers," acting out what he sees around him. For his efforts, relevant adults will bestow rewards and administer punishments. A reward indicates successful control over his environment, approval; a punishment is failure at achieving a goal, disapproval.

This kind of growth behavior continues into adulthood. As more and more relevant people come into the environment, there are more roles to play. Teachers and peers, as well as parents and storybook heroes, begin to exert an influence, and all kinds of modifications are attempted in language behavior. Throughout adulthood the pattern is repeated. We tend to alter our language to suit the group we are in or the group we wish to be in. As we find it necessary to change our language, our personality will also change. So closely related are language and personality that one cannot change without attendant change in the other. This means that every interaction will have some effect on us. Communication coming in and communication in response is neither simple nor trivial. Thus, close interactions in small groups can be examined by looking at language, and behavior in small groups can be improved by alteration of language.

The Small Group and Personality

Small group interaction may be looked at as a set of impacts on personality. Each person comes to the group as a distinct individual with a fund of traits, beliefs, values, and goals. Whatever adjustment is made in those traits, beliefs, values, and goals represents an alteration in personality. Part of the alteration is self-programmed, for a good part of the talk that goes on in a small group is as much to convince the person who is talking as those he is talking to. Each member of the group will display his personality through his talk and his responses. As the group becomes synthesized, as consensus is reached, talk will sound more and more alike, members will become more and more compatible. Over a long period of time, each member will tend to develop a style, acceptable to the other members of the group, that will denote the position he holds or role he plays in the group. Personality will alter distinctly to accommodate others in the group. When the member leaves the group, he will carry with him some of the change that came about through his participation.

The phenomenon of addressing the self in spoken language is an intriguing one. The Russian psychologist L. S. Vygotsky developed the concept of "inner speech" as a basis for a theory of language development. According to Vygotsky, the child first begins to vocalize, then associates vocalizations with external things. He then proceeds to act out social situations by verbalizing his way through them. Thoughtful speech and behavior develop as he internalizes this rehearsal type of speech. For example, a small child will very often pretend his way through a social situation before he attempts it. He will define an imaginary protagonist and talk things out with him, then find the real person and behave as he did at rehearsal. This act is equivalent to the kind of rehearsal that goes on in the minds of adults as they think their way through a transaction in advance. The oral test applied by the child helps him to determine in his mind whether he is capable of carrying out the transaction he plans. The mature adult will have to determine the limits of success and failure before he attempts to apply rhetoric to a socil situation. As the situation becomes more and more purposive, more preplanning and analysis is necessary. But the small group does not provide advance planning time for the transactions that go on, and so it is sometimes necessary for participants to talk their way into and out of positions, exactly as the small child does. This Vygotskian concept may help to explain why so much talk is necessary in the small group.

It is also clear that talk carried on in the small group has modification of the behavior of others as its goal. It has already been noted in the previous chapter that virtually all talk may be considered rhetorical for it seeks to bring about a change in the person who hears it. In this sense, talk is a competitive activity. Furthermore, if we consider that even talk for purposes of convincing the self has behavior change as a goal, it is hard to conceive of nonpurposive talk, even in nonpurposive situations. Each person seeks to exert some mastery and control over every transaction, and, as we have noted, each person seems to be satisfied or pleased with the transaction as the outcome tends to be in line with his own goals. The purposive activity in group discussion attempts to control the personal goal seeking by imposing a group goal around which the participants can synthesize their own goals, and thus it seeks a mutual "victory."

Norms Governing Limits of Transactions

Competitive activities, in our culture, are controlled by a set of norms. There are certain activities that are clearly barred.

Torture, extortion, threat of violence or violence itself are considered signs of antisocial behavior and a set of laws have been developed by society to prevent and punish their use.   These devices, known to the ancients as "inartistic proofs," are not permitted in a social transaction.   However, any transaction may have its intimidating features, depending on the power of one or more of the participants.   Conversation between a subordinate and a superordinate may be characterized this way regardless of how calm it may appear.   If one party has the power to punish or reward, deference will usually be shown by the other party, or he must be prepared to take the consequences.   While use of pressure by a superordinate may be considered "inartistic," our social norms permit this kind of activity, and thus some parties to transactions can anticipate being losers from the outset.   Nevertheless, many succeed in "winning," at least partially, by adjusting their goals to accord with those of the authority figure.

It may be necessary, however, to do considerable adjusting of personal goals to avoid the attendant loss of self-esteem that seems to be inextricably bound up in such transactions. Employer-employee and student-teacher interactions are characteristic of such unequal combats.   A student wins only when the teacher defines his win as a win for teacher as well.   Most students have discovered that even the most permissive and understanding teacher can be "driven to the wall" and forced to use the power of his office in order to win an interaction.   Most students further understand when to stop pushing, and to accept modest victories.   Teachers, however, sometimes misunderstand the capacity for defeat on the part of some students and attempt to force them into a position of total capitulation, leaving no out for salvation of self-esteem.   The teacher who punishes and then attempts to compel verbal apology provides an example of this sort of activity.   The student has the alternatives of capitulating and suffering the loss of ego, or resisting and feeling the total force of the system come down on him.

The situation is not quite the same between the boss and employee, since there is no legal compulsion for the employee to stay employed on a particular job.   Employees who perform tasks of considerable importance to the company may, indeed, find themselves in a stronger bargaining position than the administrator, who may be easy to replace. The lower a man is in the hierarchy, however, the less bargaining power he has, and if he has reached a state where he no longer feels capable of finding other employment, he too must give in and concede the victory to the other party.

Ostensibly, the theory behind small group discussion is equalization of combat. The participants are held to be on equal terms. This is not always the case, and as participants who hold different positions on the scale of authority are brought together there may emerge the establishment of authoritarian controls that impede the flow of talk. The rhetorical devices may be employed more to influence the authority than to achieve the group goal.

Norms of Language Use

The relationships of parties to any verbal transactions may be understood through examination of the norms of language usage. The impressions they receive from the people around them help them to understand their strengths and weaknesses in participation. The way friends, parents, teachers, and other relevant persons in their environment respond to them gives them notions about the amount and type of control they are able to exert over others. The child who wins in the family may discover that the techniques he uses at home are worthless with peers. It is necessary for him to adjust his linguistic output if he wishes to retain friends. If he is willing to sacrifice friendships, he may retain his verbal behavior. If it is necessary for him to defer to the peer culture, however, he may intensify his attempts to win at home, and demand more and more victories, thus forcing the parents into a compensatory subordinate role.

Language behavior in the small group is conditioned initially by previous experience and is stylized by the kinds of victories the participants have previously won. Each member will seek a position in the group that will enable him to utilize his customary style. Often there are conflicts for position. Two compromisers may find themselves in combat for time as each seeks to play the desired role in juxtaposition with the others. Two dominant personalities find it difficult to share a participant role. Part of the confusion of small group interaction lies in sorting out the roles and enabling the members to develop modifications in style that will permit them to participate in such a way that their victories are maximized without necessarily forcing others into defeat.

Cognitive Style and Language

The cognitive style of the participant is also reflected in his language. Each individual may have learned a method of working his way through a problem. Some may seek inspiration; others may free-associate. Some may seek some kind of external authority for solutions; others may work through the problem rationally. In the small group, there is likely to be as much confusion because of differences in cognitive style as because of verbal technique. Those who seek inspiration or authoritarian leadership often find themselves in conflict with those who wish to work step by step for a rational solution to the problem. To add to the confusion, the achievement of consensus depends on orderly procedure. There must be a good deal of time permitted for sparring and experimenting, learning the technique of discussion, before individuals will settle into a productive role. It is for this reason that prescriptions about how to behave in the small group are relatively worthless. The words that might be said about what is desirable in a group are descriptions of what has happened when a group has done well. They are only relevant when a group has learned to do well, and the individual members have achieved appropriate roles. And it is precisely to these people that they are redundant and unnecessary.

While there is nothing that can be done about previous training of individual participants in a small group transaction, there is a considerable amount that can be done about their behavior once they enter into the group. Because the group begins to function as a microculture it can establish its own norms, which can influence the behaviors of the participants. What goes on in the small group, furthermore, can influence the external life styles of the participants. Thus we find that the Madison Avenue style influences the home life of admen, professors are professorial at home, and so on. Vocational groups are particularly influential cultures since they are primary economic units, and roles attained in the vocational group tend to be sustained to the extent individuals are rewarded by their group participation.

Interaction and Personality

The concept of impact of interaction on personality is most eloquently discussed by Ernest Becker (*Birth and Death of Meaning*). Becker asserts that the human ego is developed through speech. The child learns who he is by performing, playing roles, and practicing at interaction. Through these activities, he learns to assess the responses of others and determines strategies for dealing with the responses as he interprets them. In fact, Becker refers to the Oedipal transition as being linguistic rather than sexual. The helpless infant becomes a mature adult once he ceases to be symbolically dependent on others. This he does by acquiring the symbols and meanings that others use and reshaping them to make sense in his world as he sees it. He develops symbols that are meaningful to others and thus is able to play the game of transaction; he begins to compete for actual victories, often employing the same styles of those around him at the outset, and then altering his style depending on what he is rewarded and punished for, until he achieves a personal, idiosyncratic style of behavior. Often, he does not understand what victory is, so his concentration is on styles of using communication rather than on goals of communication.

A child who is not exposed to language, or who is denied the opportunity to play at developing language, ususally becomes deficient in some form of verbal output. The child who is consistently punished for language use learns to avoid interaction and finds it very difficult to develop sufficient skill to participate in the life game. Often these language-deprived individuals will seek vocations that do not include interaction, and it is to their dismay that they learn that there is hardly an occupation that does not require interaction in some way. Further, children must learn that it is possible for them to succeed at communication. Their own concept of self is a direct function of the number of times they can successfully exert their influence. Once again, inartistic proofs are permitted to the very young. Sometimes displays of temper and thoroughly egocentric displays of will are sufficient to obtain a victory. As the child grows older, however, he must learn that he seldom can win at the expense of others, and he learns to take into account the goals and wishes of those around him. Once he learns this, he becomes a rhetorician, though perhaps not a very skilled one. The "cons" younger children use are transparently egocentric, but the fact that he elects to "con" rather than become angry indicates that he is beginning to understand the basic rules of human transaction.

Maintenance of Self-Esteem

There are some adults who have become very skilled at interaction. These usually have very high self-esteem and considerable control over their verbal output. Self-esteem is the image of the self that is held in the phenomenal world. It is, of course, made up of information that comes in from the outside. The individual who is capable of developing and maintaining self-esteem without outside information is "schizophrenic." He is not in contact with the world at all. Too much self-esteem, however, may produce a bore. The individual who is incapable of understanding that he has lost in a given case proceeds with his linguistic output regardless of the responses of others and frequently becomes irrelevant as the others learn to ignore him.

We cannot lose sight of the competitive aspects of the Oedipal transition. The child initially seeks to use symbols to maintain a comfortable environment. He next learns that it is necessary for him to lose a few, to take into account the fact that others are contending to have their needs met also. Most of this he learns by "competing" in a small group, either a family or a peer unit. Movement from the family tells him that others are not as devoted to his needs as are his parents, and he begins to mature his style. He discovers that if he can phrase his demands in terms that are satisfying to others, he will have his demands met. In so doing, he begins to learn to meet the rudimentary demands of others. The interaction of groups of young children is characterized by much shouting, fighting and pummeling. There does not appear to be much order to the transaction. The child who takes his ball and goes home when he cannot pitch, however, learns that he cannot play the game alone and thus he loses, rather than gains, personal satisfaction. He may then elect to bargain, to pitch part of the time, and permit the better pitcher to do it part of the time. He may learn, finally, that his role is not that of pitcher at all, but simply that of ball owner, a role that, if acted out graciously, will give him sufficient reward so that he feels part of the group. Thus, he learns to exert rhetorical control.

The impression is often given by those who disseminate advice on how to participate in small groups that it is possible to subordinate personal goals to those of the group. This really does not appear to be so. Small group interactions do not always have happy outcomes. There are a number of cases where one or more members refuse to accept the group solution and continue struggling for their own ideas even after the solution has been put into operation. (It is for this reason that conflict resolution devices such as majority rule were developed.) Such personal rebellions occur when it is impossible to find anything in the group attainment that will satisfy personal needs. Regrettably, in teaching group dicsussion in the classroom it often appears that personal desires can always be subordinate to group goals. This is because the classroom situation is quite unrealistic, and it is the act of subordination that makes the individual look better to the teacher. The individual must discover the nature of the conflict between self and group in a real context, when he has something at stake.

Once again, we must consider the proposition that "the group" is an abstraction. We infer the existence of "group" from the behavior of the people in it. What really goes on in group interaction is the search for a kind of plan or program that will satisfy the people involved. It may represent a least common denominator or it may represent a solid commitment. But consensus cannot involve the clash characteristic of the democratic process, for at that point, the group becomes an arena or an electorate. Thus, group becomes an ad hoc definition. If an aggregate of people does what is characteristic of "group action," then they may be termed a group. Looking at group this way tends to resist the compulsive expectation of behavior that results when we define group merely by the number of people present in the room. The essence of the whole business, of course, is the impact that the various members have on each other. If they can mutually affect each other so that common ground and common decision are established, then the group output is usually both satisfactory and workable. If they clash, this does not mean that the output will necessarily be inferior, but it may mean that they are unable to function together as a group. Clash results when the rhetoric of conciliation and consensus fails. Interestingly enough, failure may be both unconscious and volitional. There are individuals whose beliefs are so strong that they are unwilling to make the concessions necessary to arrive at consensus. These people may consciously subvert conciliatory efforts, or they may sincerely convince themselves that they are working toward consensus despite the fact that their resistance is manifest.

The Group and the System

Using this ad hoc definition of group—a group exists when an aggregate of people demonstrate their capacity to achieve consensus or who perceive themselves as cooperating—we can stipulate some behavioral criteria for analysis of behavior of interacting people, using the concept group as an evaluation criterion, rather than a finite definition. For example, when people interacting polarize themselves and engage in verbal combat around a single issue, they cannot be considered a group. Such combat is clearly identified when the possibilities for choice are limited on an "either-or" basis. In order to make decisions under these circumstances, it is necessary to vote. The act of voting implies that there are winners and losers, the losers reserving the right to attack and seek revision of whatever decision was made at some later occasion.

The definition could be extended to include aggregates of

people who experience conflict about issues or personalities, but who agree that they are seeking consensus as a goal. It could be further extended to include aggregates that agree on a goal but not necessarily on a method or procedure for reaching it. It might also include aggregates of people who agree that they ought to have a goal, though it has not yet been stipulated. Finally, it could include aggregates like persons seeking education or therapy together, for whom some professional has determined a goal, which may be collective or individual, and toward which the interaction is directed.

Employing this kind of definition keeps focus on both output and procedure. Procedure includes not only collective steps taken to achieve output, but the elements of the collective steps, that is, the individual interactions of the participants. Thus, the mere presence of five people in a room might not constitute a group. It would not be necessary to show concern about interpersonal hostility, unless it could be demonstrated that such hostility impeded the transaction toward a goal agreed upon by the participants.

Perhaps it would be helpful to contrast the notion of group with the notion of system. We have placed great stress upon the idea of interaction. We've done so because to understand the nature and the significance of the interaction process is basic to understanding the entire communication process. To the social scientists interaction is as fundamental as is the molecule to the chemist and the neutron to the physicist.

Though interaction exists in time and space it is not necessary to be burdened by events from all time and space. Interaction consists of, or takes place in, a relationship that a human being has with another human being or with other human beings *or* with objects in his environment. A single relationship is atemporal. It may be affected by previous interactions but it is itself something that occurs once and never again.

It would present real difficulties if we could go no further. Every act, every word would have to be conceived as a single unrelated phenomenon. It would be impossible to interrelate them into anything that even approaches understanding.

It is possible to extend our conception of these interrelationships so that we conceive of a set of interactions as a system.

Admittedly these are also abstractions. They are useful because, though our interest is in the set of relationships that are occurring between individuals and the significant objects in their environment at a given time, the observations do not include each participant's entire history of interaction and thus not his entire personality.

But it is very useful to be able to think of a set of interactions as a system. When a strange boy walks into a room where three close friends are having a rollicking good time, they may appear relatively unaffected by the stranger but he is certainly aware, however distantly, of them. He becomes part of the universe of symbols in that environment. Certainly the people in the room do not comprise a group because they are not in a state of interdependence. But they are also more than an aggregate since each participant in the system is affected by the others around him. The three may be a group; the newcomer may be seeking to join them. But physical propinquity alone does not make the four of them a group. This does not happen until the newcomer is permitted to share the norms the other three employ.

When the concept "social system" is used, it is in this context. It has direct meaning to the observer since somewhere he must draw boundaries around his observations. He must decide what is relevant and what is not relevant. This is not a travesty however. The participant also selects, classifies, categorizes objects—human and nonhuman—and receives the communications—verbal and nonverbal—that are part of the immediate environment.

It is in the context of social systems that roles are enacted. The role therefore is an immediate thing to some time and space. Permit an analogy. A specific brick in one context is part of a wall. That same brick could also have been part of a walk, or a street, or a chimney. It could have different relationships in the different systems of which it is a part. If that same brick was part of both a wall and a fireplace, it would have two different sets of relationships. To understand it, we would have to understand the role it played in the fireplace and in the wall. Perhaps it appeared peculiarly placed. The placement could not be accounted for either by its function in the fireplace alone, or in the wall alone, but its placement could be understood by understanding its dual role.

The same process happens with humans. A supervisor plays his role of authority or leader in front of the people he supervises. However, in another context, he may be subordinate to someone else, a person also concerned about the people being supervised. It is necessary for the supervisor to please both superordinates and subordinates. Consequently, his behavior could not be understood by looking at him in either role alone. To understand why he behaves as he does, he must be viewed both as supervisor and supervised. Consider how complex this becomes when we examine the multiple roles all humans must play. They might, simultaneously, be father, scout leader, committee chairman, member of a religious congregation, son of a domineering mother, and so on. Whatever role is being played at a given moment cannot operate independent of some influence from the other roles.

In the same way are social systems made up of roles. Roles in a social matrix are interrelated but not necessarily interdependent in their goals and objectives. Only if this latter point is reached does a set of interacting roles become a group.

This definition of the group could be extended, without a great stretch of the imagination, to include participants in any interaction, for, in any given case, shared time and space involves those who share it in some sort of investigation of what they might do with the time and how they might participate in the interactions. Individuals who do not find profit in the interaction might drift off and participate elsewhere. Those who achieve consensus on what they ought to be doing might then be said to constitute a group. From this perspective, the concept of "stake" becomes important to understanding the behavior of the individual in the group. For example, a participant in social conversation may have little stake in the outcome. If he is either bored or threatened by what is going on, there is nothing to compel him to continue to participate other than his feeling of obligation, responsibility, or desire. If he sees himself as basically submissive, he may choose to remain present, despite the threat of the interaction, for to leave would require more inner strength than he can muster. If he has a particularly strong self-image, he may seek to take control and direct the conversation to topics he finds less threatening and more amusing. If he is functionally autonomous, it may matter little what is said, and he may choose either to remain present and ignore what is going on, or if choice is possible, he may seek another group which might provide a more stimulating interaction.

Participation

As the compulsion to participate increases, the stakes go up and the attendant impact on personality increases. An interaction with classmates, for example, can only be partly temporary. During the time span allotted to the course, it will be necessary to confront the same people at the same time and place. Failure to appear for such interaction may result in a lowered evaluation from the authority-teacher; thus it is necessary to appear. If the matter is further complicated by the threat of an evaluation of "participation" to be given by the authority, success at interaction becomes necessary, and tension may increase, particularly in the individual who feels incompetent to deal with those present or uninterested in the outcome. The undergraduate who finds himself in a class largely peopled by graduate students may display this kind of tension. He may feel intellectually inadequate; he may not be sure he is being evaluated on criteria different from those used on the graduate students. He may feel a singular compulsion to demonstrate his adequacy in order to earn a high evaluation, or he may feel hostility to the others in the group that may impel him to want to "show them up." In any case, his self-esteem is on the line, and, despite the ostensibly cooperative demeanor of the situation, he is engaged in vigorous competition for survival both academically and in his own estimation of self.

Pressures become even greater in a vocational situation. To the extent that the individual perceives himself threatened economically, or perhaps recognizes challenges to his position in some kind of established professional hierarchy, the outcome of his transactions becomes more important. In a vocational setting there is no finitude for the transaction. The student participating in class knows the date at which the need for his participation will end. To end a vocational participation, however, requires finding another position, as well as overcoming the apprehension of the unknown that may militate against seeking another job. Involuntary ending of participation may come when the authority perceives the employee as ineffective. Thus a double threat is imposed, one internally, the other externally. To alleviate fears on both counts requires intensification of efforts to achieve "satisfactory" participation, however that is defined in the mind of the individual.

In each of the above cases, a kind of hypertonia may be possible. Success in interaction may be impeded by desire for success in interaction. Thus, the struggle to find a comfortable role in the group process becomes all-important. The discovery of a role demands an "understanding" both of situation and of self. Deriving this understanding is based primarily on individual perception and interpretation of perception, the acting out of which may be termed the participants' "interaction personality." This personality may be changed internally or externally in the struggle for an appropriate role. External change comes from the actions of other participants, and internal change comes from interpretation of those reactions.

There are at least two possible reasons for anxiety and personal distress during interactions. One comes from the internal understanding of inability to achieve one's goals. The other comes from input of negative evaluations (or evaluations interpreted negatively) from the other participants. Both tend to reduce ability to respond to what is going on by forcing the participant back into an internal world of interpretation. The more he retreats from the reality of both interaction and group goal, the more likely he is to subvert consensus.

Consensus and Individual Perception

One of the major difficulties in getting a group of people to achieve consensus lies in the realm of perception. Each person enters interpersonal interaction with a unique set of perceptions. The concept "phenomenal world" helps explain this. "Phenomenal world" represents the sum total of perceptions, experiences, and symbols that is possessed by a single human being. No matter how similar a set of life experiences may be between two persons, each phenomenal world is presumed to be essentially different. The slightest difference in physiology will affect differences in perception. The most minute difference in perspective will also alter information received. Communication takes place, however, as similarities or points of contiguity are discovered in phenomenal worlds. Consensus may be regarded as a process of synthesizing relevant portions of the phenomenal worlds of the participants in a discussion.

The infant begins to construct his phenomenal world at the time of his first perceptions. The moment he becomes aware of specifics in the "buzzing, blooming confusion" of his life, he begins to prepare the phenomenal world that represents the world in which he will live and react. The act of communication can be considered as an attempt to push part of a phenomenal world into the phenomenal world of another person. In order to do this, the child must learn to symbolize, but, as he learns to symbolize, the symbols themselves begin to affect his perceptions and thus alter his phenomenal world. Words, particularly words that represent feelings, convey only limited similarity. What one person feels when he is "embarrassed" may not be the same as what another feels. The word is learned situationally in context. Thus, for one person it may have particularly strong meaning, and for another be almost irrelevant.

Developing a Style of Communication

The child begins to exert influence over his world, first by responding to it, and then by communicating with it. He gets an image of himself as a communicator depending on the success or failure he has. He discovers that some activities have little effect, while others seem to get him what he wants. Thus he develops a personal style of communication, which is modified when necessary depending on the way people respond to it. The transition, for example, from high school to college will demand some alteration in style, but this alteration may not be drastic—it will depend upon how closely the relevant audience in the college resembles the relevant audience in the high school. A shift from college to vocation may demand more change. A person who is in contact with reality and is capable of receiving cues and interpreting them correctly will adjust when and where necessary in order to cope most efficiently with the audience he has before him. But, as we have already noted, the problem of interpretation is most difficult. It is difficult to utilize the feedback information we get when we speak with others. Hence, the phenomenal world will tend to influence the way information is interpreted. If in his phenomenal world the individual is an "effective communicator," he will tend to interpret cues positively and reinforce his own behavior. If he regards himself as ineffective, only the most dramatic positive response will convince him that he has had any success at all.

Each evaluation he makes, however, results in a revision of his potential to act both in a given situation and in general. His potential to act is represented by the repertoire of types of acts he has at his disposal. It may also be represented by the number of roles he is prepared and equipped to play and the effectiveness with which he plays them. All of this taken together may be considered an operational personality. It is the part of him that others see and respond to. Ability to control anxiety and respond definitively may make a person appear effective to others. Their response to that perceived effectiveness may, in turn, make the individual more effective as a communicator. By the same token, however, indefinite and weak presentation may evoke negative response from others, regardless of how definite and convinced the person may be inside. This means that it is necessary to have both strength of image internally and the ability to express that effectiveness so that others will perceive it and evaluate it positively. Both mental set and skill are essentials to effective communication. Both are also functions of "personality."

The way the cards are stacked for disagreement, it is amazing that people can get anything at all done when they interact. It is clear that people who appear to have common goals can clash over the methods of achieving them, and that people can agree on a course of action despite the fact that they have drastically different goals. Part of the agreement that is reached comes because each party to the question has the privilege of interpreting what he hears in his own phenomenal world. Thus, since the future cannot be seen, each man has the opportunity to make the future look as he wants it to look and react accordingly. Part of the agreement also comes from the desire for immediate approval. When the trend in a group seems to be toward consensus, then resisting consensus usually evokes negative evaluations from the other participants. There may also be a small residue of agreement that comes because there is real harmony on both goals and methods. If this were the case very often, however, there would be considerably less surprise about the results when a program was initiated.

The design of the phenomenal world is such that it helps to overcome the physiological inferiority of men. The capacity to contend against hostile environments comes to man largely through linguistic means, and these, in turn, are products of the individual phenomenal worlds. There can be considerable synthesis on a course of action if the threat or problem is specifically perceived. Thus, in confronting a hostile army or a predatory beast, there needs to be little discussion about whether it would be desirable to defend against it. In cases such as these, the first person who suggests a methodology becomes the general and has the privilege of carrying it out. He may deploy the others as he sees fit. If, on the other hand, the threat is neither immediate nor clear, it is necessary to get a clear image in the various minds of just what it is that action is to be taken against. On this level, it is possible that each participant will perceive threat uniquely, that is, each discussant pictures in his own phenomenal world what it is that he is concerned about. Any proposed course of action must be relevant to this perceived threat if consensus is to be reached. It is often easier to find a solution that fits all the different threats than it is to say what it is that is bothering the various members.

Hostile behavior and clash can be easily evoked during the proposal stage of discussion. If a member does not perceive that a solution meets the need as he perceives it, he may feel personal threat. It is rarely clear to him that the person who made the proposal may be seeing the "world" differently. It often appears more obvious to conclude that he displays no concern about things that really matter, or even that there is a personal vendetta expressed or implied in the solution. The situation may be analogous to the feelings of the head of a mail room whose fellow committee members decide to purchase mailing machines, which will phase him out of existence. He may take the decision as a personal threat and be unable to fight back, for he may perceive himself as playing some other role in the company and hence not wish to jeopardize his status or his role. He has, in effect, elected the role of "expansive man of goodwill," or "good loser." Appropriate representation of this role may communicate a "bigness of spirit" not really there, and if a sufficient number of discussants may be made to feel some guilt about phasing a colleague out of a job, they may, in turn, elevate him to a still higher position.

Strategically, whether he is conscious of it or not, each group participant is playing for optimum position. He seeks a role that will maximize the positive cues he receives from the group, and he seeks an outcome that will give him the greatest "payoff" on his stake. The extent to which he succeeds or fails in achieving these goals determines, in part, his subsequent behavior. In short, each interaction he undergoes will make some change in his operating personality. Each experience he has contributes to his repertoire of possible behaviors.

Furthermore, unless our participant is entirely schizophrenic, he will depend upon others to confer his identity upon him. In other words, he will seek an image of self through observation of the responses he receives from others. He may find it necessary to defend against negative cues, or he may be able to expand through ingestion of positive cues, but who he is depends upon receipt of outside data. The interpretation of the data depends upon what he possesses in his phenomenal world, but each input and interpretation of input will alter his phenomenal world. The development of personality is really the response of interaction.

The homeostatic drive operates strongly in the individual as he operates in a group framework. He will tend to seek groups that best accommodate to his personality, and he will remain active and productive in groups that reward him for his behav-

iors. Once he begins to feel comfortable with a specific group
of people, each new person entering the group represents a
threat to him. That newcomer must adjust himself to the group
"mind" in order to feel comfortable, but to a small extent, at
best, the group must accommodate by seeking a role for the
newcomer. Since each newcomer has the potential to seek any
of the available roles, each member finds his homeostasis within
the group threatened by the new entry.

This tendency toward suspicion and rejection of newcomers
has serious ramifications, particularly in groups operating in
establishments that depend on group decision for their output.
Many companies have discovered that efficiency and productivity can be seriously disrupted when new employees come on the
scene. While it may be entirely unconscious, there appears to
be a tendency for the newcomer to protect his individual role
before showing concern for the group or organizational goal.
For this reason, a number of business establishments have tried
to find methods by which employees who have to work together
can get insights into their own personalities and behavior and
the impact they have on others. While many of the methods
employed have not been particularly successful, the concept is,
of course, a worthy one.

The concept of phenomenal world, then, enables us to see
how the individual must synthesize his personal goals with the
ostensible goals of the group as he understands them in order to
work toward effectiveness. It must be understood that no
matter how objective one might try to be in analyzing behavior
and activity, in the final analysis response will be to subjective
perceptions, which help explain some of the unpredictable oc-
currences that characterize small group interaction.

The Quest for Role

The communicating personality develops as a result of responses to it. Seldom can these responses be to the individual
qua individual; most often they will be to the role the person is
playing. Each observer of human behavior must fit what he
sees into categories useful to him in interpretation. Initial
contacts do not convey much information about individuals as

persons, but information of a sort can be gleaned if the behaving person can be understood in the role he is apparently playing. Once the role has been observed and interpreted, it is possible to make exceptions to the evaluation by direct observation of the person.

As a group forms for the first time, each member is seeking some kind of pattern of behavior, consistent with his previous behavior, that will evoke approval from the other members of the group but also consistent with the standard of behavior within the group. The initial stages of group activity are characterized by much "fooling around." Attempts to "get to the point" are customarily thwarted, because it is not yet clear to the members what the "point" is. At the end of the interaction members may discover that they have adopted ideas that were presented during the first fifteen minutes and wonder why they just didn't accept them and have done with it. But the degree and quality of acceptance differs at the various stages of group activity. At the beginning, real agreement is impossible because the various participants have not made their commitment and developed their stake.

Leadership is a good case in point. Even if a leader has been appointed by some external authority, there will be a testing period in which various members attempt to set themselves in various leadership roles. Someone will assume direction of the task, someone else the maintenance of solidarity. The appointed leader may be partly able to assume these roles, but until he is "ratified" in his position, his leadership will only be minimal. (Unless, of course, he has the power to reward and punish, in which case his leadership will be characterized by his becoming the focal point for the individual rhetorics of the members.)

To ascertain the most appropriate role, members will run through a series of stylized activities, often as they have done them in the past. They will act as they have acted. They will need time to do this, and to interpret the responses to their actions, so that they can make slight modifications in their activity. In the first stages of group development activity is usually polite and reserved. A feeling of frustration and boredom may come from sparring verbally without accomplishing anything. The members will intensify their behaviors, seeking response, for failure to receive response is frustrating. As they intensify their own actions the feedback they receive is also intensified. The signals they receive permit a more explicit formation of further actions. Gradually, they will emerge playing definitive roles.

What goes on in the role-seeking in small group interaction is similar to what the child does as he develops in the family unit. Within the family, the child will test various role commitments against the parents and siblings. Sometimes the parent will withhold judgment while siblings respond with vigor; sometimes the pattern will be reversed. The child will have defined in his own mind just what he can gain from each, and his repertoire of behavior will mature into behaviors calculated to win responses from mother and father, and activities to carry on when the whole family is together.

In the initial testing period with peers, the child will attempt those devices that have proved successful for him, but in order to sustain his position with peers, it may be necessary for him to develop a personality which differs drastically from what has been effective in the home. For the mother and father he may have adopted a good student–good boy role, but with peers he may have to accept the role of a court jester, for the intellectual role may be accorded no value by the children on the streets. If he has succeeded in learning how to dominate parents, he will initially strive for dominance with peers.

In the group, those people who have won success and are known as leaders elsewhere will usually vie for leadership—for control over others—in the present group. Some will be quite blatant in asserting their ascendancy, while others will play more subtly. When any group, especially a "blue ribbon" group, is brought together, the first group task is to arrive at consensus about the hierarchy or ranking of roles and statuses. This is not an easy thing to do, for if the various members have won reputations as leaders, they will attempt to sustain this image of self by assuming some leadership role in the present group. Particularly when the groups are drawn from diverse segments of society with little previous contact, there will be no objective criteria on which to base decisions about the hierarchy. Many sociologists and social psychologists hold that values are what people hold as desirable or "good." These desirable things may be unspoken and unconscious assumptions made by the individual. They are part of the "cultural history" that the individual brings to the interaction situation. The more firmly the person holds these values and the more different they are from those of others in the group, the more carefully must the testing period be approached. And yet, it may be possible in such groups to divide the leadership tasks in such a way that everyone can have "a piece of the action," a role.

Because every activity carried on in the small group is perceived and evaluated by others, and because the evaluation is transmitted back to the performer as a response, each individual must carry on some "reality testing" before he can feel secure in a role. In a sense, he is trying to master a "script," a set of verbalizations that will confer upon himself some identity which is acceptable both to the others and to him. Each person tries to master some lines that serve to enhance his self-esteem because of the response they evoke in others. The first resort is to cliché, and consequently much of the initial talk in group interaction may be considered "phatic communion" as the various members try to sniff out the positions and commitments of the others in the group. Gradually, however, each person seeks to become adept in some role. Presumably it will be a role that serves the group ends as well as personal ones, but it appears that personal commitments transcend those of the group, and it is possible for a member to adopt a role that subverts the group purpose, to become an "opposer," or "severe critic" if it serves to swell his estimate of himself.

Part of developing this script is to determine limits of behavior. The individual must not only hit upon a role of appropriate quality but he must determine how hard and how long he is to play it. Quality, in the first instance, is determined by relevance. If a member seeks to play a role that the group does not value, he will achieve no status, regardless of how well he plays his role. If his customary method of winning approval is to provide information and the group does not want the information, he finds his patience wearing thin, and distressing activities beginning to materialize. This is a position in which college professors often find themselves when they try to participate in community activities. The professor has been rewarded, both with pay and honors, for the information that he dispenses in his classroom and in his scholarly articles. When he encounters a group that has all the information they care for, he may have to adopt the role of rebel in order to find some position that is tolerable in the community group. Thus, many professors are attracted to extremist causes just to attract the attention of the community by doing something that they regard as relevant.

The problem of mobility is also intrinsically bound up with role. To change groups will necessarily mean modification of role. True modification of role demands attendant personality change, and so the initial attempts to play the role demanded by a new group will be awkward. Once again, responses to the new role are necessary, and adjustment must be made to the responses. Sometimes, in seeking membership in a new group, a person may overplay, and be penalized accordingly because of his excesses.

Thus, each person, in all of his transactions, is in search of propriety, the proper role, the proper method of playing it, at the proper time and with the proper audience. Failure to receive expected rewards means loss of face, and reduction in self-esteem. Reduction in self-esteem means limitations on the repertoire of effective behavior, which in turn modifies the operating personality so that it is less effective. Saving face represents a minimal goal in transaction. Each of us seems to develop methods by which we can indicate to others that our self-esteem has not been damaged. Even when the attack has been direct and vital, there are few who will admit that they "goofed" in playing out their role. (Interestingly enough, most people will declare that they do not play roles and that they are entirely consistent in their behavior regardless of who is participating around them.) One of the most difficult things to do is to criticize our own behavior. Usually, when we indulge in this activity, we come up with an evaluation highly favorable to the self. Much of our analysis and introspection time is spent in such self-justification.

Too many frontal attacks, and too much overt hostility, cannot be handled effectively and so, in addition to methodolo-

gies of indicating that our own self-esteem has not been damaged, we usually equip ourselves with ways of demonstrating to
others that we present no threat to their self-esteem.   Concern
for the role of the other is an important rhetorical device in
small group interaction.   As long as it is clear that the other
person offers no direct threat to our own role, it is easy for us to
support him in the playing of his role.   The adept player will
have a series of verbal formulae that he may use to enhance the
self-esteem of others.   A person may, for example, not agree on
the ideas of others, but temper the attack by showing that he
understands the reason for the ideas and respects it.   He may
even go so far as to label his own attack as personal and selfish,
and most of all he will seek to level his arguments against the
ideas rather than the individual who presents them.   When this
line is crossed, however, the interaction is fraught with peril, for
it is possible to withstand an attack on ideas, but very difficult
to avoid fighting back when one's self-worth is attacked.
Furthermore, most of us are so caught up in our own ideas that
we cannot get clear whether someone is attacking our words or
our personality.

The simple learning of techniques of conciliation is not sufficient to sustain satisfactory role projection in an interaction.
There are commercial "systems" of personality development
that seek to substitute verbal ploys for internal commitment.
The learning of the words, however, is irrelevant, for a role too
heavily stylized will appear to be a sham and will evoke the
same hostility as a more direct roleplay.   What each person
really seeks is a kind of behavior that can honestly present the
self in relation to others in such a way that even disagreement
must be carried on with respect.   Control over language is
critical in developing that kind of role.

Verbal Manipulation

According to Becker, the proper phrase properly delivered is
the highest attainment of human interpersonal power.   It is a
form of control over others that very few men have been able to
achieve.   The ability to handle verbal manipulation in many
contexts affords the maximum opportunity for control.   This in

turn confers the greatest capability to protect and expand self-esteem. (Remember there are some forms of power that are nearly absolute but that are not the "highest attainment of human interpersonal power." Use of a gun to obtain submissiveness is one of these.) While it appears to be impossible to be able to exert this kind of control in all contexts, there are some humans who achieve such skill in verbal manipulation that even in situations which threaten them they are able to protect their self-esteem sufficiently to appear capable.

The small group confronts the individual with a constantly changing series of contexts. Within a group context it is possible to experience virtually every kind of social interaction, ranging from the deep intimacy of friendship to the mortal verbal conflict of the debate arena. There are few able to maintain their control throughout this constantly changing panorama of events. In order to gain the maximum contribution from the individual, the group context should afford each person the greatest possible opportunity to fulfill himself, protect his self-esteem and win his goals. The paradox is that the interactive process will not allow all persons to assume the kind of leadership role that might best assure him the accomplishment of these goals. To the outsider, the leader appears to have the control. To the insider, however, the leader can appear to be under constant threat. There is some reason to believe that the leader has even less opportunity than the ordinary member to attain his goals. If the interaction is successful, the group is often given the credit, but failure is generally attributed to defective leadership.

It is hard to determine what the word "proper" means in Becker's context. It may refer to what is legitimate within the operation of that entity known as group, or it may refer to what is compatible with the goals and values of the individuals, or it may mean something between those extremes. Proper could refer to "social usage" exclusively, but it appears that proper means accomplishing personal goals, including enhancement of self-image, without jeopardizing the quest for self-esteem by others.

One way to determine what the elements of "proper" might be would be to observe how people interact, classify their behavior as successful or unsuccessful, and then examine the elements of the personality of the successful behavers. Attempts at this sort of analysis have resulted in long lists of qualities—"goodwill," "enthusiasm," "optimism," "critical judgment," "sense of humor," "courage"—which read actually like some sort of membership oath and bring us no closer to an understanding of how a "successful" interactor should interact.

We might say that what we are after is a situation where the words of each individual evoke the maximum positive response, while minimizing threat to the ideas and values of others (listeners). Here we would be talking about optimum use of rhetoric in the group transaction. Following this path to the logical conclusion would lead us to believe that personality as reflected in group interaction can be analyzed in terms of rhetorical success or failure. But the question then arises, "Who is the audience for the rhetoric?" The context affords the answer— the rhetoric is directed both internally and externally. The participant in social transaction must persuade others that he is a person of worth, and he must use the information others transmit back to him to convince himself of the same thing.

Most communication proceeds through the interchange of words. Words, we have already noted, carry both denotative and connotative value. They may be reinforced by nonverbal cues, but we have already demonstrated how tenuous the interpretation of these phenomena are. The saying of words permits either a complementary or contradictory action by listeners. If the tone of a statement is appropriate, that is, if it satisfies both the personal and social criteria of the listener, it will evoke a complementary response or supporting action. If it threatens the self-esteem of the listener, or if it seems to the listener to threaten the stake he has in the group process, the response will be contradictory or conflicting. It is not entirely clear, however, that complementary and supportive responses are always desirable. In seeking a group solution, excessive harmony may encourage the internal feelings of the participants, but to the extent they are committed to a group goal they must consider themselves to be failures. There must be sufficient contradiction to permit examination of the various issues and proposals that are presented to the group, but support for the personal worth of the individual member must be sustained.   Part of the social bargain consists of developing contradictions around carefully controlled patterns.   Thus, the social group will map out limits of contradiction, and it may even prescribe a pattern that contradiction must follow.   The process of majority versus minority, with the issue to be resolved by vote, characteristic of the democratic process, represents one such solution.

Attack and Defense

Sensitivity in social interaction is not easy to come by.   The young child makes many faux pas and gaffes.   When mother tells him "not to stare at Aunt Sadie's scar," his eyes are drawn to it like a magnet.   The repercussions may help convince him that the physical infirmities of others are not proper objects of attention.   He learns eventually to ignore obvious weaknesses, despite the fact that these weaknesses could be exploited to reduce the effectiveness of those that have them.   But the normal standards of proper behavior prescribe that the person who attacks another because of physical infirmity draws the antagonism of his colleagues and thus reduces his effectiveness.

Attacks   on   personality   are   supposed   to   be   subtle. Presumably, people are supposed to be humble and self-effacing in their interactions.   Supposedly, if each person played this game, "truth" would win out.   But there is very little chance of suppression in the urge to employ rhetoric, and personal weaknesses are the easiest of all to exploit.   The school teacher, for example, capitalizes on the weaknesses of her students.   The capability given to her by the system to criticize the child helps her maintain her power.   In a small group with peers, however, the norm is to concede qualities in the other person.   In some cases, criticism can be administered merely by failing to point out a personality quality as a virtue.   "Smith is kind and moderate, Jones is kind," implies Jones is immoderate, and he, Jones, knows it.

One of the main problems affecting institutional progress is that it is hard to get a satisfactory critique of the vocational behavior of an employee.   Such criticism, it is presumed, makes the person who gives it vulnerable to attack.   In most groups the rules of interaction demand that hostile comments be restrained unless they are absolutely necessary, and even then they must be tempered.   Blame must be placed on systems and inanimate objects, not on people.

There is a basic therapeutic reason for attempting to ban negative comments.   The essence of therapeutic communication is that a direction for change should not be pointed out unless a method for change and assistance is also available.   People cannot and will not modify behavior at the direction of another, unless the other is very important to them, and unless the change can be effected without jeopardizing fragile self-esteem. The kinds of criticism offered by writing and public speaking teachers, for example, often fall on deaf ears, because if the student were to accept the suggestion he would have to concede his own lack of worth.   Those who are committed to change in advance for reasons of their own are able to understand criticism and interpret it as part of self-improvement.

Bombardment of a person with hostile stimuli may, however, convince him of his lack of worth.   There are a great many people in our society who are apparently capable and yet who do little, because they are convinced of a lack of worth. Parents, peers, and pedagogues have combined efforts to defeat the personality.   It is clear, for example, that excessive attention to manner of speech may cause stuttering.   It is equally clear that overstressing any personality trait may give rise to hypertonic concern about it.   Studies of communication reticence indicate that it is easier to withdraw from interaction or to behave sociopathically than it is to ignore or adjust to negative input.

Most of us have negative qualities and know it, and we are able to fend off attacks by raising certain warnings in the conversation.   The obese man may make it clear that he finds talk of diets unpleasant.   The black man may interrupt the telling of racial jokes that denigrate him.   The woman with a faulty complexion will change the subject when the beauty parlor appears on the agenda.   The nonathlete will not participate in discussions of golf and will expect to be given an opportunity to change the subject.   The present supervisor will warn off the employee who talks too much about the virtues of the past supervisor. By the time we reach adulthood, most of us are mature enough to catch these warnings and avoid subjects that may threaten the self-esteem and personality of the other people around us. Some, seeking power at any cost, may exploit these weaknesses and use them to destroy.

But the control of tension-producing situations—"you stay away from my taboo subject and I'll stay away from yours"—gives a degree of stability to interaction. There will be, in most groups, a tacit acceptance of certain taboos, and the person who raises such a topic does so at his own risk for he is likely to incur sharp sanctions from the rest of the group. Sometimes this is unfortunate, for the topic made taboo may be crucial to the solution of the problem. Thus, a group of professors may make certain assumptions about their qualities and avoid discussion of the "publish or perish" system, when it is precisely that system which contributes most heavily to the "problems of teaching at our school."

The effective communicator will show three basic traits in response to the standards opposed by the group: (1) he will be able to sense and avoid forbidden topics; (2) if he happens to hit on one accidentally, he will be able to change course and "get off the hook," and (3) he will be able to cope with others who tread on his forbidden ground. The sensing process seems to develop as a part of social conditioning. David Riesman refers to it as "radar" that indicates the acceptable and unacceptable in a social grouping. But our internal radar is not infallible. Conditions change; academic tenure may be perfectly acceptable as a topic in a group of professors—until it is denied to one member. To dwell on it after that could be highly destructive, and particularly if a member were to comment on how easy it is to get tenure, and how tenure protects the system from incompetency. The person denied could feel a deep sense of threat, and will give some cues to the group. If he is unable to cope with the verbal threat, he may elect to leave the group. In any case, his self-esteem will have been seriously injured.

Consideration of verbal interaction as an investment procedure offers some insight into the development of these social rules. Each comment made to another is an investment of self and seeks some kind of gain in self-esteem. The gain is derived through interpretation of the response of the other. A comment that appears to be approved by the group is more valuable than a comment that is ignored or attacked. The comment-investment we make is calculated by examining personal and group goals. If status with the group outweighs commitment to the issue under discussion, our comments will be directed toward winning social approval. If victory on the issues is the goal, we will employ various rhetorical strategies in order to gain acceptance of our ideas. Solicitation of goodwill is the imperative, for we tend to participate to maximize our *ethos,* to raise the possibility that we will appear to be credible sources to those who hear us.

We have already noted that the process of response to the remarks of others is inferential and affected to a large extent by the condition of the phenomenal world of the viewer. Thus, if John Smith (a "D" student) turns in a good paper, we can assume it is plagiarized, while if Bill Jones (an "A" student) turns in a bad paper, we can attribute it to an "off day." Our response is to the image we are led to by the inference, not to the life-fact, which we really cannot get at.

This process of inferring can be divided into three elements. It appears that when we examine the remarks of another person:

1. *We look at intent.* Is the speaker trying to enhance himself? Is he seeking to further the group goal? Is he seeking to do something from which we will benefit or from which we will suffer?
2. *We look at attitude toward self.* How valuable does the person think he is? Does he demonstrate a sense of worth? Is he so deferential that doubt is cast on the merit of his remarks? Is he of sufficient worth to warrant including in the rules of the interaction game?
3. *We attempt to discover his attitudes toward ourselves.* What does he think of me? Is there any reason to believe he is an ally? An enemy? Has he conceded my worth in some previous transaction? Do I have reason to feel guilty about my reaction to him?

In general, we will support the individual who seems to be supporting something from which we will profit. We will tend to support the person who appears worthy, convinced, and strong or who seems to express a set of values we hold to be important, and we will tend to support the person who seems to be willing to support us when we need it. Furthermore, we will tend to seek close association with people who seem to satisfy these three criteria in our own minds, and we will tend to avoid and ignore those who do not. The subgroupings that develop in the interaction process are usually organized around these lines. We can assume that much of the hostility and wrangling that breaks out in a small group will center around these personal questions. We can often observe a group which appears to be in total agreement about an issue engaging in an argument about what appears to the outside observer to be trivial. The answer, of course, lies in the attitudes the members have toward one another, in the unspoken dictum, "I hate you so much that if I find you on my side I must reexamine my premise to determine whether I am on the right side."

Inability to find supportive answers to the questions we ask about others may lead to the adoption of a "suspicion" role. Failure to convey to others information that would lead them to find supportive answers about you may lead to them relegating you to an "ineffectual" or "incompetent" role. Consistent assignment to these kinds of roles can have a disastrous effect on personality. Many people now classified as mentally ill became that way because the information they received about themselves from others pushed them inexorably into that role. More general, however, is the phenomenon of people avoiding interaction because they recognize it as a situation in which they cannot win. They develop a conviction about their own behavior and use this conviction to justify avoidance of others. While it is no great problem if you are unable to participate well in some kinds of interactions, it is disastrous if you can participate well in none. The real problem, of course, is that our judgments of people are based on inferences derived from grossly categorized experiences, and consequently it is most likely that the person who functions differently in any way from the accustomed norms will be ignored or treated with hostility. This is most frequently noted among people from other cultures who try to interact and do not know the prevailing style. The typical pattern is to reduce them to marginality, unless, of course, they have some peculiar charm or high reputation, which would make the group elevate their deviation to high status. We will accept from the "mad, Hungarian professor" what is entirely unacceptable from the Hungarian janitor, even though it is essentially the same behavior and something characteristic of the Hungarian culture.

When we observe and evaluate the behavior of others, it is virtually impossible to check our conclusions against "life-facts." To do so would mean to find some way of penetrating the mind of the other person, and this is clearly impossible. Basically, there are certain assumptions we make and act on that prevail (according to our fiction) in all human confrontations. For example, we think we can tell how another person "feels" by observing his behavior in interaction. When a person says he is for something we assume that he will vote that way when the time comes. When he says he likes golf, then we ought to be able to find him playing it. When he says "I like you," we expect this to be translated into positive, supportive actions. Sometimes, it is possible to get beyond the words and observe cues that tend to negate the words, but this is only possible when we are quite familiar with the behavior style of the person with whom we are interacting. Once we do know the nonverbal style, however, the contrast between verbalization and nonverbal performance may be a source of humor, and can be used by the skilled performer to enhance his prestige and influence. Unfortunately, the person who does not know the style may not be able to recognize irony and humor and may find himself trapped when he takes the words literally. We are willing to concede the capacity for sarcasm to people we know well, but we cannot make this concession to people with whom we are unfamiliar, or who outrank us in a status hierarchy. For them, sarcasm, humor, or irony are unacceptable until we have learned the extent to which we can trust their words to coordinate with their behavior.

We can see only the outward signs of behavior. We are not, normally, willing to accept testimony about something if it does not seem to square with what we have seen.   Many skilled platform speakers are quite nervous as they approach their audience but their skilled performance does not convey nervousness to the listeners.   Listeners will not believe it when the performer tells them that he was uneasy during the speech. They are more likely to rely on their interpretation of what they have seen, which may have been evaluated as "confidence" and "smoothness."   If the speaker convinces them that he was nervous, we feel that he should have acted nervous, and if he did not act nervous, he should not tell us he was nervous.

We tend to believe that performances should be effortless.   A person who is uncomfortable when he talks and shows it tends to make his listeners uncomfortable.   A speaker who has to make some effort to deliver his lines and cannot conceal the effort evokes a hostile response, despite the honesty and sincerity of his statements.   We are unable, of course, to introspect about our own uneasiness when we speak and tend to want those who speak to us to conform to ideals.   Thus, very often, groups will tend to undervalue ideas that are not spoken with conviction and fluency, and to adopt ideas that are expressed with facility and vigor, regardless of their quality.

After close association, it may be possible to get beyond the style and discover the person, but unfortunately, most of our contacts are too fleeting, and so we tend to seek the kind of polish that most people, including ourselves, cannot deliver.   It is for this reason that strong self-esteem is essential to the person who wants to succeed at communicating with others. The likelihood is very great that the bulk of the listeners to anyone will not be terribly attentive and responsive.   There must be enough strength to carry on from the beginning to the end of the remarks and to find those positive cues that exist, otherwise there will be personal pressure exerted to evade interaction at the next opportunity.   Discomfort is contagious. Listeners can convey it to speakers and the reverse, and listeners can pass it on to other listeners.

The position of the uncomfortable person in the group is most unfortunate.   He knows that he cannot perform with the kind of facility that is expected of him, and yet he knows that he may have to perform.   Some who feel chronically uncomfortable may seek panaceas in the form of short courses, interaction skills courses, and the like, but all they really acquire is a facade, easily penetrable the first time an unexpected situation arises. Skill can be best imparted through encouragement, and here a group that really seeks optimum performance from all can generate activities designed to encourage those who have qualms about their participation. Attempting to live up to the goals stipulated in the textbooks on discussion is even more frustrating, for a person who had all those attributes would be the universal leader. Warmth and acceptance can do a great deal to expand personality and encourage participation, and this is particularly important for the person who has not been habitually encouraged. Our schools can do little to support the growth of interpersonal skill, and teachers themselves, with their tendency to concentrate their criticism on performance criteria, tend to make most of us apprehensive about interaction of any kind. Stage fright is not confined to the public platform. There are many who feel it any time they enter a transaction at which something is at stake. Some insight and empathy, however, can be derived by looking at our culture and what it does to the production of interpersonal communicators.

Influence of Culture on Communicative Personality

The broad study of a culture tends to blur the individual transactions of the people who make up the culture. The concepts of "culture" and "society" are aggregate terms made up of the norms of the multitude of interpersonal relationships. One of the criteria of a culture is that its members understand the meanings of signs shared in interpersonal situations. One way to discover the dominant patterns of a culture is to seek out the modalities in communication between the people who live in a geographic area or who share a way of life. A culture then would be represented by an aggregate of people who have a communication style in common. The broader the culture, the less commonality would exist between the people in it. Each culture, furthermore, is made up of subcultures, the populations of which are more and more alike. Within a main culture, individuals can seek out the subculture in which they feel comfortable. The individual may seek the culture that represents his personality style, or he may adjust his personality style to fit the culture he wishes to belong to.

Another way of looking at a culture is through common symbology. Those who belong to the same culture have a symbol system in common, or know a set of verbal games that they play with each other consistently. The word "game" used here does not refer to a sport or recreation, but to regularized transactions, played as a sort of routine, almost to display commonality within a culture. Those who share a culture defined this way share connotations. In the United States, for example, the difference between middle-class and poverty-class cultures might be demarked by the connotations of words like "school" and "police." For the middle-class child "school" may mean excitement or boredom, but it is also a safe place, approved by his whole society. For the poverty child school may refer to a prison-like condition. Similarly, "police" may be immensely threatening to the poverty child, while the word represents a "community helper" to the small middle-class child. Unfortunately, it appears that as the middle-class child grows up, he adopts the poverty definition of police.

Because of variations in meaning and because of the use of words in one tier of society that are not used on other levels, we can define poverty and middle-class as different cultures. Their language reflects their behavior, and in turn it acts upon their behavior, so that common action and common talk become more and more difficult. It is even more painful in our society today, for in the relations between black and white we apparently use the same vocabulary, but the meanings we give to the words appear almost to lead to inevitable clash between the races.

Regularities in verbal transactions define the social units that make up a culture. There are transactions indigenous to family, school, peers, social groups, and economic units. Each person will belong to a number of groups within the culture, and the commonalities will be greater within groups than between them. That is, homes will operate in similar fashion, but they will differ from the operation of work units. Once a communication style has been mastered, for example, family communication, it is relatively easy to employ it when in contact with other families in the culture. By the same token, vocational patterns will be similar between places of employment. But it is necessary to learn several styles because of the differences between home, social, and economic units. Slop-over of one style into another context may seriously impair skill in transacting. In short, the lion in the office can be the lamb at home, and he must learn to play both roles with skill.

The individual will undergo considerable dissonance and ambiguity as he attempts to learn ways to alter his style so that he can appear adept in the various subcultures in which he finds himself. Inability to make appropriate transitions, or perseverating the behaviors expected in one social unit in another, represents an aberration that may be classified by others as "mental illness." There is a basic psychiatric aspect to interaction with others in groups. Many authorities now regard mental illness as an evaluative classification rather than a disease. We may define behaviors that are potentially dangerous to the self and others as "mental illness," but we also tend to define behaviors which run clearly counter to expected behaviors as mental illness as well. The evaluation is conferred from the outside in, but each evaluation tends to reinforce and support the aberrant behavior. Thus, interaction within a group can induce mental illness. In addition, the group holds sufficient power to reinforce and support so that it can offer the cure to the disease it causes.

To ascribe to some person or to some position authority over an act or action is common in all human societies. In Western (particularly American) society this is commonly done through the constitution and bylaws of the numerous organizations. Authority is the *right* conferred by the members on a person (or social position) to act in given circumstances. Thus the president has the right to open a meeting. The treasurer has the right—possibly with some limitations—to write the checks. Any group can confer on others or on positions the right to do certain things. A father has the right to discipline the child. It is not written in a family constitution but it is real and unmistakable nonetheless.

In other cultures the positions that are ascribed authority are much more numerous and the authority ascribed is much more explicit and pervasive than in ours.   In South Asia the eldest family member often still has the right to pass on the actions and activities of all family members.   He approves marriages, jobs that family members take, decisions over acquisition and disposal of land, educational choices of sons and grandsons, and so on.   Penalties for deviation are clear and explicit.   Probably the cruelest penalty is to be excommunicated from the family circle.   One's choice is clear—conformity means survival; deviation means destruction.

The behaviors permissible or not permissible in the current social structure of the United States are not so clearly laid out. It is often unclear what a reward or penalty is.   The boss may invite the employee to his home because he sincerely feels he wants to get to know the employee better and because he likes him.   From this standpoint, the invitation is a reward.   The employee, on the other hand, may be apprehensive about his skill at interacting with a power figure and may regard the invitation as another means by which the boss can "fatten his batting average."   From this standpoint, the invitation might be a punishment.

We learn both our language style and our scale of rewards and punishments from the cultures in which we are raised, and we expand our knowledge within the cultures in which we participate.   Movement from group to group calls for adjustment of personality and behavior and this in turn calls for adjustment in a phenomenal world.   In some cases only minuscule adjustments are necessary; in other cases, major personality changes are required for survival in transition.   The capacity for change in phenomenal world and personality is controlled by the degree of openness that remains in the phenomenal world. The man who is constantly receiving stimuli and is relatively nonrigid in his interpretation of them stands a better chance of being able to change rapidly enough to survive in a number of social groups.

One very important aspect of learning diverse interpersonal behaviors is the type and strength of the cultural affiliations that a person brings with him into each of his many groups.   The individual usually cannot find it possible to extend his behavior beyond the limits transmitted to him by his cultures. Self-imposed moral restrictions are very influential in learning diverse behavior. To the extent that various moralities are firmly rooted, deviation from morality cannot be tolerated. Hence, the individual would be disqualified from participation in those groups that tended to violate moral codes held very strongly. This holds true, even if the behavior is inapposite and nonrewarding. For example, the peer culture holds that it is not moral to "rat" on a friend. Parents, however, expect to hear of deviant behavior on the part of one child from the siblings. The child who refuses to tell the parent "who did it," or who does tell the teacher which of his friends did it, may suffer sanctions. Even so, he may not feel the penalty, for his moral code may be so strong that it can sustain him through the negative responses he evokes. For most of us, however, excessive violation of the norms of one group means expulsion from the group, and attendant damage to self-esteem. Even when the moral code is firmly rooted, it is hard to escape the feeling of inadequacy and despair that comes with rejection by a group. The morality may sustain, but apprehension levels in subsequent interactions with similar groups will be materially increased. The man who cannot understand why he is being rejected, however, is likely to suffer most from the rejection, and the damage to his self-esteem is almost unrepairable. He is the obvious candidate for the mental hospital.

Our personal values—the assumptions, implicit or explicit, we make about what is good or bad—are made from contacts we have had with persons around us. These values represent our primary loyalties. But there are many primary loyalties that we may have and the one which is called to the fore today and used as a justification for a particular action today may be different from the one used as a justification for the same action tomorrow. They do, however, sustain us through many intolerable interaction situations.

The ethnic immigrants who came to the United States around the turn of the century were accorded no great status by the society. They were stigmatized and rejected by those who had arrived here before them. The force of the social and cultural group, however, was strong enough to permit these people to make significant economic and social progress, which resulted in their admission to the dominant society. The man who held a high office in his ethnic lodge could more easily take the rebuffs and insults sent his way by his more Americanized vocational associates than the man who had no such status in a meaningful group. To an extent, this is the problem that affects the Negro today. Transition is slow and painful, and it is made even more arduous because there are few strong forces which confer honor and dignity within the home community.

The person who cannot discover a group that will give him rewards suffers from the greatest destruction of self-esteem, and eventually may cease to function as a viable personality. There seems also to be a tacit respect given to nonconformity as long as the particular brand of nonconformity is accorded respect elsewhere. Thus, the citizen of a foreign country may deviate from some norms and be given honor for it, while the same man seeking citizenship in this country would be expected to conform to all norms. Within a task group, the person who seeks social goals may be a very popular figure even though he is not being paid for his socialization, because socialization is accorded reward elsewhere in society.

Interrelationships with others are essential to determination of personal effectiveness. We discover this very early in life. Becker, for example, points out that early peer contacts are crucial in learning to deal with others. We learn from our friends how to protect the individual self without damaging the self-esteem of the people with whom we interact. If we do not have this experience, our capacity to interact is severely impaired. Through our peer associations we learn to make reciprocal agreements—"if you don't give me a piece of your candy, you can't swing on my swing." A harmonious group concedes to each member a bit of potential for idiosyncrasy and receives in return individual conformity with the major norms of the group. The search is to preserve the self-esteem of all the members. Some, of course, need more preservation than others. Some will never learn to defend their self-esteem, perhaps because of unfortunate events at home or in school, perhaps because they have no real contribution to make.

The not-so-effective group devotes a great deal of its time to attack and defense. The members spend an inordinate amount of time injuring and then attempting to repair the self-esteem of others. In fact, a viable role within a group is the attacker–supporter, who first injures and then seeks to mend the injury, deriving expansion of his own self-esteem by his ability to be "big" in relation to those with whom he has fought.

Self-consciousness about group relations tends to indicate that they are not so healthy. Humans are not particularly aware of individual parts of their bodies until they begin to hurt. Once a toe has been stubbed, we become acutely aware of the existence of the toe. By analogy, excessive concern for improving interpersonal relations may indicate that they are not all that they should be. Concern about what others might think and about personal image in the group may indicate a threatening situation, in which attacks are made upon one another. Groups that are goal-directed and which have developed mutual devices for protecting each other in transaction are not particularly concerned with psychiatric introspection. It is still questionable whether there is any direct action that a group can take to improve relations among its members.

Mental Health and the Small Group

If the notions about mental health and illness offered by the new psychiatrists (Becker, Szasz, Merloo, Ruesch, and others) are correct, then the small group can be examined as both a "cause" and a "cure" of personality deviation. If we are to accept the diagnosis "mental illness" as a social evaluation, then we ought to assess the cultural context in which it exists, and the nature of the communication that leads to both deviation and the evaluation of it.

An individual personality will expand and become strong as its manifestations and activities are rewarded by the people around it. If we start with this premise, then we can infer that the person who "loses" consistently in interaction is going to find himself becoming less and less relevant, more and more marginal in his relations with others, until he finally finds it necessary to opt out of transaction entirely. He may elect to draw into a shell and refuse to participate in normal interactions (or he may restrict his interactions only to absolutely essential ones). He may also decide to "defeat" those that have been berating him and make a massive attempt at dominance of social transaction. In either case, the norms of society in general, and of most subgroups, accord no value to his behavior. We expect people to participate as the situation warrants, and we expect them to show some concern for permitting us to behave as well. Thus, both excess withdrawal and excess domination appear to be abnormal.

It is easy to ignore the person who withdraws and this is usually what happens. He admits few stimuli in, remarks are not made to him, his wishes are not taken into account. He may share the same space with the others, but he is not actually part of the group for he has signaled to the others that he is either not interested or not capable of contributing to the common goal. The lack of stimuli is his punishment. He begins to lose identity, both with himself and with others. But, basically, what he seeks is someone to reach out and pull him back into the group. The society, however, cannot seem to make the effort. The quiet child in school is ignored, regarded as not-so-bright, left alone, until finally he fades away. The quiet adult is looked at with curiosity because "still waters run deep," but if wisdom is not forthcoming on demand, he is written off with "stagnant ponds are full of scum." The efforts made by the quiet person to reenter the mainstream are often ineffective. His long withdrawal from interaction has atrophied his technique. He speaks with hesitation, conveys little credibility, is fair game for interruptions, and, in most cases, he is heard politely and the conversation then passes on, leaving him out, despite whatever wisdom he might have had in his words. He is easy to bully, easy to intimidate, and he knows it. His whole phenomenal world is full of images of failure that mobilize themselves to cause him to fail again and again. Eventually, he is moved outside the pale of society and is left to fend for himself, alone in his world.

The person who seeks dominance and control is punished by direct conflict, sometimes by expulsion. Sometimes attacks can be reinforcing: "I am important enough for them to mobilize all that hostility against me!" However, a person can tolerate only so much hostility without forcing either withdrawal or a state of sociopathology so strong as to represent a threat to any group that comes in contact with it. The demand for a role of leadership not fulfilled by the group can be fulfilled in the phenomenal world. It is possible to build an inner world where success is always certain, where truth and justice (represented by you) always win, and where no other person has any worth at all. Such people are often the organizers of extremist organizations. They surround themselves with followers, often the quiet, timid people, who are perfectly willing to submit to authoritarian leadership. From this base they can lash out at the system that expelled them and thus obtain their revenge. Or, in some cases, they can take refuge in another identity behind the walls of a mental hospital.

The foregoing should not be taken to mean that a group can bring about this kind of behavior in one or two interactions. All the typical group can do is take the person as he comes to it and react accordingly. The pressure of business, the need to get decisions made and programs operating, makes it virtually impossible to take time out to administer "therapy" to those who are not working to serve the group end or who do not conform to the group notion of acceptable behavior. Most of the so-called "inadequate" people got that way long before they began to participate in group activities. They are the product of home, school, and peer cultures, and vocational and interest groupings cannot be expected to nurse them back to health. By the same token, however, there is no need to make their condition worse. There may be a useful job with status that the man who seeks to dominate can do, and there may be an opportunity to solicit opinions from the quiet man. In short, there is a bit of therapy that can be administered by the small group that just may possibly begin to redirect the cues and interpretations of the "outcasts."

Experts in mental health have determined that the small group is a highly effective device for the administration of therapy. The group is employed to reverse the process that made the individual ill, to provide him with support, if that is needed, to give him status, or an opportunity to "sound off."

In general, when we deal with the question of mental health, we must also deal with the problem of "marginality," or just how "in" or "out" the individual is. Each small group that has been together for a while will develop a set of verbal ceremonials that differ from those of any other group. One group might indulge in sarcasm and personal cutting, which may seem very threatening to a stranger or newcomer. Another group may utilize ethnic humor, which might bewilder or antagonize someone unfamiliar with the pattern, particularly if his ethnic group seems to be under attack. If the stranger is to become a permanent part of the group he will have to learn to accept these norms, and also to participate in them. Sometimes, anxiety about belonging will force a newcomer to overdo the ceremonial. This will stamp him as unusual and will evoke penalizing behavior from the group. There is no particular guidance that can be given, either. The ceremonials are often so deeply rooted in the interactive behavior that they cannot be written down in a handbook of behavior for new members. Presumably, however, experience in interaction will enable the new person to pick up the cues and behaviors, and he will learn to do them through practice.

This kind of problem is also characteristic of the clash that comes when two main cultures are brought together. It is easy, for example, for blacks and whites to misunderstand one another. Their cultures are different, and the word "different" does not imply any sort of infuscation. It is hard for the middle-class white to determine if a black man is friendly or hostile. Behaviors that are normal for the black seem unusual in terms of white culture and are easily misinterpreted. By the same token, the black man may interpret white behavior as hatred or apathy. The connotations they place on words differ, and words that are quite acceptable in one group may be offensive when used in the presence of the other group. In general, we might assert that a set of norms which differs from our own is always threatening, at least for a time, for it is a living example that life can go on in a value framework different from our own. Part of our self-esteem is rooted in the values we attach to our group. To find that our group behavior is not representative of a broader norm tends to pick away at self-esteem. People who operate differently because of their different norms must be regarded, initially, as unimportant or odd, until some understanding of the reasons for their behavior is reached.

Cultural transition is thus made difficult, because it requires more than occupying a place or performing a skill. The Negro who moves into a white neighborhood finds himself immersed in a completely new set of norms. If he accepts them too readily then he must deny his antecedents, and if he refuses to accept them at all, he is not accepted in the neighborhood. The same is true of the white teacher confronting a black class.

Moving up in an occupational hierarchy also presents this problem of adjusting to norms. A man who participates in workers' activities and then is moved to a supervisory job encounters a number of difficulties as he tries to familiarize himself with his new culture. He may be more comfortable with his old style, but to remain rooted in it will deny his opportunity to assert supervisory control. Sooner or later this marginality must be dropped, and the man must settle on a role, for if he does not, his ambivalence will force him into actions disconcerting to both groups in which he seeks to maintain membership, and he will be penalized in two places rather than rewarded in one. There does indeed seem to be a correlation between marginality and mental illness.

The concepts of status and role are important in considering the psychiatric implications of small group activity. The ethological studies seem to indicate that human beings, like other animals, seek possession of a clearly demarked "territory" that they will defend against interlopers. For the human "territory" is represented by a position in the social system. Territory is developed in the symbolic terms, "status" and "role."

Status refers to a position in a ranking of members made by members. It indicates the preference of the others for advice, control, or leadership of an individual and it is dependent on others. Role may be elected, tried out, and tested by the individual, but the status received for that role is conferred by the other members of the group. Role represents choice; status represents evaluation. Role represents position; status represents the function of position. Status directly affects role in that high status may be interpreted as reward and low status as penalty. Thus, some sociologists refer to status–role as a singular concept. Once a high status has been achieved, the individual struggles to retain it. Holding on to a status position becomes a more important preoccupation than doing the group task or fulfilling obligations under the employment contract. Even when the individual is clearly unfit for the status conferred, he will struggle to hold it. Often men will compete to push themselves into positions knowing that they cannot possibly fulfill the obligations of that position. The trappings of the position, the uniform, the privilege, become such important considerations that movement downward in the hierarchy strikes a severe blow at self-esteem and tends to impede the operation of personality and the selection of new roles. Most high executives understand that when they have outlived their use in a particular position, they will be moved into one which carries with it the same status, even though the role is considerably less influential.

Roles refer to the way the individual plays out his status position. He may be a "good leader" or an "ineffectual leader," a "democratic leader" or an "authoritarian leader." Role can be described in terms of activities that can and cannot be carried on to remain consistent with the impressions others have received. As people begin to respond consistently to a role, the self-image becomes more clear and there is little ambiguity about behavior. The individual knows how to behave and how to act. When role becomes blurred and obscure it may mean that the individual is rising or falling in the hierarchy. Part of the determination of self-image and the attendant evaluation of self made by each of us comes from analysis of how well we are doing in our role, and answering the question of whether we have received sufficient status reward for our activities. In short, we want to know if our role is "paying off." If it is not, we must find reasons. Sometimes these can be found in the behavior of others; sometimes in discovery of personal inadequacies. But, in any case, if our role activity is not paying, self-esteem has been injured and adjustments must be made. If we can adjust to a role that provides more rewards there is no problem, but if our role shift results in a steady decline of status, there is the possibility of our withdrawal from interaction entirely.

The individual who interacts with others under any circumstances has his personality on the line. He can expand his self-esteem and his capability to cope, or he can, in the words of Eric Berne, have his "backbone shrivel." It is the most basic of all competitive transactions, and the entire symbolic life of man is spent learning to cope with the kind of rhetorical situations man finds himself in on a daily basis, even though he may be unaware that he is employing rhetorical strategies. From the standpoint of the observer, it is hard to determine just why people act as they do, for we cannot know what exists in their phenomenal world. Perhaps the dictum of Arthur Combs and Donald Snygg is the wisest to follow: "All behavior is rational to the behaver at the time of behavior." That is, a man acts as he does because it is the most appropriate response available within his phenomenal world as that world is at that moment. One instant later it may be perfectly clear that the action was not wise or prudent, that it evoked negative response, that it created more problems than it solved. That means that more data is put into the phenomenal world.

But whatever goes into the phenomenal world is refracted by the phenomenal world. Earlier we pointed out that the question of interpretation of feedback cues is resolved by self-image. Any response given to a speaker can either be in harmony with what he expects or not; or, he may interpret it as in harmony or not, depending on how strong his self-image is. Responses are consistently misinterpreted, as are projected messages. That is why it takes so long to develop an appropriate role and to achieve a position in the status hierarchy within a group. It is only after careful observation of an individual's behavior over a long period of time that it is possible to make some sensible interpretations of that behavior. When this familiarity comes about, however, group norms tighten, and it becomes more difficult for the group to accommodate new members or to alter its style of approaching problems. The group will seek to support the homeostatic drive of its members. Thus, the whole process of group interaction represents personality development, and the group has it in its power to contribute to the mental health and the mental illness of each of its members.

Humans are notoriously dependent on each other for survival. Nowhere is this more important than in the development of personality. When we communicate with others we communicate a whole self, and when we adjust our communications we must also adjust our self. So personal to us is communication that it represents the total self. It is the only way we "get to" other people in the world. One way to understand the vital nature of communication in interpersonal transaction is to examine it through the conceptual framework offered by Hans Vaihinger. His philosophic constructs are built around the proposition that man builds a world inside his own head made up entirely of fictions, for this is all that man can possess. However, he must act "as if" the fictions were true life-facts. To the extent that his behavior accords with what others perceive as facts, it may be deemed successful, and to the extent that behavior gets him into trouble, awkward situations, or results in failure, it may be classified as unsuccessful. In any event, man can do little else but act on what he perceives as successful. What is referred to as "empirical data" is little more than confirmation of fiction by others.

Classifying Impressions

The world inside the head is made up of impressions in memory of sensory perceptions together with words and evaluations. The words point to the sensory impressions and are the substance with which such impressions are communicated to others. The evaluation determines the way impressions are manipulated, resulting in the selection of courses of action. Presumably, the most effective personality is the one that can bring the impressions in the head into some measure of concordance with the world as others see it. Such a personality would also have the capacity to adjust his internal world as more data is put into memory and as more words are learned around which impressions can be reclassified.

The symbols possessed by any individual are limited in number, but sensory impressions are virtually unlimited, which means that in order to communicate, impressions must be sorted. Words are the keys to the sorting process. In doing the sorting, however, intrinsic and unique qualities of individual's sense perceptions must be left out, and much of the classification is done around prototypes. In our consideration of people, for example, it is impossible to keep in memory the peculiarities of behavior of all the people we have encountered. Those who are significant to us remain in memory in relatively full figure. Others are classified according to whatever seemed to be more relevant at the time; perhaps by occupation, religious commitment, race, physical appearance, and so on. Continued contact with individuals enables us to remove them from their categories, but this kind of contact is only possible with a limited number of people. Hence, in many of our interactions what we are really doing is projecting a stereotyped image of our self to a group of stereotyped people. For most purposes, this works well enough to enable us to function, to adjust to new situations, and to bring off a sufficient number of victories to warrant moving ahead. It breaks down when the categories to which we are responding are not viable or sensible, that is, they do not concur with categories developed by others. It also breaks down when we try to force those people with whom we have close contact into categories, or try to make others conform to categories built around those whom we know well. To make each employer into a father image or love object, for example, might be considered a sign of mental distress.

In a sense, our manipulation of internal image is a probabilistic activity in which we take the present situation, compare it to various situations in which we have found ourselves, assess the quality of our own behavior under those circumstances, and then select a behavior appropriate to this situation. Experience and input help expand the categories to which we can respond. Sound evaluation of effect helps us choose a precise course of action. In a way this description is quite similar to the description of the human problem-solving apparatus in operation offered in *How We Think*. There John Dewey pointed out that the typical person first feels a difficulty, then defines it, then examines various solutions to it, then selects one, and then puts it into operation. The third step, examination of solutions, is perhaps the most complex, for this involves us in "feeding forward," that is, developing goals and expectations that determine for us how successful our actions were.   Activity that does not satisfy expectations or which evokes responses that we do not expect disturbs our data-processing apparatus, tends to disturb our capacity to make choices in subsequent situations.   Thus, personality is constantly under modification during each and every interaction.

It is for this reason that we are concerned with the role of individual personality.   If we assume that personality is holistic, somewhat more and somewhat different from the summation of the elements in it, we are confronted with a dilemma as we approach the study of and participation in the small group.   As we observe and analyze the small group, it is imperative that we separate out elements of personality that are amenable to empirical measurement, so that we can develop generalizations about small group behavior.   When we participate, however, we are dealing with total humans and they cannot be expected to behave precisely according to those generalizations.   Each participant in small group activity develops a relationship with each other person.   The relationship is affected by the personality of the participant, the activities of the group, unanticipated events, pressures from others in the group, and so on.   Each man starts in the group as "his own man" imparting meaning to events and acting on the meanings.   The evaluations add up and interact, and as each participant develops a "history" of participation, the equipment he uses to make the evaluations changes, so his assessment process is now an interaction between previous knowledge and present circumstance.   To the outside observer, acts can be classified into categories and explained, but to the participant acts come naturally, rationally, and are based on the operation of the phenomenal world.

It should be clear that throughout this exposition we have been dealing in abstractions.   The substantive knowledge about human interactions is limited, and in no case can it ever be as firm as knowledge about nonlive entities such as electrons or durum wheat.   What we hope to do is discover some premises on which our "guesses" about human behavior can be based.   It is quite a bit easier to make predictions about the behavior of people in general and groups in general than it is to make predictions about how people will respond in a direct act of participation.   There appears to be no set of rules that can be offered for individual behavior, exactly as there is no system for refined analysis of group behavior.

Status has been examined from a number of perspectives. We have suggested that we could derive some propositions about it from examination of the territorial drive in animals.   We have looked at role as a form of homeostatic mechanism.   We have suggested that norms could be derived both from examination of a specific group, and also from an examination of the culture in which the group exists.   Each time we select a proposition to govern our analysis, our perspective must change to fit the proposition.   If we are investigating from a cultural perspective we may lose sight of some individual transactions, and if we are observing individual behavior we might not do so well in drawing conclusions about the culture.   There does seem to be a general proposition that covers both analysis and participation in human interaction; that is, man tends to solve his problems through interchange of language.   Solutions to difficulties are sought internally through the process of thought, a main part of which is symbol manipulation.   Man governs his dealings with others through the use of symbols.   Our internal world is symbolically based and our actions in relation to others are carried on with symbols.

Symbolic Behavior and Animal Behavior

Another perspective that may be taken is to attempt to apply the propositions developed by ethologists to human symbolic interaction.   Students of animal behavior declare that all animals seek (1) survival, (2) homeostasis, (3) territory, and (4) stimulation.   They point out that the behavior of animals can be best understood by grouping their activities under these categories, identifying each activity with the goal it seeks to serve. Broadly the analysis can be applied to human interaction patterns.

Survival, for example, is best ensured for humans through the development of complex social institutions designed to protect the species. Humans are essentially frail; cultures include the elements that protect the human against predators and the elements. The institutions of society are held together with a symbolic–communicative adhesive. Order of the society proceeds through a normative system. Language is used to connect the men. Without common language there can be no common culture, and of course, without common problems leading to common culture, no language will develop. It is irrelevant at this point to decide which came first. The fact is that they are inextricably connected. Thus, social survival, familial survival, economic survival, and physical survival require that we understand rules expressed through a system of symbols and that we know how to use the system of symbols to carry out the rules.

Our position in the status hierarchy, both within subgroups and in the main society, suggests to us the parameters of our behavior. We defend positions, for position carries with it the amount of honor we are accorded by others, and in most cases it also carries economic survival. Some of our behavior, which we may later classify as irrational, was perfectly rational at the time, for it was a defense of our psychic territory, a response to a threat to our status.

Each animal seeks to get the clearest understanding of the world in which it lives. In short, it tries to work out relationships to its surroundings so that it will know what to expect. Man is very little different. We want to know what we can do and cannot do at given times and places, so that we can make personal judgments about the nature and extent of our behavior. We want to know that topics are taboo with a given group of people, and we want to know the rules by which we must play to seek whatever it is we want from others. Identification of our role in the group provides us with information on which we can base such judgments. Defining our role presents us with a range of action choices which we can examine in each situation. The ability to shift roles to suit differing ecologies is characteristically human. The animal can only play one role, while humans can play roles as parents, students, friends, and many more. Failure on our part, however, to shift our roles appropriately, will result in failing in our objectives, and so it becomes imperative to know "where we stand."

Stimulation is sought often through interchange of symbols. We alter roles, play for different statuses, interact merely to dispel boredom. We use language as play, and sometimes we seek hostility and conflict in order to provide some excitement for ourselves. Learning, particularly, comes to us as a result of our desire for stimulation. The compulsion that we feel to learn new things and methods will provide us with material we can use to change our goals, develop new roles, and achieve new status.

We should be able to examine any given behavior in a group as it seeks to serve those four ends. A critical comment may be motivated out of desire to solve the problem and "survive" economically. It may result from a perceived threat to status. It may be made because the role demands it. Or, it may come just because someone wants to have "fun." Thus, one possible way to study the small group may be through the animal analogy.

The Cybernetic Analogy

Linguistic constructs may be examined as a random intersect of words spoken, or as a complex of word possibilities in which mathematical interactions take place, helping us to predict what others will say and how we can respond. A mathematical theory of games might serve as a model within which the communications dimension of human interaction can be studied, in other words, a stimulus can evoke certain other behavioral responses, each of which has a different payoff. The response anticipated is the response that affords the highest payoff to the person making it, and thus can be expected and prepared for. Alternatives of behavior can be blocked out into flow charts, with various tracts to follow depending on the kind of response a remark evokes.

Viewed in this light, interaction becomes part of a mathematical formula, which can be built into a complex program for the computer, a program that should produce sound predictions of what will occur next in a group. Our actions could be classified as to the extent they approximate the optimums established by the program. Anxieties could thus be predicted and prepared for, and thus avoided. We would be able to exert rhetorical control by adjusting our "feedforwards" to the optimum output and working through the steps of the program according to the calculations.

While this may seem to be a "cold" way to understand human behavior, there is reason to believe that such programming may be at least partly valid. Certainly there are observable regularities in human behavior that can be mapped. Even if all human behavior were entirely random, it would still be possible to plot curves of the behavior that occurred most frequently. For this reason, a "mathematical" or "cybernetic" approach to the study of the small group holds some promise for deriving some basic generalizations. Unfortunately, the direct application of this system to the behavior of individuals in the group does not seem quite so promising. In the give-and-take of interaction, there really is not the time to plot probability curves before behaving.

The Phenomenological Approach

This approach seems to hold much promise for understanding the person who is participating in the group. It provides a model that is useful in understanding past behavior as well as for plotting future behavior. Using the "as if" approach, we can examine the sources of our communications in many dimensions at once. This results in a phenomenological view of personal behavior that takes the holistic nature of the group transaction into account.

Through introspection, we can examine our own values. Conscious awareness of the process that goes on inside our heads can enable us to look at our own behavior and try to determine what it is we are after. We recognize, of course, that what we verbalize may have no connection with our real goals. Our expressed attitudes often come to us through social exigency —we express ideas because the others around us have expressed them. They meet a social need, but they may not be connected at all with our personal value system. Our behavior offers a much better clue to what it is we value. Discovery of our own values assists us in the development of a personal rhetoric for behavior in the small group and in any interpersonal transaction.

Much of the dissonance in our internal world is a result of the question that arises about how real our expressed attitudes are. We may have been influenced by our social group to support the educational propositions expressed in A. S. Neill's *Summerhill* and suddenly find ourselves speaking up at a P.T.A. meeting in support of a more authoritarian approach on the part of the school. We may express our belief in discipline and rigid administration of the home to our friends and feel conflict about our apparent lack of concern about the activities of our children. We may discuss the number of hours we plan to spend studying and even outlining the method we are going to use, and then move on to the nearest beer hall for an evening's recreation. If we raise the question, "What are the real values?" we get nowhere. The values only exist inside and one way to approach the question is to separate the personal goals and values from those imposed by the society or the group. We are equipped with loyalties of greater or lesser degrees to home, family, school, peer group, work group. It is not possible to think out in advance which of these has superordinate control over the others. Would we sacrifice a trip with the family in order to do extra work for the boss? Would we drop our father's religion in order to marry a girl of another faith? Would we vote the death penalty on the jury and still hold our membership in the American Civil Liberties Union?

The recent integration movement has confronted a great many white people with this kind of confusion. The "liberal" creed has been one of "tolerance" and goodwill. It preaches that all men are equal and those who hold to it tend to feel that they would have no difficulty interacting with people of other races. Their record proves it. They have been at cocktail parties with students from African and Asian countries; they have entertained in their homes classmates or professional people of the black race. They are dismayed to discover that their confrontation with the "ordinary" member of the race fills them with repugnance. The "man of the streets" unsettles them.

This was not what they had bargained for.   The first bastion of defense is rationalization, arguing that tolerance and goodwill are possible only when everyone is educated up to a certain level.   Who then will do the educating?   If it is not possible to face the ordinary member of the group, then the responsibility must be given to someone else, or shucked off, or it may be necessary to avoid the question entirely and turn attention to other matters, avoiding contact but still expressing the creed, or it may be necessary to find a new creed which better describes the value, or it may be necessary to revise the behavior to fit the creed.   Whichever of these choices is made indicates which values are most important.   If the man elects to revise his creed and rationalize away his prior commitment to "tolerance," he can infer that his loyalty to economic class or race transcends his commitment to "democratic principle."   If he overcomes his initial repugnance and succeeds in interacting well, then he can infer that his commitment to "racial harmony" transcends his commitment to the values of his race and social class.   In any case, the "truth," however we can get at it, is internal, revealed only to the individual and only inferred by the outsider, and not available either for comment or measurement.   If you want to discover how a man's phenomenal world is laid out, it is necessary to watch his behavior as well as listen to his words.

Another way to approach this problem of conflict in the phenomenal world is to examine the various roles that are available for the person to play.   The role he holds most important, that he values most, that has ascendancy in his phenomenal world, is the one that will govern his choices of behaviors.   For example, a medical doctor who clearly defines his prime loyalty to the norms of his occupational group will play the role of doctor in his social and political encounters.   It will not be too difficult to discover the nature of his value structure.   The question is, will he be able to understand that he is primarily acting out his professional role as he makes his choices?

The performance of role creates our personality, and if we bungle we are destroyed.   Somewhere in our phenomenal world is an image of ourselves, which we project into the future as we make decisions about our behavior.   For most of us, this image is obscure, we are not fully aware of what it consists of. In fact, it is exceedingly difficult to know very much of it, but systematic investigation of the kinds of choices that are made can result in some understanding of our value system as reflected by our self-image. Understanding of the phenomenal world offers a fruitful way of discovering something about your own behavior and the behavior of others with whom you interact.

Propositions about Personality and the Small Group

The fragility of human interaction cannot be overstated. We cannot afford to underestimate both the destructive and thera-peutic powers of the small group. Through group interaction we may become strong and productive human beings, or we may be crushed and relegated to the scrap heap of society. Participation in small groups calls forth from us our basic animal behavior as well as the most sophisticated of human activities, the capacity to communicate.

Communication lays out the context for our behavior in a given time and place. Our personality, in fact, is built on communications and our potential for responding to them. Our plans for behaving are always constructed out of past data projected into the future. We estimate present conditions only in terms of what we have already experienced and what we can construct out of what we have experienced. When we examine our actions, we must look at them as past events, and conse-quently can rarely, if ever, get at the motivations for our behav-ior at the moment. The same is true for any general investiga-tion of communication behavior in small groups. The measurement is either what has happened or what people be-lieve about what has happened. The present moment escapes us, and the future is a mass of probabilities. The process of communication infuses our actions and the actions of those around us with meanings. We build our own personality and contribute to the growth of the personalities of others through the simple and ordinary act of communication. We do this all the time, whether we are aware of it or not, and when we attempt to do it consciously we are playing the role of teacher or clinician.

Our life in contact with others is a constant process of spinning a linguistic self-system and placing it in relation to our understanding of the self-systems of others. Through this process of interaction, we become human. Becker has said, "Speech is not merely a part of human behavior or merely integral to it, or simply the most important aspect of it. Speech is everything that we call specifically human because without speech there would be no true ego." In order to relate the past to the present and future, the human must fix himself at each moment in relation to the other people around him with a precise verbal designation of himself. Whatever this designation is, "self-system," "ego," "self-image," "personality potential," it means "I" and it is what controls the interaction with others. We form the "I" through contact, and we know ourselves through the experiences we have in communicating with others. The only sensation that comes to us from inside is information about the state of our own bodies. Thus, we might legitimately conclude that interaction with others in groups represents the most pertinent elements of human life for study, it is the most human of all our acts.

We have, in this chapter, elaborated a number of ideas about how the group can be viewed in order to develop generalizations, as well as how the individual can view the group in order to improve his capacity to behave in it. Some summary of those propositions is now in order.

1. *Anxiety affects humans as it does all animals.* Anxiety seems to be present in all higher animal organisms. In man, anxiety is elaborated verbally and is deeply bound up with identification of self and in projection of personality. The loss of either role or status can induce a relatively severe anxiety. Both role and status result from interaction; consequently, skill at participation with others is essential to prevent anxiety from overpowering the self and reducing it to ineffectuality.

The small group, thus, can both enhance or reduce self-esteem; facilitate mental health or induce mental illness. Learning control over interaction is imperative in avoiding severe emotional disturbance. The inability to interact satisfactorily with others is considered to be a main symptom of mental illness by psychiatrists, and part of retraining to "normal" health is instruction in how to interact with others.

2. *The responses we receive from others are the main buffers to anxiety.* Our individual conduct is largely motivated by the words we hear and the signs we see in interaction. Our successes and failures are determined by the effectiveness we demonstrate in getting others to move in line with our own prophecies and commitments. We employ rhetoric, artistic proofs, to motivate human behavior. Our use of rhetoric is rooted in our own image of self, which provides us with information about what we might be able to accomplish and the methods available to us for doing it. Since the rules of our democratic society restrict our attempts at motivation to communication and interdict the use of threat of force, our interaction with others may be construed as a competition, in which we "tot" up a won–lost record. The man who discovers he can win victories by motivating behavior in others is rewarded and thus improves his skill. The person who suffers consistent defeat and frustration finds his arsenal of verbal potential seriously reduced.

It is for this reason that it is virtually impossible to develop a system of instruction in behavior in the small group which will "guarantee" success. Success in interaction implies successful personality, and personality represents the totality of a life experience, hardly something that can be provided in a classroom, three days a week for fifteen weeks. The uniqueness of human behavior is compounded by the factorial manner in which relationships increase as one individual proceeds to interact with others.

While some of the techniques applicable to the speaker–audience situation may be germane to the small group, the problem of confrontation remains, exemplified by the fact that speakers and listeners can reverse roles, and the speaker is given little opportunity to develop a "fiction" about his success. He must live with the responses he receives and he must adjust to them at once. Thus, the scorekeeping in the small group is more effective and direct, and, consequently, the possibilities for failure and anxiety are somewhat greater in the interpersonal transaction. However, by the same token it is difficult for a man who speaks to a passive audience to discover whether he has won or not, while in the small group victories are obvious. Thus, the small group has the potential for elaborating or reducing self-esteem.

The rules of interaction in the small group are quite different from those that apply to the platform situation. The communicator in the small group is not a performer, for he does not occupy a stage as he would in a more formal situation. Rather, he plays a number of roles, one for each member of the group, and he is evaluated according to the expectations that others have of his behavior. To be effective, he must be able to vary his role and meet the expectations of the others. Thus, the need for variation in role, while fitting group norms, is exceedingly high, and tensions placed on the speaker are that much greater. Each dyad that emerges in small group interaction represents a potential success or failure. The development of the reification "group" may be relatively simple for the person who observes and analyzes outside of the interaction context, but it is hard for the participator to generalize about "the group." He must respond to Joe, Tom, and Bill, one at a time.

The potential threat is clear to those who participate, for it is hard to find people willing to take the responsibility of leading, and even more difficult to find people who can do it well. Most people attempt to find a comfortable role, one in which they can respond in a kind of general way to the others. While they may win nothing great this way, they minimize their potential loss. To attempt to control behavior of individuals in small groups represents great risk, for a leader can be deposed and feel the consequent reduction in self-esteem, even if the leader is appointed by an outside power source. In the small group participants have the privilege of evaluating their fellows as "irrelevant," which represents the deepest threat to ego and self-esteem.

3. *Finding a method for studying the small group is difficult.* Most studies of behavior of individuals in groups have been done through some kind of controlled experimentation. Attempts at measuring what happens in "live" discussions have not proven too fruitful. As a result, many of the generaliza-

tions about small groups are the result of studies done under "laboratory" conditions. Confirmation of the findings in life situations depends on careful observation, but there has been no opportunity to replicate most of the studies in real conditions. There is the constant question of how large is the gap between the findings of experiments and the operations of a specific person in a given discussion.

On one hand, in this book, we have tried to examine the generalizations that have been made about small groups. On the other hand, we have tried to give some advice that might be useful to the individual that has to participate. Often there has been conflict between the advice, and it is hard to reconcile this conflict. Rather than keep the reader in a state of dissonance, we must make it clear that despite the fact that many people have been studying small groups, there is a great deal we do not know. To approach the question of personal behavior, for example, takes us into realms in which we can only speculate, theorize, and attempt to cull through personal experiences and observations. This has often been referred to as the "clinical method." What is needed to improve our understanding of individual behavior in the small group is a series reporting the personal experiences and feelings of participants in small groups. It is on the feeling level that we most lack data, and this is the level that is the most difficult to get at in any formal sort of way.

We have attempted to avoid giving directive advice about behavior, but we have made one generalization clear, that is, the participant in a group discussion is engaged in a rhetorical task despite the concept that the small group is supposed to be engaged in a cooperative activity. The nature of the human is to attempt to assert control. If this can be recognized and kept in mind during participation, it may be possible for an individual to regulate his own behavior so that he can be more successful in his interactions.

We have given considerable advice about what a group ought to do in order to live up to its various obligations. We have discussed problems like consensus and output, indicating that the group per se is judged by what it accomplishes, rather than by what it does for the mental health of the participants. We must, however, fall back on the notion that "group" is an abstraction developed for ease of manipulation in thought. The possibility of definition is so great that it is unwise to assert that if four or five people occupy the same place at the same time and talk with each other they form a group. The purpose of the interaction determines the nature of the obligation, and no definition of group should omit some examination of purpose. The group is judged by how well it achieves its goal. The individual in the group is judged by the way he helps achieve the group goal and by his own personal effectiveness at interaction. Thus, a "good" group, may have ineffective participants in it, and a "poor" group may have effective ones.

4. *Examination of groups as they fit into a larger culture is an effective mode of analysis.* By fitting small groups into a cultural context, it is possible to apply a system of probabilities to develop generalizations about expectations in small groups. The concept of norms, for example, has been adapted from the study of culture and applied to the small group. Examining a culture in general, it is possible to observe some regularities of behavior, the development of certain "rules" of procedure. It appears that similar rules or norms emerge in the small group.

Furthermore, general norms of a whole culture have an effect on the individual participation of people in groups. To the student of the small group the individual is the object of primary study. It is hard to find him as we study a whole society, and so it is necessary to examine aggregates of individuals and specify modalities of behavior. The same kind of analysis can be made in a small group, where the individual is regarded as an object of primary value interacting with other meaningful objects each of which can be valued. This perspective enables us to identify norms, specify roles, and delineate the structure of relationship, or relative status. We can then generalize about a small group, or about small groups in general, depending on whether we use an inductive or deductive process to analyze our data.

5. *Each human participant in small group activity is seeking a sense of identity.* The individual finds out who he is in relation to others. The communications between members of a group take on deep meaning and become something more than a means to an end or a technique by which people solve

problems.   The group problem represents only one preoccupation of members of small groups.   Each of them is trying to
derive what he can, personally, out of the interaction.

A fruitful method of analysis of individual behavior in the
small group is to look at possible gain or loss in self-esteem to
explain behavior carried. For the participant, an understanding
of how his own behavior might support or threaten others can
assist him in selecting more appropriate behavior, designed to
maximize the goodwill extended to him by other members of the
group.

Once again, a broader area contributes ideas for the study of
the small group.   An examination of the theories of child
development leads to the conclusion that the individual in the
small group goes through essentially the same states of development of self-esteem as a child developing through home, school,
and peer culture.   As the child seeks situations that reward and
enrich, so does the group member.   As the child seeks "victories" so does the small group member.

6. *The kind of behaviors permissible and available to the
individual develop from his role and status in the group, both of
which contribute to the development of personality.*   It may be
somewhat unconventional to take a rhetorical view in examining
the small group.   There seems to be confusion, however, between the goal of the group qua group and the personal goals of
individuals.   There can be no question about the fact that an
individual cannot subvert his own desire to exert influence over
others.   The personal drive to "win" may be associated with the
group goal, but it will only be so associated when the individual
can perceive potential gain for himself by doing it.   Individuals
struggle for roles that will be most comfortable and predictable,
that provide maximum satisfaction, and they seek status which
maximizes their control.

Role and status taken together provide the range of behaviors
that can be utilized in seeking future goals.   Successful playing
of a role and achievement of status goals provide the individual
with more choices about behavior.   Unsuccessful playing and
lack of achievement reduce the number of choices he can make.
Thus, skillful participation in the small group depends on prior

success and failure; individual behavior can be also be examined in this context.

7. *There are many theoretical constructs to choose from in looking at and participating in small groups, but the activity must be regarded as primarily holistic.* Small group behavior can be considered as a function of social norms, or it may be considered a summation plus of individual behaviors. Role may be considered from the standpoint of group needs met by individuals, or individual goals achieved thus shaping the group. Status, too, may be considered from the standpoint of what is needed in the group or what is needed by the individual. Individual behavior can be considered as a game, a cybernetic process, a psychiatric fulfillment, or a premeditated rhetorical act (among others).

Small group activity may be measured by graphs, charts, attitude scales, evaluation questionnaires, or quality of output. Members can be asked to express their personal satisfaction or lack of it. Reports can be subjected to content analysis. But whichever of these ways is selected, part of what we are looking for is omitted. Somewhere in the interaction, and in what it does inside the individual, lies the real essence of human interaction, and we cannot yet get at this with any known instrument. Thus, each participant in and student of the small group must rely to some extent on his personal experience and feeling as he attempts to explain behavior or to plan it.

A Final Word

We have moved far in this discussion from the conference room and the formal planning meeting. We have looked at the relationship of individual to group to society, at the process of rhetorical control, at internal data-processing and the effect it has on the individual. We have clearly not, in this chapter, used a "behavioral" approach to our investigation of the small group.

On one hand, we can take the "hard-nosed" view that the only thing we ought to be concerned with is the output of the group, and on the other hand we can show serious concern for the self-esteem and fragile personality of the individual. It is hard to be cybernetic and psychiatric at the same time, and this represents the real "bind" in trying to understand the phenomenon known as the small group. A company vice-president may not be concerned about the "mental health" of his employees, yet it is important to him for it tends to control the quality of the decisions he might expect. A group therapist may not care particularly what his clinical group gets done, but what they think they have to do will have considerable to do with their mental health. Throughout our investigation of the small group we must be concerned with the nature of the group and the individuals in it. Modes of study must be discovered that will enable us to look at final output, process by which it was achieved, and individual contribution to the process. We cannot omit concern for the internal effect of the whole procedure on each individual, for this will affect output, process, and individual contribution in the next discussion. Thus, we are involved in one of the most complex and challenging studies available to man, the study of how man relates to man, how well he does it, and what he gains and loses in the process. This is the essence of the discipline known as "small group study."

EXERCISES

GROUP ACTIVITIES

1. Work out with your group a technique of discovering "norms" in operation. See if you can come up with norms for the following interactions *as they are carried out on your campus:*

    (a) Norms of competing for a grade in a large lecture-type class. In a small face-to-face interaction class. In a laboratory class.
    (b) Norms for talking with your academic adviser.
    (c) Norms for carrying on a disciplinary action.
    (d) Norms for functioning of student government committees.

(*e*) Norms for socializing on Saturday night.

(*f*) Norms for talking socially with professors.

2. Now examine faculty interaction on your campus.   See if you can isolate some norms of their behavior.   Discover the kinds of language they use on and off campus.   What are their norms for decision-making?   How are the rankings established?   How is high status conferred?   What are the various roles played by faculty members?   What are their interaction patterns?   How are rewards and punishments determined and administered?   (Do this exercise at your own risk.   You may discover too much!)

3. Determine how your language changes with each change of role.   Is there, for example, on your campus, a mini-language, a language used only by students that is largely unintelligible to faculty and other adults?   Develop a lexicon of this language.   Show where and when it is appropriate to use it.   Detail the kinds of people who use it.   What are the sanctions for using it at the wrong time?   What kinds of roles does use of this language characterize?   (It might be interesting, if you have time, to communicate with other campuses and get groups there to work on this project also, so that you may have a chance to compare mini-languages.)

4. Develop a handbook of advice to participants in committees in your student government.   Tell new committee members how they can succeed in the hierarchy, how to vie for leadership, how to get their propositions adopted, how to make friends, and what kinds of communication styles they may and may not use.   Make sure that what goes into the handbook is behavioral advice.   Don't talk about sincerity, enthusiasm, goodwill, critical demeanor, or anything like it.   Above all, don't advise them that they will get out of their participation precisely what they put in.

5. See if you can discover the norms that exist in your class for receiving and interpreting feedback.   How can you determine what the instructor is thinking?   How do you determine whether you are in good standing with other members of the class?   List all the possible behavioral cues

emitted by the various members of the class and interpret what they mean evaluationally when you are speaking to them. If you make separate lists, how similar or different are they?

6. Using the material you generated in exercise 5 above, see if you can develop a method for critiquing participation in small groups in your class. Remember that the purpose of a critique is to improve participation behavior. What kinds of behaviors will you look for that you will classify as "effective," and what kinds will be classified "ineffective?" See if you can develop a statement suitable for distribution to the next group of students that might take the course.

7. Conduct a discussion on the topic, "annoyances in communication." Develop a list of the kinds of behaviors that make you hostile, indicate what they mean to you, and the strategies you use to counter them. From this, see if you can generate a set of norms about typical communication behavior with your peers. What topics and styles are taboo? Why are they forbidden?

8. There has been much talk lately about movement of black people from poverty to the middle class. Assuming the "middle class" is a kind of group and has characteristic communication styles as well as the usual set of norms, prepare a dossier of advice for a black student, your age, who plans to "move up" into a more affluent society, and participate with you in whatever it is that you do. How do you think this advice will strike him? Is there any advice you can come up with for middle-class whites about the way they respond to interaction with blacks?

9. For the benefit of next term's class, come up with a plan for observing, analyzing, criticizing, and improving small group interaction in the class. Be sure that you use Dewey's "Five Phases of Reflective Thought" to guide your thinking. In fact, you might have half of the group generate rigid agendas and have the other half just go through a discussion. Then compare your results and procedures.

10. Just how much reliance should be put in the ethological principles specified in the preceding chapter? Do you

think human beings are animals, partly animals or distinctly nonanimal? Can you come to a consensus with your group, and also indicate specific behaviors that you would classify as "animal" and "human?" If you accepted the proposition that "humans are symbolizing animals," what difference would it make in the way you viewed human interaction?

INDIVIDUAL PROJECTS

1. Examine some of your past contacts with others. In what way has your life been changed because of influences exerted on you by relevant people in your life? What was the nature of their activity and what was the nature of the change? How do you think you have affected the people around you? Is there anyone you have changed? Is there anyone you are trying to change? If there is, in what ways are you trying to bring about the change and what are you trying to get them to change to?

2. Now a little more introspection. To what extent do you "talk to yourself," "rehearse your lines" in preparation for social situations, or daydream your way through stresses? Has this activity been useful to you? What does it indicate about the "as if" nature of your phenomenal world? Incidentally, you might try to put pen to paper and write several paragraphs or pages on the topic, "What My Phenomenal World Looks Like to Me."

3. Have you changed since high school? What can you remember about your interpersonal behavior in high school compared to now? Were there any differences in the way you felt about yourself and your relations with others?

4. Who are you, in your own eyes and in the eyes of others? Send a questionnaire around the class in which your fellow students answer the following questions:

(a) Name three people you would prefer to socialize with.
(b) Name no more than two people who you would prefer as group leader.

(c) Name the most intelligent person in here.

(d) Name the person who has most influence with the professor.

(e) Name the person who has most influence with the class.

(f) Name the person you would want responsible for organizing a "good time."

(g) Name the person who most consistently impedes the progress of the class.

(h) Name no more than two people you would prefer somewhere else.

Now try to guess who will receive the most votes in each category. Include yourself in this guessing. Have a committee tabulate the results and compare them with your own conjectures. It might be a good idea, now, to meet in groups and see if you can decide why the tabulation came out the way it did, and to examine your own conjectures about the outcome.

5. How do you go about examining the remarks of others? How do you determine what the other person's intent is? What gives you information about the way he thinks about himself? How can you determine his attitude toward you? Meet with your group and come up with some guidelines for making this kind of evaluation.

6. What threatens you? What makes you anxious? What do you fear when you participate with others? How do you go about managing your fears? Can you meet with your group and come up with some advice to others about sources of interpersonal anxiety and how to manage it?

Selected Bibliography

Some of the more influential books in generating ideas about phenomenology and human interaction are Hans Vaihinger, *The Philosophy of 'As If'* (London: Routledge and Kegan Paul, 1965); Ernest Becker, *The Birth and Death of Meaning* (New York: Free Press, 1962); and *The Revolution in Psychiatry* (New York: Free Press, 1964); and Arthur Combs and Donald Snygg, *Individual Behavior* (New York: Harper & Row, 1959). While none of these is on the small group, per se, they are filled with applicable propositions about the meaning and impact of human interaction.

The Vaihinger book is a classic and exceedingly difficult reading. Perhaps more than any other book encountered by the authors, it clarifies the matter of "fictions" to which we respond and lays the groundwork for the study of phenomenology as it applies to human interaction. Ernest Becker approaches human interaction from the standpoint of a psychiatrist, and shows in detail the influence that the spoken word has on human behavior, and indeed, how important communication is in the interactive life of all of us. The Combs and Snygg book is also a classic of its kind. It lays the groundwork for the examination of the behavior of the individual in a group setting and uses perceptual psychology and phenomenology as its framework.

For those of you who wish to pursue the ideas concerning the individual in the small and large group and in society, there can be no better introduction than that of David Krech, Richard S. Crutchfield, and Egerton L. Ballachey, *Individual in Society: A Textbook of Social Psychology* (New York: McGraw-Hill, 1962). You will find the language (the terminology) some-what different in *Individual and Society,* but the premises upon which that book is written is not unlike ours. Specifically, the complexity of the individual's phenomenal world is clearly delineated.

There are other books on social psychology that will set slightly different perspectives that may be more meaningful to some of you. Try especially Alfred R. Lindesmith and Anselm L. Strauss, *Social Psychology* (New York: Dryden Press, 1956); Tamotsu Shibutani, *Society and Personality: An Inter-actionist Approach to Social Psychology* (Englewood Cliffs, N.J.: Prentice-Hall, 1961); and others that your instructor might be able to suggest.

An analysis of the group is available in the lucidly written *The Human Group,* by George C. Homans (New York: Harcourt, Brace & World, 1950). For a good conceptual treatment of the way in which nonpurposive group interaction affects group structure, particularly ranking and leadership, this account is a classic. For those interested in a broader and more traditional sociological perspective, assuming you've not already had one, see some of the basic sociology texts. They will give a good introduction to the concepts commonly used. For those who wish to explore the concept of the social system there are a number of sources each of which will lead to others. The George Homans book, *The Human Group* (*op. cit.*) is a good beginning. Also see the first chapter of Charles P. Loomis,

Social Systems: Essays on Their Persistence and Change (Princeton: Van Nostrand, 1960).

There are many good ideas about human interaction in the writings of John Dewey. The book most directly applicable to the study of the small group is *How We Think* (Boston: Heath, 1902) in which he spells out his "five phases of reflective thoughts." Another source of original ideas is Dewey's *Art as Experience* (New York: Minton, Balch, 1934).

Perhaps the best of the communication-oriented books on small groups is Franklyn Haiman, *Group Leadership and Democratic Action* (New York: Houghton Mifflin, 1951). Another, earlier, work is James McBurney and Kenneth Hance, *Principles and Methods of Discussion* (New York: Harper & Row, 1939). A more recent and highly readable work is Gerald Phillips, *Communication and the Small Group* (Indianapolis: Bobbs-Merrill, 1966).

For those who might wish to explore the world of communication more avidly, we would recommend you look first at Edward T. Hall, *The Silent Language* (Greenwich, Conn.: Fawcett, 1959). Here communication is discussed as forms that are real, meaningful, but not obscured with the entities we call words. This you'll enjoy.

There are a number of compendia of journal articles available for someone interested in delving into the research that has yielded the generalizations on the small group. See, for example, Paul Hare, Edgar F. Borgatta, and Robert F. Bales, *Small Groups: Studies in Social Interaction* (New York: Knopf, 1955 and 1966); Eleanor E. Maccoby, Theodore M. Newcomb, and Eugene L. Hartley, *Readings in Social Psychology* (New York: Holt, Rinehart and Winston, 1958). Others are Dorwin Cartright and Alvin Zander, *Group Dynamics: Research and Theory* (Evanston: Row Peterson, 1960); Barry Collins and Harold Guetzkow, *A Social Psychology of Group Processes for Decision-Making* (New York: Wiley, 1964); Josephine Klein, *The Study of Groups* (London: Routledge, 1956); and Joseph McGrath and Irwin Altman, *Small Group Research* (New York: Holt, Rinehart and Winston, 1966). For a more systematic collection of propositions related to the small group (and to many other aspects of human behavior) you should see Bernard Berelson and Gary A. Steiner, *Human Behavior: An Inventory of Scientific Findings* (New York: Harcourt, Brace & World, 1964). See especially chapter eight.

For a general overview of the problem of studying the small group, an excellent source is Robert Golembiewski, *The Small Group* (Chicago: University of Chicago Press, 1962). This book provides an organized exposition of the kinds of research that have been done in small group interaction and explains in detail the various styles of investigation available to the student. Another treatment of groups that will place much of the research and observational work in perspective is W. J. H. Sprott, *Human Groups* (London: Penguin Books, 1958). Not many of you will wish to get into the various social psychological theories which have underscored experimental work on small groups. However, you can get an idea of some of this literature in Gardner Lindzey (ed.), *Handbook of Social Psychology*, Volume I: *Theory and Method* (Reading, Mass.: Addison-Wesley, 1954). There in the first 258 pages are the range of ideas that have, even in this day, formed the basis of perspectives of small group and human observation. These articles cover stimulus-response (by William W. Lambert), cognitive (Martin Scheerer), psychoanalytic (Calvin Hall and Gardner Lindzey), field (Gardner Lindzey) and role (Morton Deutsch and Theodore R. Sarbin) theories.

For more information on ethology and its potential influence on the study of human interaction, Robert Ardrey, *Territorial Imperative* (New York: Atheneum, 1966). This is written from the standpoint of the student of natural state animal behavior, and it outlines the particular animal needs as they relate to the human. There are also some good chapters on the implications of these propositions for the study of human society. Another good animal behavior book is Desmond Morris, *The Naked Ape* (New York: Harper & Row, 1968). Although this book is written for popular consumption, Morris is an excellent zoologist and his writing is cogent. He uses considerable imagination and originality in translating his information into human terms and showing its impact on human behavior. His more recent book, *The Human Zoo* (New

York: McGraw-Hill, 1969) may be even more cogent.

For information about the small group from a psychiatric perspective Eric Berne's *Games People Play* (New York: Grove Press, 1964) is enjoyable, but even more pertinent is his *Structure and Dynamics of Organizations and Groups* (New York: Lippincott, 1963). A more traditional psychiatric overview can be found in W. R. Bion, *Experiences in Groups* (New York: Basic Books, 1961).

For application in the classroom, a good source is Mary Bany and Lois Johnson, *Classroom Group Behavior* (New York: Macmillan, 1965) or Herbert Thelen, *Dynamics of Groups at Work* (Chicago: University of Chicago Press, 1954).

A good sociological treatment, replete with complicated but highly useful diagrams, is Timothy Leary's *Interpersonal Diagnosis of Personality* (New York: Ronald Press, 1957). This book, written before Leary's psychedelic experiences, provides an original treatment of the problem of personality as it is affected by interaction with others.

Other Works Cited

Arnold, Mary (Ed.), *Health Program Implementation Through PERT.* San Francisco: Western Regional Office, American Public Health Association, 1966.

Asch, Solomon, "Studies of Independence and Conformity," *Psychological Monographs.* 1956, Vol. 70, No. 9.

Bales, Robert F., *Interaction Process Analysis: A Method for the Study of Small Groups.* Cambridge: Addison-Wesley, 1950.

Berne, Eric, *Games People Play.* New York: Grove Press, 1964.

Berne, Eric, *The Structure and Dynamics of Organizations and Groups.* Philadelphia: Lippincott Co., 1963.

Bruce, Lenny, *How to Talk Dirty and Influence People.* Chicago: Playboy Press, 1965.

Flavell, J. H., *The Developmental Psychology of Jean Piaget.* Princeton: Van Nostrand, 1963.

Kierkegaard, Sören, *Fear and Trembling and Sickness Unto Death.* Garden City: Doubleday, 1954.

Mead, George Herbert, *Mind, Self and Society.* Chicago: University of Chicago Press, 1934.

Meerloo, Joost, *Conversation and Communication.* New York: International Universities Press, 1952.

Neill, A. S., *Summerhill*. New York: Hart Publishers, 1964.

Parkinson, C. Northcote, *Parkinson's Law*. Boston: Houghton Mifflin Co., 1957.

Peter, Laurence J., *The Peter Principle: Why Things Always Go Wrong*. New York: Morrow, 1969.

Riesman, David, *The Lonely Crowd*. Garden City: Doubleday-Anchor, 1953.

Ruesch, Jurgen, *Therapeutic Communication*. New York: W. W. Norton, 1961.

Szasz, Thomas, *The Myth of Mental Illness*. New York: Harper–Hoeber, 1963.

Vygotsky, Lev Semyonovich, *Thought and Language*. Cambridge: M. I. T. Press, 1934.

Whyte, William H., Jr., *The Organization Man*. New York: Simon and Schuster, 1956.

Index